RED MEMORY

Tania Branigan is the *Guardian* foreign leader writer; she spent seven years as the *Guardian*'s China correspondent. Her writing has also appeared in the *Washington Post* and the *Australian*. *Red Memory* is her first book.

RED MEMORY

Living, Remembering and Forgetting China's Cultural Revolution

TANIA BRANIGAN

faber

First published in 2023
by Faber & Faber Limited
Bloomsbury House
74–77 Great Russell Street
London WC1B 3DA
This export edition published in 2023

Typeset by Faber & Faber Limited
Printed and bound by CPI Group (UK) Ltd, Croydon, CR0 4YY

A CIP record for this book
is available from the British Library

ISBN 978–1–78335–265–4

Printed and bound in the UK on FSC paper in line with our continuing
commitment to ethical business practices, sustainability and the environment.
For further information see faber.co.uk/environmental-policy

2 4 6 8 10 9 7 5 3 1

For my parents,
Nong and Keith Branigan,
with immense gratitude and even more love.

The Cultural Revolution ended [decades] ago. Obviously it is not acceptable that we comment [on] the resentment, right and wrong of the former times. So just let us review some photos about it . . . The historical sense of the paintings is for remembrance and forgetting.

Pack of 'Red Memory' playing cards, bought in Beijing

For the health of a single individual, a people, and a culture the unhistorical and the historical are equally essential.

Friedrich Nietzsche

To destroy a country, you must first destroy its history.

Xi Jinping, quoting the Qing dynasty scholar Gong Zizhen

PROLOGUE

> These two matters are not finished, and their legacy must be handed down to the next generation. How to do this? If not in peace, then in turmoil . . .
>
> **Mao Zedong, in his last months, on the Cultural Revolution and forcing the Kuomintang to retreat to Taiwan**

Ice sealed the lakes at the heart of the city and colour had leached from the streets and skies, smog dissolving into cloud: the horizon was just a memory. The ginkgos in the park were ink tracings now. Pet dogs wore thick jumpers this morning, and had scuttered past with a stony resolve I recognised. Though I was indoors again, still swathed in layer on layer of wool, the cold continued to insinuate itself. Soon it was bone-deep. These industrial buildings to the north of Beijing, once used to manufacture armaments, were beloved by artists for their bare concrete walls, lofty ceilings and expanses of glass, all of which contributed to the studio's mortuary chill.

I'd heard that the paintings were large, but that hadn't prepared me. Each was two and a half metres high and, hung on the walls, dwarfed me further, so that I was the one under scrutiny. At this scale, and monochrome, even smiles were somehow sombre. On first sight, the images were almost photographic. These faces had the same fated quality as pictures of missing children, as if they too anticipated what I knew awaited them. Step closer and the clear lines scattered into a flurry of brushstrokes; smeary blotches and swipes of ash and charcoal. The pictures both dominated and eluded. The paint was thick, encrusted on the canvas and stuck here and there with bristles. I stepped back again and recognised some of the faces inspecting me. A celebrated author, behind heavy glasses. A glowering actress. Communist heroes. Others were unfamiliar. Famous, infamous or unknown, all were painted in precisely the same way, at the same immense scale. There was tragedy here, and villainy too, but the painter drew no distinctions: 'Even if they are bad people, they are still people,' he said.

He was an unassuming man, bundled in a fat black vinyl jacket and marmalade-coloured sweater – an outfit a student half his age might have worn, but which he carried off easily. He drew on cotton gloves to hunt through the stacks for the canvas I'd requested, then pulled out a frame and bore it to an easel before untaping the cover. A face emerged, unyielding, though with a trace of a smile: benign? Triumphant? Chairman Mao gazed out, and I gazed upon him. I was used to him in grand dimensions, from the giant portrait that still hung on Tiananmen, the great red gate in the capital's heart. It was startling that the others matched him as I looked around. There were over a hundred pictures in all, but one was missing, Xu Weixin told me: the very first portrait he had drawn, as a child. He had grown up in China's far north-west. He had liked his gentle teacher, Miss Liu, so was shocked and shamed when it all erupted and he learned of his naivety – she was, they warned him, a class enemy: the daughter of a landlord. Outraged at the discovery, he steeled his heart and did the right thing, used his pen, pinned the hideous caricature to the blackboard, and still remembered, as if it were this morning, the moment she walked in and saw it, and how the blood drained from her face. She understood already what it might mean, what might follow. He was too young, but grew up fast. Soon he would see them burning pictures and breaking Buddhas, beating people with sticks and metal bars.

He would hear the screams, and listen to the silences that followed.

He didn't dwell upon his tale, though his memories were 'very, very vivid'; he outlined it efficiently. 'You were eight . . .' I began. I was only checking the details, but he took it for a different kind of question, about his culpability, or perhaps a reassurance he hadn't wanted.

'Of course, I was responsible. It's only a question of how big or small my responsibility was.'

Big enough that, all this time later, he'd devoted five years to these giants, spending days on his ladder to define a hairline, shape a brow. Each of Xu's subjects had played a part in this madness, as victim or perpetrator; often both. Some of them had whipped up rage and hatred. Others had died in the struggles. Painting them helped him take responsibility, he said; they were tied to that first picture, for which he still felt guilty, but which had helped him to understand how people could turn upon each other. He thought that others, seeing his work, might begin to understand too.

Modern China had bred outspoken artists, fond of provocative statements – giving the finger in Tiananmen Square; sculpting Mao riding bareback on a pig. Xu was not interested in provocation, or statements. He didn't satirise forced demolitions, boast of eating foetuses or simulate sex. He held a good position at one of China's most prestigious universities. His very medium, oil painting, was conservative. Even once I'd heard about his childhood, his commitment to the portraits was surprising – almost peculiar. He hoped that one day they could hang in a museum, confronting browsers who might, perhaps, be forced into reflection, and in facing their past help their nation to move forward. But the difficulties of his project were encompassed by its title, the careful *Chinese Historical Figures* with its telltale addendum, *1966–76*. Those were the dates of the Cultural Revolution: the decade of Maoist fanaticism which saw as many as 2 million killed for their supposed political sins, and another 36 million hounded. They were guilty of thoughtcrimes: criticism of Mao or the Party or its policies, or remarks that might be interpreted that way. Others, like Xu's teacher, were guilty by blood, their parentage enough to condemn them. The hysteria, violence and misery had forged modern China, but the movement was rarely mentioned these days. It was not utterly taboo, like the bloody crackdown on Tiananmen Square's pro-democracy protests in 1989. In the past it had been discussed more widely, although never freely. But by the time I arrived in 2008 it dwelled at the margins, biding in the shadows. Fear, guilt and official suppression had relegated it to the fringes of family histories and the dustiest shelves of records.

Xu had been able to show the pictures together just once, in Beijing, a few years before – 'a ghostly experience,' recalled Carol Chow, the daughter of one of the subjects. She had stood face to face with the father she could not remember, the father who had died in the tumult, now painted like a memory, as though he were frozen in time. After all I had heard, I wanted to see him too. Xu brought out the picture at my request: I saw a handsome young man in a fur-trimmed jacket, with quizzical eyes and the hint of a smile upon his confident face – too confident, perhaps. Zhou Ximeng came from a long line of distinguished scholars and himself excelled at every stage, topping the class throughout his studies. For centuries, education had been the key to social advancement in China. In the Cultural Revolution it could mean ruin. To stand out was not an advantage. A mob of Red Guards, Mao's youthful political vigilantes, seized him for a passing comment, holding him prisoner in a village not far from Beijing. He was twenty-seven, recently married and newly a father, but his daughter believed he had reached a point where his life seemed beyond his control. 'You had to first renounce yourself, and then renounce your family and friends. I think, when he got to that point, really, he just closed up.'

Chow, then just a few months old, would never see him again. Her father would briefly escape his captors, to throw himself in front of a train. Three decades later his mother would kill herself too. The night before, the family heard her call out in her sleep: 'Ximeng, Mummy's coming –'

It was Chow's story that brought me to Xu's studio. I had heard it from her husband, an investor and astute political observer; we'd met for lunch at an Italian bistro, where we ate grilled sandwiches, swapped gossip and picked over recent developments in Beijing. Then, over coffee, he mentioned a trip that the couple had made a few years before, to the village where Chow's father had been held. The farmers had been kind enough when the family returned. They still remembered the young man from all those years ago. They recalled how quiet he had been that morning. They spoke of recovering his body from the tracks, and burying it close by. But they dismissed the family's quest to reclaim him – struggled to even comprehend it. Too many bones from those days lay jumbled in the soil. How did anyone expect them to know which one of the bodies was his?

It was a cruel tale, but not the worst I had heard from the era. Perhaps that was why it haunted me. I knew that the ten years of the Cultural Revolution, which ended only after Mao Zedong's death, were savage, unrelenting and extraordinarily destructive. The violence and hatred terrorised the nation, annihilated much of its culture and killed key leaders and thinkers. The movement was an emperor's ruthless assertion of power, which Mao directed and set in motion to destroy opposition within the Party. But it was also an ideological crusade – a drive to reshape China's hearts and souls as he had transformed its politics and economy. People were to be remade or removed. At his spark, an equally ardent mass movement blazed up. Thanks to these contrasting, sometimes conflicting aspects, it was truly universal. Its victims included Mao's two heirs apparent and some of the country's most revered artists and scholars, but also schoolchildren and impoverished farmers in remote provinces. No part of the land remained untouched; no part of the people unscathed. The campaign was bent upon spiritual purity, and the true realisation of the perfect communist society, erasing the bourgeois contamination which had tainted the Party – and the country it ruled – since taking power in 1949. It drew upon idealism and hope. It was also fired by banal grudges and personal ambition, as people seized the moment for their advantage. The frenzy of the movement obliterated temples and relics and closed schools and universities. It tore apart families and friendships.

Yet until that lunchtime conversation, the Cultural Revolution had been history; a jumble of terror and absurdity, sadistic violence and stylised propaganda films, with ballerinas porting bayonets. I knew the facts but hadn't truly grasped how recent this all was, nor how close. Though I'd read accounts of the era, its horrific excesses – which extended, in places, to cannibalism and mass killings – belonged in another world. However documented, however graphic, they were too terrible to be quite real. Chow's story jolted me. This was prosaic in its horror, and only an arm's-length away – so immediate it came up over coffee, so commonplace that people wondered why you'd bother searching for a body. It was a woman not much older than me who had lost her father before she could crawl, knowing him only as a handful of photos and stories. It was a woman who lived each day in the consciousness of that absence – so that, although now a mother herself, she could not imagine what it would mean to have that space filled; she would be, she thought, another person entirely.

This wasn't history. It was life.

— II —

It is impossible to understand China today without understanding the Cultural Revolution. Subtract it and the country makes no sense: it is Britain without its empire, the United States without the Civil War. Unfortunately it is also impossible to truly understand the movement. Mao's erratic nature, changing tactics and deliberately cryptic pronouncements; the political intrigues at the top of the Party; clashing interests and motives at all levels of the movement; the many stages through which it rapidly passed; its sheer scale – each one would make it hard to decipher. Together, they make it in many ways incomprehensible. It might be seen as many movements in one. In parts it looks similar to the terrible genocides of the twentieth century. In some regards it echoes Stalinist purges, but with enthusiastic mass participation. What made China's slaughter unique was that people killed their own kind, and that the line between victims and perpetrators shifted moment by moment. Unlike other tragedies under the Chinese Communist Party, it was all-encompassing.

Mao's control of his party had been weakened by his Great Leap Forward, a breakneck industrialisation campaign and collectivisation of agriculture. It led to a catastrophic famine which killed as many as 45 million and was reined in by pragmatists in the Party, including his assumed successor Liu Shaoqi and Deng Xiaoping (who would, much later – after Mao's death – become the country's paramount leader and set it on the course of radical reforms, letting loose the market forces which created the China of today).

Mao's response to the failure of his plan, and the dissent it had caused within the Party, was a dual campaign to re-establish his absolute authority and remake China's soul, harnessing the masses to override the rigid Party structures on which he had depended and to eradicate all opposition. He relied upon his minister of defence, Lin Biao, one of the chief instigators of the personality cult; Kang Sheng, the Party's feared security chief; and others, notably those later called the Gang of Four – a handful of radical Party officials and his fourth wife, Jiang Qing. She had never forgiven the Party leadership for sidelining her, and had scores to settle. But the Chairman's ground troops were the Chinese people – and, most of all, China's youth. In the first phase of the revolution, the children of the Party elite became Red Guards: groups of young zealots who swept through Beijing, and then other cities, launching vicious and sometimes murderous assaults, forcing people to demonstrate their loyalty to Mao and attacking 'old culture': temples, books, traditional clothing. Even the former palace of the emperors – the Forbidden City, at the heart of Beijing – escaped unscathed only thanks to the personal intervention of the premier, Zhou Enlai. The destruction and violence quickly escalated, targeting the Five Black Categories: landlords and rich farmers, counter-revolutionaries, 'bad elements' and rightists. In Daxing District, on the outskirts of Beijing, entire families were murdered.

Many senior figures egged on the early assaults on officials, unaware of how far this campaign would go. But soon they fell prey to Mao's disfavour and his desire for more radical change. A second wave of 'rebel' Red Guard groups formed after delegations of cadres were sent into schools and universities, sometimes reining in the youth and at other times urging them on. Liu Shaoqi, whom Mao had once chosen to succeed him, and who had recently spearheaded purges, was now ousted himself. The children of top leaders, having peacocked as Red Guards, were disgraced, persecuted and detained. The confusion deepened as rebel groups turned on each other over minute differences, ideological or otherwise. Fighting exploded into something closer to civil war in places, with pitched battles as factions sought to outdo each other in their devotion to Mao. The People's Liberation Army too succumbed to the political convulsions.

Within a couple of years, with his absolute authority over senior leaders once more established, and shaken by signs that the turmoil was spiralling further than even he desired, Mao was ready for a return to order. The PLA took charge and the Red Guard generation were exiled to the countryside in their millions. Chaos was replaced by stagnation, but the terror remained and killings surged as citizens were condemned as traitors, spies or corrupt by revolutionary committees: new political bodies initially intended to replace the centralised Party bureaucracy but in reality dominated by the PLA and long-standing cadres.

— // —

This second part of the Cultural Revolution was superficially more routine than the first, with some sense of normal life returning: schools reopened their doors, and banned books circulated in secret. China began its rapprochement with its great foe, the United States, indicating that it was looking outwards once more. But this phase was in some regards even more confusing and turbulent than the earlier stages. In 1971, the fall from grace and mysterious death of Mao's new heir apparent, Lin Biao, detonated many people's faith in the movement. Either the great and wise Chairman had erred terribly by promoting him – or he had struck down a man who had served him loyally. Lin was celebrated for his slavish devotion to Mao: if, as now claimed, he was a vile traitor, could anyone's fervour be trusted? Lin's death also meant the ebbing of military control. Struggles for power were bitterly contested at every level and in every place, often as Mao's favours shifted from one faction to another, erupting sporadically as attacks on imagined conspiracies or similar campaigns. Only his death – and the ousting of the Gang of Four shortly afterwards – would put an end to the turmoil.

Even China's supposed ideological brethren struggled to make sense of this mess: North Korean officials derided it as 'a great madness, having nothing in common with either culture or a revolution'. In many ways the Cultural Revolution marks the apogee of Maoism, in its ruthlessness and its belief that Chinese culture could and must be transformed. But it was far wider-ranging, more confusing and multifaceted than earlier movements.

China is scarred by loss and violence on a staggering scale. The nineteenth-century Taiping Rebellion killed over 20 million people, roughly the global toll of the First World War. The brutal Japanese occupation of the 1930s would lead to 15 million deaths. The famine brought by 1958's Great Leap Forward caused perhaps 40 million. The Cultural Revolution's death toll is almost modest by these grotesque standards, yet it consumed the country in its entirety. No workplace remained untouched. No household remained innocent. 'Complicity' is too small a word – comrade turned on comrade, friend upon friend, husband upon wife and child upon parent. You could build a career on such betrayals, until the currents shifted once more and the victims turned upon you. Such intimate treacheries and abrupt reversals rent the very fabric of China, Confucian ideals of family obedience and newer Communist pledges of fraternity. Your own crimes were equally unpredictable; the most 'sinister' aspect of one supposed conspiracy – targeted in the late sixties – was that even some of its core members were unaware of its existence. Sycophancy was no protection, especially for those at the top. Devotion to Mao was the only means of advancement; to wield this political weapon too effectively earned his suspicion as well as his approval.

Maoism was supposed to be the cure for a chronic sickness. It had been diagnosed by Lu Xun, who, in the early twentieth century, abandoned medicine to save his nation through literature.

He'd been shocked by a photo of a Chinese crowd surrounding a compatriot the Japanese were about to behead as a spy. They had come to enjoy the spectacle, he wrote: 'All physically strong bodies, yet displaying expressions of apathy . . . Citizens of an ignorant and weak nation, no matter how healthy and sturdy their bodies, can serve as nothing more than subject matter for or spectators of meaningless public displays.' It was identified again a decade later, by the sociologist Fei Xiaotong: 'The problem of selfishness in China is really more common than the problem of ignorance or illness. From the top of society to the bottom, no one seems to be without this shortcoming.'

Yet Maoism had left a greater void in twenty-first-century China. It had destroyed the moral architecture that existed, however flawed, and attempted to replace it with hastily erected constructions (devotion to Mao; radical egalitarianism; a commitment to communism above all bonds of family and friendship) – which were then razed too.

There are cruel and callous people everywhere, and there will be no shortage of them in a country of 1.4 billion. In my seven years there, I was as often amazed by generosity and courage, sometimes at enormous personal price, as I was shocked by indifference or inhumanity. What was missing, perhaps, were the structures of value and practice, and the opportunities which those created to do the right thing – to stop and help a stranger without risking outrageous medical bills; to access help oneself, preventing the kind of violence and spite that come from desperation. But a nation always sensitive to slights from others was far quicker and harsher in judging itself. Around me I heard the hum of shame, from people who in other ways were outspokenly, even aggressively patriotic: *Chinese people are too low-quality. The masses are terrible. The Chinese are numb. There is no individual conscience. There is no core belief – no core at all;*

just a sickness of the soul. Asked the country's most pressing threat, the Chinese opted for 'moral decline' over poverty or crime. You heard the diagnoses every day: a crisis of trust; social decay.

'Our society is ethically hollow,' wrote one survivor. 'If we trace these problems to their roots, we are likely to find them in the Cultural Revolution.'

— // —

The man who had unleashed it still surveyed his nation from Tiananmen. Mao Zedong Thought was enshrined in China's constitution. The centres of power stood apparently untouched as the country they controlled raced on. Leaders resided behind vermilion walls, as the emperors had. Close by, stately political gatherings convened at the Great Hall of the People. In November 2012, I would sit below a red-carpeted dais there as Xi Jinping said that he had accepted the baton of history: the leadership of China. It was what we then assumed to be a once-in-a-decade moment, the Party having replaced Mao's tyranny and caprice with a bureaucratic schedule, choosing its leaders by consensus and replacing them every ten years. Xi's assured manner stood in contrast to his earnest rhetoric. His speech was brief, but suffused with the years gone by. The son of a revered revolutionary, he spoke of an inherited duty and an onerous future mission – 'weightier than Mount Tai', words borrowed from Mao, who in turn had drawn on an ancient chronicler.

'History is made by the people,' Xi added, echoing Mao again. He was twelve when the Chairman launched the Cultural Revolution. His father was brutally persecuted, and Xi himself was paraded and shamed; friends say his mother was forced to denounce him. Later, he was exiled to a long stretch of bleak rural poverty. His half-sister reportedly killed herself, following years of political pressure. This is the history made by the people. These are the facts he could not touch upon as he took his place. Since then, he has purged powerful rivals, called for ideological purity and won over the masses with his appeal to a stirring national vision. China once more is unabashed in seeking global leadership. Far from stepping aside in 2022, Xi entrenched his rule: his tenure is now indefinite – even, perhaps, lifelong. He is hailed as a helmsman, referencing the title once accorded to Mao. His drive for order is the antithesis of Mao's anarchic streak. His country is more educated, sophisticated and cynical. History does not repeat itself. But, they say, it rhymes.

Back in 2012, observers understood his talk of history to magnify his vision of the 'Chinese dream', bringing the nation wealth and power worthy of the annals. We should have taken it more literally. Xi is more conscious of the uses and disadvantages of history than any leader before him, bar perhaps Mao himself. In late 2021, preparing for his norm-breaking third term, he rewrote the Party's past, issuing a new account of its hundred-year record. But even within six months of taking charge he had warned the Party that 'historical nihilism' was an existential threat on a par with Western democracy – as if its control of the world's most populous nation and second-largest economy, mightier than ever abroad and buttressed by massive security at home, might be imperilled by its ghosts and their stories.

What if he was right?

China was driven in the truest sense: propelled into the future by the forces at its back – and by one above all. Hundreds of millions lived out its consequences (broken families and broken minds; an individualistic urge for survival; the rush to cut-throat capitalism; deep cynicism) without ever discussing it. Many of those were unborn when the movement ended. It existed for the most part as an absence, like its victims, making itself evident in what was not said, not seen, not recorded, not recognised. So many had died and suffered. The country was a crime scene; all that was left were the chalk marks and onlookers keeping their distance. Even those drawn to it, as if against their will, stepped carefully round the outline.

— // —

So much had fallen into obscurity as China charged ahead. Its pace was exhilarating and relentless – intoxicating to outsiders like me, drawn by its energy and power; both thrilling and overwhelming to insiders. I had arrived in the year that Beijing was to host the Olympics, as a correspondent for the *Guardian*. There was no better place to report on: this world was rich with possibility. Ordinary lives were crammed with incident, jostled into action. Week by week my notebooks filled with flamboyant tycoons and dogged activists, factory girls and farmers; with explosions, corruption scandals and China's first gay beauty pageant. Everyone was on the move – leaving the fields, moving cities and jobs, finding religion and losing old friends; striving, struggling, pinning hopes on whatever lay ahead: a new building site, PhD or pyramid scheme. Just keep going. Just keep up. There was no time to look over their shoulders. Jobs and marriages, homes and neighbourhoods vanished in a moment. The noodle shops and cheap grocery stores near our flat began to empty; one evening I came home from work and only debris remained. The wasteland brooded across the road until I went away for four days and returned to find a park. By then I was used to the disappearances, but this materialisation threw me and for a moment I thought I had lost my way. There were paths and benches, lofty trees, swathes of turf and beds bright with flowers – a landscape painted into hurried existence. The grass was a smooth, assured green from a distance, but once I ventured in, the lumps underfoot betrayed the rubble I remembered. For even as the bulldozers erased Beijing, whole streets disintegrating under their advance, the past, or at least some version of it, persisted. Miles of courtyard homes had disappeared, but crabbed pomegranate trees grew pregnant each summer in the corners that remained. The cleaver-sharpener called out for trade as he bicycled past a Lamborghini the colour of Bird's Custard. Adverts urged the middle classes to treat their fathers to cosmetic dentistry, with the ancient-tinged injunction to demonstrate *FILIAL PIETY OF TEETH*.

Even the great events and figures in history were within touching distance, so close it felt almost surreal. A survivor told me of her ordeal on the Long March – the gruelling 1930s retreat which brought Mao to pre-eminence – in the war against the Party's great foe and rival, Chiang Kai-shek's Kuomintang, nominally the government of a splintered China. An octogenarian recounted dances and card games with top leaders in the early forties, with everyone joking and teasing each other. ('Mao played too,' he added. 'But no one cuffed him around.') A photographer described how she had captured the moment Mao declared the founding of the People's Republic in 1949 – and how the premier, Zhou Enlai, had grabbed her shirt to stop her falling off the rostrum. The daughter of Mao's secretary remembered the friendly 'uncle' who would take children out for a ride upon his jeep. The lawyer appointed to defend Mao's wife Jiang Qing at the Cultural Revolution's end recalled her defiance and the shortcomings of her trial. This proximity had an almost fantastical quality to me; all the more so as the leaders on whom I reported were more remote than ever. There had been a time when the Party occasionally found it useful to grant access to burnish its myths, and Mao and Jiang both expounded at length to foreign journalists they had chosen. In the 1980s, before the massacre of pro-democracy protestors, top leaders met the small foreign press corps from time to time. But by 2008, when I arrived, such interaction was unthinkable. I had spent the previous three years as a political correspondent in Westminster – a peculiar realm, far stranger to me than China, but one in which it was part of the job to lunch ministers and other senior figures. Here, we toiled for crumbs from a distant table. Even extracting a response from a ministry's press department was an arduous, frequently vain endeavour.

That was a minor frustration. A greater one was germinating. I knew that news mattered, here more than anywhere; that the truth counted, or as close to it as one could get – rarely quite close enough in China. Yet as I chased from one event to the next, and as story piled on story, a dissatisfaction percolated. I'd begun to suspect that in telling these truths we missed others as important. Above all, we wrote about the moment, and everything that had led to it. As reporters we focused on action, not on the long, slow accretion of time which followed. We portrayed each purge or disaster as the last link in a chain, the outcome of decisions and errors, circumstances intended and unforeseen. But everything that truly mattered lay on the other side. It was as if, when a world was upended, we imagined that it might simply be righted, heedless of what it really meant for lives to go on and on, a year, a decade, half a century later. When a life crumbled, you might simply reconstruct it, brick by brick: a Lego house for plastic people, dusted off and ultimately unscathed, ready to start again.

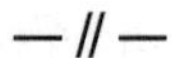

The story of the futile hunt for Chow's father crystallised my growing unease. I began to sense the Cultural Revolution in almost every subject I covered, and to realise that, like the long-dead young scholar, it was a silence, a space, that made sense of everything existing above or around it. It was the decade that cleaved modern China in two; the pivot between socialist utopia and capitalist frenzy, between merciless uniformity and pitiless individualism. Its end marked the decisive turn away from Maoism, so thoroughly discredited by the toll it had taken. Its radicalism arguably birthed the pro-democracy movement of the 1980s but also contributed to the crackdown which ended it. It is inscribed not only in China's economics, its politics and its culture but deep in hearts and minds – so deep that many did not realise it was graven there. It explained a tycoon's drive, a film director's caution. It shaped unhappy families, the expectations of romantic love, the grasping for money, both bitterness and hope. It was the defining moment for the country.

Its submergence unsettled me. Though you glimpsed it, you could never quite hold it in view. Many survivors never speak of it at all, including to their families. They are still protecting themselves, and protecting, too, their children. But even – or especially – in silence, trauma is carried through the generations. Without speaking a word, parents may transmit their pain and fear to those whom they love best. An unnamed loss can still shape their lives, and their children's, and those of their children's children: traumatic history 'violently intrudes upon the present, creating a sense that the tragedy keeps repeating and there is no escape,' writes the psychologist Elena Cherepanov in her work on the transgenerational legacies of totalitarianism. Victims and perpetrators struggle to live with what happened and what they did. It is written in their bodies, as it is in the body of the nation: 'China and the Cultural Revolution – it's like meat on bone,' a historian told me.

I wanted to understand not only what the Cultural Revolution had done to China but how it was still shaping it. The subject has not always been as sensitive in China as it is today, and remarkable research has been done within the country, despite the risks, often by those who survived the era. Plenty of books have been brought out in Hong Kong, which used to have spirited independent publishers, as well as outside China. But the memoirs and histories I read perplexed as much as enlightened me. They never fully answered my questions: not about what had happened, and how, and why, but about how the country lived with it, what it meant and why it mattered now.

At some level it seemed incomprehensible that hundreds of millions of people ignored ten years of their lives that had shaped them profoundly. Some have not been allowed to discuss it. Some fear the practical repercussions of raising it. Some simply cannot bear to address it. Others hush as if it were a curse, so powerful that its very mention darkens current peace and prosperity. It is, to them all, unspeakable. And so the Party and those it rules have conspired in amnesia. A decade has disappeared.

Over time I would come to find the silence less striking than the burgeoning attempts to break it. To speak out invited trouble: if the Cultural Revolution had taught people anything, it was the need to keep your head down – to avoid any form of distinction or attention. Yet online, or in more daring publications, Red Guards began to talk about their past, or families spoke of those they had lost. A significant number regarded the revolution with nostalgia, as a time when rural communities had made real strides in culture and production, and when workers had been respected. Others spilled secrets they had hidden for decades: their fears, their guilt, their culpability. The echoes grew. The internet had given some a new space to share stories they would already tell, but others were triggered by the conversations they heard. Even English-language state media wrote calibrated, careful pieces on the growing discussions.

I began to track these hints and clues, but I did not want to write a book. It felt absurd to have China as a 'specialism' – home to a fifth of the world's population; a place of staggering social, cultural and ethnic diversity, spread across territory almost forty times larger than my homeland. Each day taught me how little I knew and how much I needed to excavate. There was a joke that after a month you could write a book upon the country (and there were a few of those); after a year you could write an essay; after five, perhaps a sentence.

Yet I could not extricate myself from the subject. I interviewed lawyers and novelists and workers; survivors damaged by their experiences, and others who yearned for the return of the era. I heard excruciating accounts of loss, happy reminiscences and painstaking dissections of abstruse political rifts. Eventually I arrived home to Britain with a suitcase of notes and books and pictures, and a sense of defeat. When I had begun, it seemed I might be witnessing a change: that hard, grass-roots effort might be clawing out room for discussion. Now I knew that the space was shrinking instead.

The lives of the people I wrote about were utterly distinct from mine, but they often seemed just a few steps away. I could see that I might have been them. My mother's family are Thai-Chinese; my grandmother, as a teenager, tried to run away to China to join the Party, frustrated by her lack of schooling and all the constraints upon an ambitious young girl. (She failed; a friend's attempt succeeded.) To have a parent from another country is to know how little you can take for granted, to understand how deeply we have been shaped by families and cultures, and so to see how easily we could be another person. A later ship, a kinder uncle, better English, and you might be there, not here. There is another you – luckier, wiser, more daring, more desperate – or no you at all.

So the smile of Chow's father unnerved me. I have led a fortunate life, as had he, and I recognise the superstitious aspect to my questions: a hope that, if I face the worst, it can't grab me from behind.

The Cultural Revolution was a time of impossible moral choices, a time when you could not do the right thing because there was no right thing to do. Worse, I recognise in it the youthful Roundhead thirst for purity. Uncertainty might have stayed me, but probably not rectitude. Why do some stand strong when others fold? Why tell the truth when a lie would be safer? What makes us able to forgive? In another place, in another time, what might we do; who might we be? This is only partially a book about China and the extremes of its history – a project that, for an outsider, might come close to voyeurism; a more cosmopolitan, respectable take on lurid true crime titles. It is, much more, about how we live with the worst that could happen and, the harder part, how we live with ourselves and who we become.

For a nation, as for the people who comprise it, identity *is* memory – a partial accumulation of events and the stories we tell about them. But memory, of course, is a work in progress: 'What we need in the present is constructed selectively by our reading of the past,' wrote Fei Xiaotong. We try to smooth these facts and instincts into some kind of coherence, tangling over the inevitable questions of what we remember, and when, and why, and who gets to decide. What happens reverberates into our pasts as well as into our future. To change our understanding of what has gone before, as events often do, is to change ourselves.

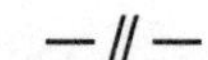

So this book is also about the secrets we keep, and the urge we feel to share. About the way that politicians can manipulate our national stories but also the part that we all play – how we collectively choose our narratives, what we include and discard, consciously and otherwise, what we emphasise or elide. It is about the judgements we pass on ourselves and others. About the battles we fight over facts and the meaning we attach to them. I had no idea, when I started, how important history would become to China's future under Xi – who began his reign with an official visit to the National Museum and within months would attack 'historical nihilism'. I had no idea, when I set out, that history would be at once fetishised and threatened. I didn't foresee the ways in which memory would be disinterred, revived and nurtured – or policed, exploited and suppressed.

But nor did I anticipate that, in my homeland, ministers would denigrate experts and politicians pursue confected culture wars, top-down manipulation masquerading as common sense and sentiment; that it would become a place where newspapers attacked judges as enemies of the people and a culture minister ordered historians not to 'denigrate the country's past' (before, in the same piece, condemning 'totalitarian moral certainty'). I didn't expect to see a West so detached from fact, so prone to zealotry, so divided, so deranged by conspiracy theories. I certainly didn't expect that, in a country lauding itself as the world's greatest democracy, a demagogue would turn to a violent mob to halt the peaceful transfer of power. Like growing up with a parent from another place, living in another land helped to teach me how little you can rely upon – how little you can count on universalities, but also how little you really know about your home or neighbours.

The more one examines the Cultural Revolution, the more extraordinary and bizarre it seems but, in other ways, the more recognisable. We are far away, in place and time. To make glib comparisons – to draw a line from left-wing students in the West to Red Guards, as some have done – is not only silly but offensive. The driving force of their campaigns could hardly be more distinct (if any analogy must be drawn, it should be to Trump and the right-wing extremism he foments); and the difference between deplatforming and murder is not just one of degree. But we are never as safe as we think, nor as good. That should be enough to trouble us. Some people still talk of democracy as if it were pregnancy – there is no such thing as a little bit; it's either there or not – even while we watch it being chipped away, or dynamited, by concerted, systematic attacks and lurching, instinctive cunning, or eroded by our own indifference or laziness. It is not so much about rules on paper, or conventions established over years, as about our own commitments – our own instincts and practices; what we are willing to accept, and what we are willing to do.

I learned more about my own country from China than I could have imagined. I had no idea, that lunchtime all those years ago, how pursuing these truths would sharpen my view; or that I would pursue them at all – it was just a story, told over coffee. Even when Chow's husband encouraged me to write an article on Xu's portraits, I did not plan to linger on the matter. I visited the studio, interviewed some of those he'd painted and their families, and fully intended to move on. Xu's subjects existed out of time, out of place, suspended in a world of their own. I had no intention of biding there. I wrote about what was new. But the book of the pictures Xu had given me, a heavy, granite-coloured slab, nagged at my attention. There was one image which kept drawing me back: more intimate than the others despite its scale. It showed a child, just on the verge of puberty. She had a schoolgirl bob and a tiny gap between her two front teeth, and the faintest anticipation upon her face. Her head was angled slightly, perhaps to catch a voice; it seemed she might be about to speak, or to think better of it. She was thirteen years old, and her name was Yu Xiangzhen.

ONE

Dare to think! Dare to speak! Dare to do!

Red Guard slogan

I knew her at once. At almost sixty, Yu Xiangzhen had the same bob, youthful face and slight figure as the schoolgirl whose portrait had intrigued me. She was neatly dressed and her straight-backed poise suggested a classroom rather than the coffee shop we'd met in – a Starbucks in a modern tower block, where office workers clattered through the lobby in high heels. Her eyes, behind her spectacles, were anxious, without the eagerness I'd glimpsed in her picture.

The painter had stumbled across her online as he looked for subjects for his series: ordinary citizens to accompany the images of actors and politicians. Since retiring from a job in state media, Yu had begun to write blogs of a kind that they would never have published, chronicling her memories of life as a young Red Guard. She had written hesitantly at first, as though she were writing for herself alone, without any sense that there were others to read what she posted on the internet. But her essays had intrigued the painter, and once they had met, his portraits kept Yu writing, rousing memories ebbed or ebbing, 'the way wind ripples a backwater'. The past floated, half-submerged, beyond reach, until something twisted and released and resurfaced, clear at last yet still ungraspable. Yu reached for these moments, tried to seize and disentangle these fragments of passion, violence and fear, but her mother and son fretted for her, and her brother, a retired official, would call her to warn that she was looking for trouble and might bring it to them all, a thought that was always in her mind anyway and tempered what she wrote – though she sounded curious rather than alarmed at his caution. There were certain things you could not say, certain lines you could not cross, even half a century later. When she got it wrong, her posts vanished almost as soon as they'd appeared.

'When people who are very close meet, like old classmates and colleagues, they sometimes talk about it among themselves,' she said. But her schoolfriends, like most of the country, preferred to think about the present: to compare notes on grandchildren, doctors and their travels. The past was painful; it was shameful; it was barely even relevant in these days of stability and wealth. Much of China was unrecognisable as the land roiled by violence – the farmlands had given way to vast factories, the city's alleys to ranks of high-rises. To dwell on the tides that had swept it before was odd and unnecessary, even perverse. Everyone else had moved on. Why not Yu?

We carried our mugs to a quiet corner table. I had read some of her posts already, but she needed little prompting; occasionally I clarified a point but her story was clear and logical. She began at the very beginning. She shared her birthday, 26 December, with Mao Zedong himself. Her family lived on the fringes of the red elite; at primary school she had sat beside the children of politburo members. Beijing, a city of millions, shrank in her telling. It was a passing detail, almost forgotten, that her neighbour had roomed with Jiang Qing in the days when the Chairman was first courting her, and that the same woman, more than four decades later, had sat in the courtroom to report on Jiang's trial for her role in the Cultural Revolution, and been startled by how black her hair remained. Such intimacy was unremarkable. Yu's grandfather had joined the Party in its earliest, smallest, most perilous days, not long before the Kuomintang oversaw a massacre that wiped out many of his friends. His daughter was eleven when she joined the Eighth Route Army, fighting the Japanese occupiers and, later, the Kuomintang. Yu's father was not far behind his wife-to-be. The couple rejoiced when the Party liberated China in 1949.

Yu was born just three years later, and dreamed of serving the people as her parents had. The future shone with promise. Her mother and father had risked everything for this brighter destiny. Mao's reading of Marx made anything possible: true believers could transform the world through sheer determination. China itself was 'a blank sheet of paper . . . [on which] the freshest and most beautiful pictures can be painted,' he urged. You did not need to wait for conditions to evolve: if you thought correctly you would act correctly and create the correct order. In 1949, that looked oddly plausible to many. The Communist Party's victory and control across this fractured country seemed itself a kind of miracle after so many decades of invasions and civil war. Chiang Kai-shek's Kuomintang government had battled warlords and the Japanese occupation as well as the Communists. But it enjoyed extensive US support – and still it fell to Mao's bedraggled band, which, though armed by the Soviets, often marched in cloth shoes or grass sandals.

For tens of millions, the early years of the People's Republic were as welcome and astonishing. You didn't have to be a Communist to prefer peace to war. The rules were rigid, poverty widespread, but the revolution meant justice and dignity. Downtrodden peasants seized the soil they tilled from landlords. Girls were protected from forced marriages. Literacy spread and lifespans lengthened. Workers took pride in their contribution; conditions and pay improved; toiling in mines and factories earned respect, not pity. Landlords were murdered in land seizures, but peasant lives had always been cheap. The anti-rightist movement forced intellectuals into labour camps, but the Party's opposition could be equally ruthless: Chiang

Kai-shek proved that it had no monopoly on autocracy. He had purged and massacred Communists in 1927; twenty years later the Kuomintang killed at least eighteen thousand Taiwanese civilians in the suppression of a popular uprising.

In 1958, Mao launched the Great Leap Forward, an extraordinary plan to transform China from an agrarian nation into an advanced economy. He would leapfrog Britain in industrial production and snatch the leadership of international communism. Households were forced to join vast communes as land was collectivised. His grand vision of abundance elicited some genuine fervour, but it was a project of such hubris it amounted to insanity. From fanaticism or fear, officials vastly exaggerated harvests; superiors requisitioned them accordingly, in at least one place commandeering more grain than had actually been grown. People were tortured or killed for their attempts to blow the whistle. It wasn't until late that year that most people saw the cracks appearing. In the cities, stomachs rumbled and faces grew waxy and thin. In the countryside, bellies swelled in mockery. People ate bark, grass, the husks of corn and eventually the dead. But as the catastrophe became clear, Mao refused to turn back.

'Even when farmers were dying of starvation, they could do nothing to save themselves,' Yu said. Her great-grandfather and other relatives were among the victims. Yet no one knew the true extent of the devastation (as many as 45 million deaths), and the propaganda blamed floods and droughts and the Soviet Union for forcing China to repay its debts. To this day, China refers to one of the greatest human-made catastrophes in history – when it talks about it at all – as the Three Years of Difficulty.

Peng Dehuai, a revered revolutionary, had already been purged when he warned of the looming disaster. But the leadership could not let the country starve forever. The president and heir apparent, Liu Shaoqi, with Deng Xiaoping and other pragmatists, undid the worst. Mao's grip was faltering at last. He feared for his power, and the posthumous denunciation of Stalin by his successor, Khrushchev, had fed Mao's paranoia as well as fuelling the Sino-Soviet split. Who would uphold his legacy? Revisionists were 'being trained as our successors . . . still nestling beside us,' he warned in 1966, in what is known as the May 16 Notification, the document setting out his justification for the Cultural Revolution. His obsession with discipline and control had always subordinated his desire for upheaval. Writing to Jiang Qing that year, he compared himself to both tiger and monkey, 'but it is the tiger spirit which is dominant'.

Mao wasn't the only one hungry for change. Discontent had been breeding beneath the surface: 'The control was as strict as if people were living inside an iron bucket,' recalled Yu. The long hours of labour and constant hunger exhausted people and sapped their ability even to complain: 'If you dared, you would be labelled as a counter-revolutionary and locked up or sent away to labour camps. Nobody dared to think, and nobody dared to speak out.' The hope which had greeted the Party's rise was beginning to wear thin. The public were growing frustrated with officials' indifference towards their lives. Mao had found a new vision to replace the shattered dream of the Great Leap Forward, and his promise to crack down on lazy and abusive cadres was genuinely popular. He pledged a great democracy in which ordinary folk could challenge officials, forcing them to truly serve the people. The ideals that the Communists had hailed for so long would be implemented at last.

Mao understood that on his own he could not see off internal critics. Instead, he would mobilise the public. Students like Yu were his pioneers: innocents enlisted in a war they could not understand. The Chairman was the Red Sun in their hearts; they grew and flourished in his rays. Each year, he rose higher in China's heavens, greater, more generous, more exalted.

And in spring 1966 Yu mustered the courage to write to him, vowing to join the army and hold high the flame of revolution: blazing words in careful characters, on the best notepaper she could find, in a brown envelope with a four-cent stamp and the inscription: *Chairman Mao (Private)*. The reply bore the red seal of the general office of the Party's central committee. It electrified her school: they were writing for the Chairman! They promised to pass on her letter! But the message was sober, even disappointing. It urged her to respect her teachers and to focus on her studies, in preparation for serving her country one day. Those thrilling, heady days of revolution were over; the Party was now in government.

Whatever his officials counselled in his name, Mao had other plans. He had already begun another round of his periodic purges. Within weeks he summoned the senior leadership to warn of enemies hidden in the Party, 'waving red flags' while secretly plotting the bourgeoisie's supremacy. Rooting them out would be a life-and-death struggle, he warned.

Ignite the Cultural Revolution! The words appeared on a big-character poster attacking Peking University's leadership: an arresting handwritten protest. Within hours, on Mao's instruction, it was read over the radio. And in the heat of his encouragement it all burst into life, scrawled white sheets blossoming across the walls of schools and colleges. Lectures and lessons were cancelled, the students freed. Raised to watch for enemies without and within, Yu was quick to accuse a teacher. Her classmates preferred action. When she saw them forcing staff to their knees, berating and hitting them, hacking off hair and emptying buckets of glue upon them, she was too disturbed to watch for long. But she was – as a child of the revolution – one of the first Red Guard recruits.

Her pride was tinged by fear: no one knew if this would be tolerated. The Party's Leninist discipline had carried it to power. It was ruthless in extinguishing any source of rival authority. But to Mao, the liberation of 1949 was only half the transformation he envisaged, and perhaps the easiest half. Bureaucratic inertia was crushing his revolution. Feudalistic ways of thinking thrived behind the facade. A new generation of oppressors had replaced the landlords: Communist cadres with the same privileges, prone to the same abuses. The Cultural Revolution was Mao's reassertion of personal control. But it was also an anarchistic upheaval. Yu and her friends were to be his shock troops. Late on a stultifying summer night, their call came.

— // —

At 3 a.m. on 18 August, summoned at only a few hours' notice, the twenty-strong band gathered outside their school. They marched in line through the night, all the way from the campus to Tiananmen Square, threading into the broadening streams down the great Avenue of Eternal Peace. As dawn broke, a million students flooded the great expanse. Red Guards took place of honour on the stands, waiting for leaders to address them. The Chairman's portrait gazed down upon them from the imposing gate. And then – it was not just senior leaders but Chairman Mao! Chairman Mao himself! Walking slowly back and forth before them, not addressing them directly but holding his hand up to acknowledge their cheers: 'Long live Chairman Mao! Long, long live Chairman Mao!' Yu watched as a girl just a few years older climbed the podium to present a Red Guard armband. The moment would forever symbolise the birth of the Cultural Revolution – the photograph and story subsequently spread across state media, so that it was remembered by millions who were not in the square that day. The rally went on and on and on, six hours of speeches and chants and exhortations, but the heat and hunger were irrelevant. This was history. Mao called young people the morning sun and they glowed in this dawn: so proud and frankly happy, surging forward for a glimpse, gripped by the moment's immensity, the Little Red Books of his quotations thrust into the air. Their voices were hoarse with crying out: 'Long live Chairman Mao! Long, long live Chairman Mao!'

Mao waved and watched. His poetry was accomplished; he was just as adept at the language of the streets. His maxims, gathered in the books that waved beneath him, are pithy: *All reactionaries are paper tigers. Political power grows out of the barrel of a gun.* But he understood that silence and absence had a force of their own. Here, above the masses, he kept that silence. The more the students roared, the less he needed to say. His choice of an army uniform spoke for him; his presence, impassive above the crowd; the speeches he presided over; the scarlet armband he accepted.

'After that, it was as if whatever we did was at Mao's order. Being a Red Guard felt like being on top of the world,' Yu said, almost glowing as she recalled it. 'All we heard, thought and studied at school was to be good children of Chairman Mao's, as if he were a god and our lives' sole mission was to be a part of the revolution.' Worshipping Chairman Mao was not a choice; it was a requirement.

Mao's Thought was 'a spiritual atom bomb': he was destroyer of worlds, and these students were to serve him. Lin Biao, defence minister and toady-in-chief, and soon to become Mao's presumed successor, told them how. He urged them all to smash the Four Olds: the ideas, culture, customs and habits of the exploiting classes. After that day, everyone Yu knew declared themselves a Red Guard. They stencilled characters onto scarlet armbands. They put away flowered cotton blouses and dug out their drabbest clothes. The numbers surged and the groups multiplied, for this was no longer the work of the elite but the mission of the masses.

'So the Red Guards began to attack the Four Olds and confiscate people's properties,' Yu said. 'On 19 or 20 August we started to go to the streets, to check all the shops, and wherever we saw anything – like Buddhas, or good-luck couplets at the doors – we ordered store owners to take them down. I took a very active part.'

Their targets were not just things, but people. Packs of adolescents encircled their prey, proletarianised long hair with scissors, slashed tight trousers, sliced the tips off pointed shoes. Victims were too frightened to resist or complain; Yu observed as a handful of passers-by cheered the Red Guards on. She didn't think it was wrong exactly, but she didn't want to watch. So she urged her friends to board a passing bus and they read to the travellers from Little Red Books: 'They gave up their seats for us and praised us.' A dry smile. 'And who would dare not to be supportive?'

The girls spent the next week declaiming Mao's quotations as they sailed back and forth on Beijing's renamed thoroughfares: East-Is-Red Road, Anti-Revisionism Street. The gangs filled the roads with smouldering heaps of foreign books, family genealogies, letters from overseas and bourgeois clothing. They smashed precious porcelain and confiscated jewels. The city was looking different already – the clothes greyer, shop and road signs destroyed, the adults quicker to lower their gaze or smile approval as the children passed.

'People could be persecuted for no reason at all,' Yu said. 'The Red Guards could just go into their houses, beat them and take away their belongings.'

The police in some districts gave Red Guard groups lists of rightists in the area, helping – or inducing – them to search people's houses and confiscate property. What looked in some ways like a spontaneous uprising was not only instigated from the top but even guided in some ways. Children were enlisted to carry out the work for which adults were, at first, too squeamish.

One night their leader summoned them: reinforcements were needed urgently. A capitalist had attacked Red Guards who were searching his house. Yu, though frightened, knew her duty and was reassured by the throng around the man's home, so large that she was sent across the street to his brother's. 'But when we saw people beating that family, and the blood, my friend and I were so scared that we hid in another room, behind a big curtain. Two girls came in, slightly older than us, both wearing their Red Guard uniforms. I saw very clearly that they were carrying something. Then they began to split their spoils – jade bracelets and pieces of gold jewellery. The way they carefully put the things in their own pockets, and the unpleasantness they showed when they spotted us, made me feel that those things were perhaps ending up as their own possessions.'

Yu spoke with precision rather than irony. Her quiet, methodical account accelerated: 'They saw us and took us back to the room where they were beating people, and asked us to take part – they gave us a belt with a metal buckle and wanted us to join in – I didn't think these people deserved to be beaten up – I grew up with a grandmother who was very kind and she taught me it was wrong to scold people, let alone beat them . . .'

Her tone was nervous, even placatory, almost as though expecting me to scorn her failure. I'd read several Cultural Revolution memoirs, thick with excuses for the authors' sins. I hadn't thought that she might account for what she hadn't done: 'I was too scared and we ran back to school. They scolded me, saying I wasn't brave enough. I felt I was, indeed, not brave enough. It was a loss of face. I didn't want to talk about it to anyone.'

Another breath. 'It was beyond my bottom line. I couldn't do it, so I had to run away. These things confused me at the time, but they were very specific matters. I lacked the basic ability to tell right from wrong. I did not fight them, and I dared not. I went with the flow and didn't give much thought to whether what we were doing was right or not. I still thought it *was* right, because everything I heard was that we needed to break the old world to build a new one.'

The targets of the raid were executed soon after, as counter-revolutionaries. The Red Guards who had beaten them stood beside Mao at his next rally.

— // —

'The horror of Red August set my hair on end – it was the utmost cruelty.' Yu knew that the revolution was not a dinner party – 'or writing an essay, or painting a picture, or doing embroidery; it cannot be so refined, so leisurely and gentle, so temperate, kind, courteous, restrained and magnanimous,' Mao had warned. But the screams of prisoners, tortured on the school campus, penetrated the dormitories and pierced her dreams.

'So I complained I couldn't sleep, to the Red Guards' deputy commander, and he asked me if I wanted to go on a tour to mobilise people to participate in the Cultural Revolution. That's how, on 31 August, I went to Shanghai. Something horrifying happened.'

She paused. 'We were taught that we had to listen to the Party and to Mao no matter what. If people were going against Mao, we had every reason to criticise them . . .'

She gathered herself. 'On 31 August I went to Shanghai with twelve of the other Red Guards. We printed leaflets saying *Long Live the Red Terror*.'

She began to speak faster and faster, and louder: 'We were looking for a car to carry us to Beijing railway station, and because I was the youngest they asked me to watch the leaflets, and I saw something so horrifying I will *never be able to forget it as long as I live*—'

Yu was shrieking. Her voice, so soft when we'd begun, cut through the murmured conversations around us, the clatter of plates and the coffee machine. 'It was dark – I was standing by the side of the road – I heard someone whispering for water and saw a man crawling towards me – from the basketball court there. He was covered in blood. The blood on his head had clotted already. I was terrified. Then I saw the court – it was almost covered in dead bodies. All had been beaten to death.'

She wasn't remembering. She was there, in 1966 again. The Yu who had grown through work, marriage, motherhood, ageing and loss had gone: I saw the schoolgirl. I waited. It was dark outside now, and the cold seeped in as people came and went through the tower doors. I pulled my coat closer around me. Without prompting, she picked up where she had left off: 'Someone found a car and we went to the railway station.'

— // —

Despite it all, that autumn was golden. That autumn was liberation. It was freedom from lessons and rules and routine. It was the hiss and clang of the trains they caught from city to city: 'They said you had to see the country to embrace the work of revolution.' Red Guards travelled free; beds and food awaited. They were heading nowhere and everywhere. The world was on the move. It was all stink and chaos, noise and bodies, people sitting on luggage racks or lying under seats so that their legs sprawled beneath Yu's feet. The propaganda brayed over the tannoy. Her comrades bawled Chairman Mao's words at each other. The windows were wedged open to relieve the sourness of sweat and pee, and at night, when everyone finally shut up and she could doze at last on hard wooden seats, the banging of wheels on rails kept rousing her. Hundreds of miles and hundreds more

– blasting through stations, shuddering onwards. They passed fields and oxen. Ramshackle towns. Peasants with baskets swinging from yokes. One of the boys taught them all to swear; cursing was red, the language of the streets. *Bastard counter-revolutionary.* She practised diligently, as she had once studied, afraid of falling short.

This was revolution. All those books they had read and the films they had seen, all the heroes they admired, who had fought and endured – who had struggled through the Long March and seen off the Japanese and defeated the corrupt, stinking Kuomintang – this was their chance to take up the banner. This was Chairman Mao's work. This was exhilaration. Yu's parents had begged her elder brother not to go, but somehow they never thought of stopping her, a girl. So while he sulked in Beijing, she roamed at whim. It was a season of exploration, sometimes delight, pitted here and there by denunciation rallies and other cruelties which she couldn't quite reconcile, sustained by the great adventure of their mission. It was both a campaign and a holiday. The trains carried them down to Shanghai, to Guangzhou and across to Kunming, with its bamboo and banana trees. On to Chongqing, its hills ghosted with fog; up to Wuhan and Xi'an, the ancient capital. To Yan'an's ochre dust, where the Party had thrived, and all the way over to Dalian, where the trawlers hauled in laden nets. It didn't matter that she was thirteen; it didn't matter that she was a girl. They were a gang, a gaggle, a flock of birds swooping here and there.

'There were no plans or destinations. We saw half the country. In later stages it just became leisure – the train stopped, once, and we asked where we were. It was Guilin, and we'd heard it was beautiful, so we jumped off and stayed there for three days and went to see all the sights. We were happy.'

She blinked and repeated, as if startled by her own thought, 'I was just – very happy. For us, the Cultural Revolution was something fun. We didn't need to go to school; we could criticise our teachers; we could go to places.'

But the millions of Red Guards touring the country had paralysed China's railway and economy: the centre had to stop it. 'So on 25 December, one day before my birthday – and Chairman Mao's – we came back to Beijing.'

— // —

Dates studded her speech, little rocks of fact amid the muddied currents. Chinese people often recited them where someone at home might have said 'one weekend' or 'that August'. Yu seemed especially reliant upon them. Chronology offered some sort of structure, a way of orienting herself. It was no substitute for an explanation, but time was the only truth there was; you could, if you used it as a footing, keep your head just above the water. There was no way of making sense of the rest of it, and even as Yu tried she seemed to realise the futility. Maoism celebrated action over thought, passion over logic, belief over reality. The Cultural Revolution's zeal, its scale, its contradictions, its switches in course – the sheer horror of it – were too much to tally, let alone interpret. It at once demanded and defied understanding.

'I would love to believe everything has both a positive and negative side, but the Cultural Revolution is an exception – it's all bad,' she said.

After so many years – after a life of work and motherhood – what had summoned her back to those days, prompted her to keep writing and asking questions? She understood that her preoccupations were regarded as eccentric. When she met her old schoolmates again, she was the one who always brought up those days. It was tolerable to friends, within reason – irksome or provocative to others.

There were people she simply avoided these days, their silence as discomfiting to her as they found her honesty.

'There's no one who thinks like me in real life,' she said.

Elsewhere, online, it was another story. The internet, despite aggressive censorship, had created a forum for the sensitive subjects that struggled to make it into newspapers in muted form and would never be raised on TV. As I learned to listen, the whispers began to multiply. Some, like Yu, found a new space to share their stories. Some were emboldened to speak for the first time. Others were jolted into words, for the further that the period receded, the more immediate it seemed. Our strongest memories are clustered in youth; decades on, people vividly recall petty cruelties and unremarkable joys from adolescence. Yu and her peers had lived through the unthinkable and their age itself refracted the past. They understood, now, what pain was, and kindness. For the first time they could see themselves in the stumbling old man kicked to the ground, undignified, whimpering, afraid. Or they wanted to set things straight at last: to leave a record, or a warning. They began to think they should tell their children, who were children no longer but parents themselves, and who needed to know their mother and father, and what life really was. Or they looked at the excess of this hasty age and shuddered, remembering when they once believed, and hoping that the nation might come to its senses and turn back at last to Maoism – while others dreaded the same prospect. They would tell me: *It's not about hatred or how evil the Red Guards were, but how to prevent it happening again – perhaps not precisely the same way, but in some new form . . . Mao's death, the fall of the Gang of Four – they were just a time-out . . . To tell you the truth, I feel it hasn't ended.*

'The consensus among most intellectuals is that it was a bad thing,' said Yu. 'But at other levels – among workers and farmers – there's nostalgia. They feel it was the best time of their lives.

If there were ten thousand Red Guards, only a small percentage of them, less than half and perhaps even less than a tenth, would reflect on what they have done. Apologies are few and far between and all those wrongdoings are unredeemed. How can we live at ease if we don't assume our responsibility to do something to wipe out the influence of the Cultural Revolution? How can we just let the wrongs, like beating people and destroying relics, go unrepented? I don't think they feel guilty; I've asked some of them,' she continued. It wasn't hard to picture her earnest, unembarrassed question. 'I think they felt lucky because they were beating people instead of being beaten. There was no sense of guilt at all. I don't think we should blame them. In the whole country there's no atmosphere of reflection. Those people who were very brutal were the same age as me, or slightly older. How could they do it? Every time we get together I look for them and ask why.'

They had wanted to divert suspicion, for they knew their own backgrounds could damn them. They were true believers, resolved to force the truth from the enemies of the people. Or they were diffident at first and held back until adrenaline flowed, and then fierce joy subsumed fear and doubt, the satisfaction of smashing the foe heightened by their righteousness . . .

Yu, after all, had believed. I thought of myself at thirteen – of all the thirteen-year-old girls I'd known. Unready. How unsure you can be at that age, and how hungry for certainty; how jealous you can be of the adult world, how suspicious, how hard to please, and yet how cheaply you can be won. How easily wounded, how slow to understand the depths to which you can scar another. I thought of the disproportion, the restlessness, the boldness and hesitance arriving with equal abruptness. I pictured Yu and her friends: more self-reliant, for sure, than I had been. But also almost entirely naive, lacking not just the patina of sophistication but even the aspiration to it. And conscientious. I knew a good girl when I met one. There was something innocent about her, even now, despite her humour and keen analysis. She hesitated, often, but she didn't falter. She was experienced enough to understand that it was better not to talk about certain things but honest enough that she couldn't, at heart, see what was wrong with the truth. She was precise in accounting for what she had and hadn't done, as fair and as rigorous as she was to others in outlining her own part and the blame she should bear for it; because in the end the enormous, impossible enigma of how the Cultural Revolution could have happened resolved to a smaller, intimate and no more answerable one: Who am I?

'In human history there could not be a worse time than this. I went through the turmoil, through this abnormal time – and I wasn't persecuted,' she said, and paused, trying to formulate her thought. 'I still feel I was, in a way, lucky to witness it.'

I had more questions now than when we had begun, but we had talked for hours already. Yu declined a lift; she would cycle home through the icy dark. I doubted her padded coat would offer enough protection. Her frame was so slight. She looked suddenly tired.

'I turn sixty very soon,' she had told me. 'There isn't much time left.'

TWO

> To determine . . . the borderline at which the past must be forgotten if it is not to become the gravedigger of the present, we would have to know precisely how great the plastic force of a person, a people, or a culture is. I mean that force of growing in a different way out of oneself, of reshaping and incorporating the past . . .
>
> **Friedrich Nietzsche**

Everyone was in a rush. As strange as it might sound to outsiders, for all the rigid constraints in China there was also an odd sense of freedom I had never found elsewhere: a punk energy, with young and middle-aged alike grabbing their moment. The lucky few transformed their lives, and millions more believed that they would any day now. I met magnates who had grown up in squalor, and ambitious officials climbing the ladder, and young men who, within weeks of leaving villages, looked as though they belonged in boy bands rather than in fields or their new factories. But none I met was hungrier or more in a hurry than an octogenarian composer. Wang Xilin was tall, broad-shouldered and still lean; slate-grey hair fell in a debonair sweep above his handsome face, which broke into a smile when he saw me. He was waiting beneath the red eaves of the concert hall, shaking the hands of friends and urging them in. The Beijing Central Conservatory of Music held an oasis amid the high-rises and crammed roads of west Beijing: a hulking new block sheltered low-rise buildings, so that behind it even the air felt softer and quieter. Willow fluff drifted in the breeze, and pink roses were growing up a fence. Swifts scissored overhead. People walked slower. It seemed out of place and out of time, more like a small town than the capital.

Wang's quartet slashed through the gentle spring evening. It was stark and angular, with sweeps of cello building into a dark, almost cinematic pursuit, agitated and relentless, then increasingly forceful, even oppressive. There was a moment's hesitation before the applause broke out. The programme notes said little of the music, focusing instead on the composer's biography and tracing his career up to his studies at the Shanghai Conservatory in 1962. The next sentence, with almost comic evasion, began: 'After the Cultural Revolution, forty-two-year-old Wang returned to Beijing in early 1978 . . .'

The blank felt apt. The Cultural Revolution's devastation was wreaked above all within the cultural realm. It isn't quite true to say it began with the release of the May 16 Notification warning that counter-revolutionaries had sneaked into the Party and must be removed, though that is usually deemed the start. Rather, the years of mass murder and oppression could be traced to a damning critique of a drama, published months earlier in the Shanghai press; Mao had personally – and secretly – revised the piece three times before its appearance. The play, *Hai Rui Dismissed from Office*, told the story of a Ming official sentenced to death for accusing the emperor of bringing disaster on his subjects. Mao and others believed the play to be an allegory: a tribute to Peng Dehuai, purged for questioning the Great Leap Forward. This assertion was in part a pretext. Follow the trail of power and influence, patron by patron, and from the playwright, himself a leading cadre, one swiftly reached Liu Shaoqi, the president and heir apparent, already in Mao's sights for turning back the Great Leap Forward. But it was also a spur to action. The May 16 Notification attacked senior leaders (later named as Liu and Deng Xiaoping) not only for refusing the proletariat's leadership but for giving 'freaks and monsters' free rein 'in our press, radio, magazines, books, textbooks, platforms, works of literature, cinema, drama, ballads and stories, the fine arts, music, dance, etc.'.

In the years that followed, the country's greatest writers, artists and musicians would be humiliated or destroyed. Lao She, one of China's foremost authors, was found drowned after Red Guards stormed his home and abused him. Gu Shengying, a brilliant and renowned young pianist, gassed herself. Wang's teacher Lu Hongen, conductor of the Shanghai Symphony Orchestra, was executed. At the start of 1966 there were thirty-five professional theatres in Shanghai; by December there was one. Private collections of paintings and relics were burned and smashed by Red Guards. Foreign and reactionary books were burned or pulped. Paintings celebrating Liu Shaoqi were a primary target in the early stages. But form was as political as content. Both style and story betrayed the artist's counter-revolutionary impulses. You did not have to read a work to judge it, any more than you had to read a person: origin was everything. If a novel was French, or a textbook American; if a person was the son of a landlord, or the wife of a Kuomintang official – they were on the wrong side of history.

Wang Xilin was one of them.

— // —

The obsession with reading and controlling culture was inscribed in the Party, and its roots lay in an older strain of authoritarianism which ran alongside China's veneration of learning. Qin Shi Huang, its first emperor, had burned books and entombed scholars – though, as Mao boasted, he had only buried 460 alive, 'while we buried 46,000'. Mao had laid out his vision long before the

Party took power, in lectures on art and literature which he gave at the Communist base of Yan'an in 1942. The Yan'an years are often regarded as the Party's halcyon era, after the bitterness of the Long March and before the perversions of power – a time of hard-working, true-believing fraternity. The leaders had lived side by side with ordinary folk in cave houses, endured the bombing raids, worn patched clothes, danced and played cards at weekend parties. But Mao had also used the time to unleash the Party's first ideological mass movement. It consolidated his supreme power, rooting out Soviet influences and a Moscow-backed rival. It set the pattern for all that would follow: the guile and ruthlessness with which he faced down challenges; the torture and killing of the Communist faithful by their own comrades; the determination to remould people through thought reform, struggle sessions (denunciation rallies), self-criticisms, systematic purges and witch hunts. It refined the use of public pressure, isolation and ostracism to break and recreate opponents before casting them out forever or absorbing them – newly grateful – in the larger group once more. Family members were urged to disown their relatives or coerce them into confessions. In its final phase, a feverish paranoia gripped the ranks as thousands of cadres were dismissed and even executed amid claims that the Party was riddled with spies and traitors. These techniques and traits, sharpened over years, would reach their peak two decades on, in the Cultural Revolution.

Mao's lectures were a fundamental part of the Yan'an campaign, spelling out how intellectuals must serve their party and shape the masses' consciousness. In a society that remained so hierarchical, and in which education had still reached so few, his demand for art that spoke to the people was compelling. He called on creators to respect and draw upon folk culture, while innovating. Yet culture was a weapon, not a gift: defeating the enemy, he noted, relied primarily upon the military and its arms. But that, alone, was insufficient; what was needed, too, was a 'cultural army', which was 'absolutely indispensable' to achieve unity and vanquish the foe.

Literature and art were components of the revolutionary machine. Art should not explore but ensure it took the correct path. The Party's task was to identify and resolve the problems of the class standpoint of creators, as well as their outlook, their audience and the work they produced. Many comrades, he added darkly, had too often strayed from the correct standpoint. Above all, he warned, 'There is in fact no such thing as art for art's sake, art that stands above classes, art that is detached from or independent of politics.' The talks rang the death knell for creative freedom. But they also birthed a new kind of art. Cultural soldiers, drilled to perfect obedience, would create new works for the masses.

Wang Xilin was one of them, too.

— // —

When I visited his home a few days after the concert, he quickly poured tea, put in both his hearing aids and drew his chair up closer to talk. 'Cultural Revolution. Beat,' he explained in English, gesturing at one ear, and grinned.

He was cheerful, vigorous and disconcertingly quick to laugh at the craziness of even the most traumatic parts of his history. I'd already realised that humour was a common defence mechanism. It was safer to treat these things lightly if you went into them at all – safer if no one could accuse you of grudges; safer not to think too hard about what they had done to you. But Wang displayed a genuine relish for his story's absurdities.

He grew up thousands of miles from Beijing, in a farming settlement in north-western Gansu province. It had been built along the road from Lanzhou to Xi'an; the only visitors were going somewhere better. There were few landmarks: a little Catholic hospital, the Protestant primary school where Wang studied and sang Western hymns, and the shabby wooden theatre. The costumes, din and clatter of the ghost operas transfixed him – but the thing about them, he realised only much, much later, was the bitterness. The good always suffered unjustly.

His father had been a Kuomintang official, his mother a traditionally raised young woman with bound feet and little education. In 1948, when Wang was ten, his father died and the family slid into destitution. There was no money for operas now; they sold their furniture to stave off hunger. One year later, as the Communist Party celebrated its liberation of China, one of its military culture and arts troupes passed through his town. Their exuberant playing lured him from his schoolhouse; by the time his mother found out what had happened, he was in Lanzhou, hundreds of miles away, entertaining the troops. His head had said no, but his feet and stomach said yes. He was given a military uniform and food to eat. It was that simple.

Wang soon grew to love his new family and the music it had brought him. There was only cursory tuition – mostly he taught himself. He quickly mastered the erhu, the classical Chinese two-stringed instrument, and also the trombone and accordion, and later the trumpet, tuba and drums. In 1955, aged eighteen, his talents won him transfer to a musical military college in Beijing. There were regular concerts: Hungarian and Polish musicians, the Red Flag Dance Troupe. He heard *Swan Lake* for the first time, and Beethoven, Vivaldi and Brahms; a little Debussy and Shostakovich. Two years later he won a place to study composition at the Shanghai Conservatory.

Once there, he did little studying. He threw himself instead into the ceaseless political campaigns. He worked with peasants in the paddy fields, dug ditches and lugged water. Soon he was head of the Communist Youth League – a tall, dashing figure who strode around the campus in his army shirt. He loved the Party and the PLA and disdained those who thought of nothing but music. When the anti-rightist campaign targeting intellectuals and cadres began, he poured scorn on the politically regressive. When another movement turned on teachers, he criticised them in big-character posters. Despite his love of Western music, he feared capitalism was infesting the campus.

And yet a tiny part of his own mind and heart resisted. As his classmates outstripped him – mastering new instruments, winning awards – bourgeois personal ambition and instincts stirred again. When a beautiful and talented pianist rebuffed him, he spent a whole night walking in the rain and weeping – he smiled, now, as he recalled his foolishness. Then he vowed to devote himself to music. For three months he worked, and by graduation he had completed his first symphony. It would not be played for thirty-seven years—

He broke off, getting up and disappearing into a back room, and after a while I began to wonder if he had forgotten me. But he came back with a two-inch stack of yellowing papers: his original score. The date that he had completed each movement was carefully pencilled on its cover. Though the spine was tattered, it was otherwise intact. It had been hidden for much of the Cultural Revolution at the bottom of a tub of rice, by a daring acquaintance who had sympathised with him.

Wang's deafness and passion dictated that all conversation be conducted at a bellow, with sudden, startling peaks; it could be hard to judge whether he was angry or merely animated. When I asked what precisely had damned the symphony – the music's style or Wang's status alone – there was no doubt. His volume shot up and his face darkened. 'They were searching houses! Do you understand or not? They were confiscating everything! It was dangerous for my friends to hide it! They didn't even know what it was! You don't understand? You children!' he snarled.

Then he laughed suddenly and apologised: 'Ask it all. I'll reply to all your questions.'

Why had the symphony not been played even in the years before or after the Cultural Revolution?

'It was still quite a tragic style – not suitable for their requirements,' he explained. 'It wasn't optimistic. All the Communist Party wanted was happy music to praise them. I liked sad music. They always required optimistic and laudatory music. Panegyrics. It's the same today. You know the Communist Party's history? They emphasise the Long March: how brilliant and marvellous it was. To me it was very sad because a lot of people died on it. But you are not allowed to say it. Everything has to be good.'

On graduation he joined the central broadcasting station's orchestra, but it was not the haven he had anticipated. There was more politics: endless campaigns like 'Learn from Lei Feng', promoting a humble soldier as a model of a selfless Communist cog in the machine. When Mao initiated the Socialist Education Movement in 1963, urging underlings to pour 'hot water' over leaders to clean them, Wang embraced the suggestion. If leaders had a good attitude they would have a warm, comfortable shower; if their attitudes were bad they would have scalding baths.

'Now I know it was Chairman Mao against Liu Shaoqi,' he added.

Wang stayed up all night to study the latest guidance. But the instructions on democratising culture struck him as ridiculous. How could a symphony orchestra, which had to perfect its mastery, be close to the masses? If you were already working in radio, broadcasting to the public, what more were you supposed to do? How could a musician's politics outweigh their artistic abilities? Bursting with scorn, he spoke for two hours at the next day's meeting. He attacked the leaders for living on politics, never working on their skills or thinking of their jobs but focusing only on the next campaign. His political record and military background spoke for themselves; he wasn't afraid.

Over a hundred staff were sitting in the room. No one else spoke.

'Not one! They had all been through movements before – they knew. I didn't. I was too naive.'

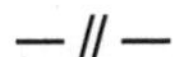

Though the rectifications had begun in Yan'an, Mao's resolve to cleanse Chinese culture intensified once he ruled the country. 'Let a hundred flowers bloom – let a hundred schools of thought contend,' he proclaimed in the late fifties. But when debate accordingly blossomed he proved less benign: the flowers were crushed underfoot. Whether from genuine shock at the extent of dissent, or because his remarks had always been intended to lure out critics, he unleashed the vicious anti-rightist campaign that rippled through Party ranks and far beyond. Leading thinkers and artists were hounded, disgraced and driven from jobs and homes. The celebrated poet Ai Qing was dispatched to a labour camp in the deserts of north-western Xinjiang, where he spent years cleaning latrines; his family was exiled with him, and his son, the artist Ai Weiwei, recalled a childhood living in a room dug into the ground. Wang could hardly have missed all this; his own sister, a low-level cadre in Gansu, was purged and denounced so brutally she went mad. But there had surely been reasons. Their brother starved to death in a re-education camp – one of tens of millions of victims of the disastrous Great Leap Forward, the cause Wang had taken up with vigour. But in

China the famine was (and still is) known as the Three Years of Difficulty; Wang never dreamed the disaster might be man-made. Nor could he imagine that the army, which had treated him so well, might turn upon him.

'It never occurred to me that my sister's problems had anything to do with me. So I was audacious, and criticised the officials,' he recalled. 'I didn't think about the results until one week later, when people said my speech was anti-Party. Then I was scared, because that was a big crime.'

The Socialist Education Movement was a precursor of the Cultural Revolution. Mao sought to remake the world by remaking people: transforming not just power structures but perceptions and inclinations. The arts were both the target of and the medium for such radical shifts. In Yan'an, Mao had dictated that literature and art must act as 'weapons', bringing people together, raising their consciousness and devastating the enemy. Revolutionary culture not only prepared the way for revolution but was a key, in fact crucial, battleground once it began. In this crudely Marxist world, bourgeois arts were not just wrong but dangerous. To build a new utopia, the masses had to destroy not only old habits and privilege but also tastes and interests.

Wang had revealed his true impulses, and now he had to be remade. First came the kindly warnings. He had stood on the side of the rightists, of course, but he was young. Shouldn't he think again? What of the army and Party's benevolence? The three thousand farmers who had toiled to support him? Wang wept with shame as he contemplated his selfishness. He penned a long essay on his mistakes and his gratitude for his opportunities. It took two full hours to read aloud, sitting on a ping-pong table in the rehearsal room. The moment he concluded his list of failings, his colleagues rose and a cry rang out: 'Criticise Wang Xilin! Wang's self-criticism is a battle cry against the Communist Party! Crack down on Wang Xilin!'

'I had been dropped into the ocean of the struggle. It was a disaster,' he said.

It was the first of ten such sessions. Each time he faced a hundred people: voice after voice excoriating him. Life outside the meetings was almost worse; no one would speak to him. Even the people who conveyed him to the sessions would communicate by note. At other times, the leaders would speak gently, even reassuringly. They encouraged him to tell them who had shared his misconceptions. It was not about punishment, after all – it was just important to get their thinking straight. After seven rounds of criticism, Wang wrote down three or four names. These were promptly denounced as the 'counter-revolutionary clique' around him. Now colleagues not only feared the taint of association; they despised him too for betraying friends.

A senior official oversaw the last meeting, the crowd hushing to catch his low voice. He had checked Wang's background: the Kuomintang father and counter-revolutionary sister. Wang had been born into a reactionary class. His eight years of service were a cover. He was a saboteur. Wang cracked. His attempts to save himself had been pointless. The elaborate process of meetings and confessions had borne him step by step to disgrace. It was a meat mincer: once you were inside, there was no way out. They ground you smaller and smaller.

He was dismissed from the Youth League and ordered to Shanxi. Those he had named as sympathisers were dispatched elsewhere, bar one, shown lenience for having lost his mother to a speeding US jeep in the 1940s. Wang's luck had turned. 'And at the start of the Cultural Revolution, because I had this history, I was the first to be criticised.'

— // —

Exiling critics and the disgraced was a tradition stretching back to feudal times in China, another respect in which the Party was happy to borrow from imperial practice. Over millennia, those who kept their heads after angering officials were dispatched to the furthest and grimmest corners of the realm. That some of them were subsequently honoured by posterity did nothing to alleviate Wang's distress.

Datong had a rich Buddhist heritage, but by 1964, when Wang arrived, it had grown into another grimy mining city. The humdrum buildings were scoured by bitter winds that blew in from Mongolia. The rightists had at least been sent to the far west together; Wang was alone. The once ebullient young man did what he could to scrape his way to forgiveness. He slaved at the toughest physical labour, volunteering to empty latrines, haul water and lug heavy loads. He drilled halting beginners in the most basic musical steps, lesson by monotonous lesson. He composed a choral work praising local cadres. The leaders were unmoved.

He saw no future. He grew more and more nervous. By early 1966 he was in a mental hospital. Six months later they discharged him; his symptoms were no better, but he was needed. The Cultural Revolution had convulsed the world outside. People were turning on colleagues and neighbours from ideological fervour, personal grudges or sheer pragmatism: you needed to demonstrate your commitment to rooting out political enemies. As Wang's name already bore a black mark, it was only sensible to choose him. By the time he was released from hospital, the posters denouncing him were up. He was taken straight to prison.

When a friend arrived the following morning to accompany him to the first struggle session, he was moved by the risky gesture of sympathy. Then, as they arrived at the stadium, his friend forced him into the melee. Wang grasped that the people who had treated him well were now harshest, seeking to distance themselves. Six months of criticism in Beijing had not prepared him. That had been refined: they'd used words to hurt him. Now abuse was daily and physical. 'Beating people was very popular,' he said, then added in English: 'Very modern!' and snorted with laughter.

The struggle sessions were themselves performances: elaborately staged, with costumes of high dunces' caps and choruses of denunciation, choreographed parades of humiliation and bodies contorted into abstract positions. Victims were posed in the 'aeroplane', with head and body thrust forward and arms dragged torturously back. The abusers were endlessly creative, placing vases inside paper hats to weigh them down and using wire to hang heavy wooden placards around necks, so they cut deeper into skin. Women wore necklaces of old shoes, since a slut was a 'worn-out slipper'. The dramatic, even thrilling rituals built to a climax of beating. Wang hunched over to show how he was forced to stand in the aeroplane position on a long, high, narrow bench alongside other victims, their heads and faces wet with spit as a crowd threw projectiles and hit them. When his shaking body could take the strain no longer, he tumbled to the ground and they battered him harder. His head was bruised, his padded coat torn by kicks and blows. The anticipation was the worst of it, crueller even than the pain and shame: sitting for hours waiting for them to announce the next victim, to call your name. Every time you heard it, you leaped from terror. 'Even now, when someone calls out "Wang Xilin!" in the street, I still have the same reaction.'

He had once thought the sessions were cathartic, believing Chairman Mao's exhortations to help the misguided correct their mistakes and to bind the others together. But the struggle sessions were not building unity, or rectifying thought: 'I wasn't helping them at all. They just wanted to beat us to death.'

His persecutors seized upon everything. Even his paeans of praise for the Party were evidence of his guilt. When he captured his production brigade's hard efforts, he had made their cheerful, diligent labour sound dismal with his heavy rhythms. He had not been celebrating their toil but accusing the Party of exhausting them.

The harshest years of Wang's life began in that first struggle session. Looking up at the posters denouncing him, he was seized by an immense, overwhelming terror. Yet at that moment something extraordinary happened: 'In that intense environment, looking around – I felt my mental problems suddenly lift,' he said. Even despair could not endure. From now on, it was all about survival.

— // —

In 1968 the campaigns stepped up. He was moved, with seven other captives, to a hut: the black ghosts' room, people called it, and they too began to see themselves as only more or less human. They crawled across floorboards riddled with broken nails while people screamed abuse and hit them. As soon as the struggle meetings ended, he would be put to work again, straining to haul his battered body, laden with buckets of water, up the icy hillsides.

One freezing night he was pulled from the shed, blindfolded, gagged, bound and dragged to a field where his tormentors forced him to stumble in dizzying circles. They threw him into a deep pit and buried him up to his neck. They pulled him out again, to beat him until the blood ran. He knew then that he would die in Datong. Many people did: 'They killed themselves – or "were suicided",' Wang said. Who cared for the life of a political enemy? Only the soft, the waverers; those who did not really believe. But Wang did not want to kill himself. He would not be vindicated: he would be just another dead criminal. And besides – he wanted to live.

He was bound and paraded from village to village, to be beaten and berated. In winter the temperature plunged to minus twenty. Hunger snarled. He plotted escape, but halted each time. He had seen the death penalty notices for fugitives; he knew that he would be tracked down and returned. Afterwards, he learned of those who had swum from Guangzhou to Hong Kong, risking sharks and drowning, and envied them. He was in Shanxi, deep in the interior, and there was nowhere to run. He did not know how or why he endured while so many broke. But he knew that one day he would tell of his suffering. He knew he would write the symphony of his story.

— // —

He was standing on a truck, about to be dispatched to the countryside for more struggle sessions, when they came looking for him. An ambitious official from another county wanted to stage a model opera: he had scoured the area for anyone with experience, and was taking Wang to assist him. One of the men Wang left on that lorry was shot soon afterwards; another, a Korean War veteran – the toughest and strongest and bravest of all – leaped into a well. Wang would not have survived, Datong folk told him later: it was an 80 per cent certainty. Had he been fortunate, they supposed, he might merely have gone mad.

No one could halt the persecution. Wang considered those who stayed away, or who watched but would not join in the abuse, good people; to turn away from victims was the greatest act of charity. In all those years he remembered just one kindness. He had endured three hours in the aeroplane position, shivering then sweating as his body protested, his head wet with spit and his throat parched. When at last the struggle session ended, an elderly woman found a quiet moment to slip him a dish of cooking water. It was warm and dirty, yet the small gesture offered one tentative moment of relief. That was goodness. Now, though he had been given a second chance of sorts, he felt no gratitude: 'I saw the darkness and evil in society. They saved me not to save my life but because they wanted to make music.'

For Mao, the Cultural Revolution's destruction was the opening act. He was as serious about creation as about eradication. Remaking the world – remaking people – required new works. The nobles and poets and graceful maidens of traditional Chinese performances made way for heroic Party secretaries and revolutionary fighters. Even as chaos and violence engulfed the land, premier Zhou Enlai laid down principles for ballet, while Mao fussed over a model opera's title. His wife Jiang Qing, once a moderately talented Shanghai movie starlet, had reinvented herself as a fearsome revolutionary who spoke of her 'art soldiers'. She blew through like a gale, interfering in everything from choreography to make-up design, and calling writers in the middle of the night to order changes to a single line. One opera was reportedly refilmed in its entirety when she decided she did not care for the shade of the heroine's red scarf.

The joke has it that the era saw '800 million people watching eight model operas'. Ba Jin, a noted author, was more scathing: 'Only a solitary flower bloomed in the garden of Chinese arts, and even then it was made of plastic.' There is plenty to mock. The Yan'an talks had laid down the artistic template, requiring literature and art to be 'on a higher plane, more intense, more concentrated, more typical, nearer the ideal, and therefore more universal than everyday life'. Heroes were ultra-heroic, the villains the vilest of the vile. Revolutionary solidarity prevailed over any obstacle. In visual arts the rules shaped not just subject matter but style and composition; in paintings, light appeared to emanate from Mao, 'the Red Sun in our hearts'. Art, and especially images of Mao, should be 'red, bright and shining'.

The media often seemed profoundly unsuited to the message. To a modern observer it is hard to imagine what lesson anyone derived from a dance piece entitled *Reversing Verdicts Does Not Enjoy Popular Support*. The disjunction can look all the more peculiar in retrospect. I once watched ballerinas arabesque with rifles in a revival of *The Red Detachment of Women*. It was a perplexing, faintly comic experience, made perhaps odder by the nostalgic warmth of the audience around me. Yet, watching a long line of soldiers advance across the stage with knife-like *jetés*, I glimpsed its genuine appeal. At their best, if only fleetingly, these works had real force and originality. They fused traditional elite forms with popular arts and new ways of staging to make works which were striking and accessible. Mass arts such as folk music were celebrated and villages put on their own performances, creating a new public space. In some ways the operas prefigured pop culture: they were instantly appealing to broad audiences and endlessly reproducible. Jiang Qing ensured that women took centre stage as forceful protagonists: not lovelorn maidens or fearful mothers but fervent revolutionary fighters.

The people who made these works, Wang included, took them seriously. His new home was Changzhi, in the south of the province: a hardscrabble place where the barely educated peasants knew nothing of arts and culture. Datong had at least been a city. But the area's political commissioner had decided that it too needed impressive model operas: 'Jiang Qing is Mao's woman,' he said. His plans were ambitious, even extravagant. He had scoured the region to assemble a band of musicians and performers, bolstered by untrained residents; all told, the new troupe numbered 120. The work was utterly alien to the local farmers. Ballet was unknown. Until the commissioner tracked down Wang, none of his band could read a score.

'It was new for them to see people who could dance on their toes, and Western instruments like violins, and an orchestra. Without forced political power these kinds of backward places would never have seen this,' said Wang. 'It was a kind of progress. Without this, they would never understand Tchaikovsky or *Swan Lake*.'

The teenage performers loathed their new boss for his strictness. He drilled them over and over. They could barely stay *en pointe*. Wang acquired a metronome and forced them to keep time as they teetered unhappily. He fused the lyrics of the model opera, sent down from the centre, with Shanxi opera tunes more apt for the area and hints of the classical techniques he had learned. The production began to garner attention, touring even outside the province and scooping up more talented musicians, giving them another chance too. Nightmares still plagued Wang, but he was less fearful now. The Shanxi operas proved a rich seam of inspiration. He was not writing the music he wanted, but he was creating again.

— // —

Oddly, Wang owed the next act of his life to Jiang Qing too. At the height of the Cultural Revolution she had unexpectedly taken up the musician Li Delun, a veteran Communist who had been branded a 'black element'. He saved himself and the Central Philharmonic Orchestra by producing revolutionary works for her. Once the turmoil was over, and Jiang imprisoned, Li devoted himself to re-establishing classical music: the Philharmonic's performance of Beethoven's Fifth Symphony in 1977 became the symbolic dawn of a new, freer age. But Li was equally passionate about searching out fresh talent, and when he heard about Wang he travelled to Changzhi to track him down and bring him back to Beijing.

Wang's piano bore framed photographs of his daughter and his parents, but the most striking image was a picture of himself in the year he returned from exile. Somehow he looked older then than he did today, and wilder: a Heathcliff with dark, disturbing eyes, his hair dishevelled by the winds, harsh lines across his face. His flat was a typical Beijing intellectual's home: a small, shabby walk-up tucked away in an old-fashioned low-rise compound. But it was light and clean and peaceful, with none of the clutter one often found in these apartments – old medicine jars, lockless keys and fake flowers, the flotsam scavenged by survivors for some future catastrophe. With its white-painted walls, plants on the balcony and peacock feathers in a vase, his home was calm and inviting. A half-written score was spread across his table and dozens of identical pencils, each sharpened to a vicious point, sat in glass jars nearby. In the bathroom a small plastic mug held his false tooth: another memento of his beatings. Since his return he had found work at the conservatory, got married and divorced, raised a daughter, but mostly he had studied and worked.

His hunger for life and art, for intellectual stimulation, was shared with millions. While the Cultural Revolution had brought limited arts to a wider audience, many felt starved of the works they had once enjoyed. Students had swapped underground copies of old European novels, or surreptitiously circulated hand-copied books. In its aftermath, everyone wanted to experience everything. The competition for higher education had always been intense; now it was febrile. When the Central Conservatory of Music reopened, eighteen thousand people applied for its hundred places. The cultural deep freeze of the Maoist era began to thaw in the Beijing spring. Banned books reappeared in people's hands. An exhibition of nude paintings drew vast crowds. Wang thrilled and shivered to blasts of Western music: not just his old favourites – Beethoven and

Tchaikovsky, Prokofiev and Shostakovich – but artists previously unknown because they had been shunned so early on: 'They really were afraid of Stravinsky.'

Avant-garde art burst forth. Daring ideas too. Students and their teachers began to debate liberalism and democracy. Foreign visitors toured the country, bringing new sounds and thoughts. While fearful Party elders launched fitful drives to curb these tendencies – targeting such dangerous Western signifiers as long hair and denim in the Campaign Against Spiritual Pollution – the thirst for novelty seemed unquenchable: 'Proper limits have to be exceeded in order to right a wrong, or else the wrong cannot be righted,' urged Gao Minglu, the editor of *Art* magazine, in a famous essay.

Wang feared it was too late to catch up; the Cultural Revolution had buried his youth. 'The more I studied, the more I hated them . . . I had an anger inside me and I wanted to learn the skills to express it,' he said.

He embarked on a concerted campaign of study: first appraising Bartók and Stravinsky, then exploring the Vienna twelve-tone techniques of Schoenberg, Webern and Berg, and finally discovering the work of Penderecki and other Communist Bloc composers. Even in his disciplined course he came across surprises. Minimalism had emerged in the United States around the time that Wang was first disgraced, but it remained unknown to him until the late eighties. He heard it out of time and place, and when he drew upon it his music did not sound like his sources but simply like himself. Like Haydn, speaking of his life at the court of Esterházy, he had been 'cut off from the world and forced to become original', an American admirer told me.

The rupture had forced creativity into bloom. People binged on the almost two decades of films, art and music denied to them. No longer did the Party decree that literature and art served the masses;

now they served modernisation. The Fifth Generation of film-makers, a series of outstanding directors, emerged: Zhang Yimou, Chen Kaige. The 85 New Wave in visual arts caused a sensation. At the conservatory in Beijing, Wang's students included a young man called Cui Jian, who would soon become China's 'godfather of rock'. And in the newly discovered discordance of Schoenberg and others Wang found a language to express his torment. His music became sharper, darker, more powerful. The dark beginnings of Symphonies 3 and 4, the blocks of sound he used to reach a climax – these were redolent of the Polish composers he had discovered. But Wang had taken what he wanted and fused it with musical intervals from those operas he had heard in Shanxi and with everything he had learned there: darkness, hypocrisy and evil.

Around him the political arguments were growing louder, more confident. Wang threw off his hard-learned caution and penned two essays criticising Maoism, the second of them as waves of student protestors occupied Tiananmen Square. His former student Cui Jian's song 'Nothing to My Name' became one of the movement's anthems.

Wang did not talk about that year, when the Party had bloodily suppressed the pro-democracy protests, killing hundreds and perhaps thousands. The massacre crushed political hopes and set back the burgeoning cultural developments. Controls were tightened. Official voices heralded a backlash against the New Wave of art. China was turning in on itself. The symphony Wang wrote that year is known only by its number, like many of his pieces. In the Cultural Revolution, nameless works were deeply suspect, seen as pretentious bourgeois indulgence; a good work should spell out its meaning to the masses. These days, perhaps leaving off the title was safer.

Wang seemed irritable as we spoke; perhaps it was the sensitivity of the period. He cut off my questions so that he could tell me about his millennium symphony. It was the second time he had raised it and I feared he had forgotten our last talk. But when I tried to say gently that we had discussed it, he grew agitated. I shifted back an inch or two.

He calmed and said, 'I didn't tell you everything last time.'

By 1999, Wang was enjoying official favour again. The darkness of the post-Tiananmen period had lifted as China embraced the free market. Officials were rushing to display their open-mindedness and innovation. Beijing's government commissioned two composers to write new works to mark the millennium: Wang was one of them. His fusion of Chinese tradition and Western contemporary music was no longer dangerously radical but impressively modern. When he thought of the years he had wasted, of the lost opportunities to learn and grow, it rankled. But he had a steady job, a flat in Beijing, a full-grown daughter. Most nights, at last, he slept through the small hours without thrashing around.

Now the authorities were to spend half a million yuan, around £50,000, to launch the finest work he had ever written. On an early morning in November, he stood in the rehearsal room, the Beijing Symphony Orchestra ready in front of him. The conductor had asked him to say a few words about Symphony No. 4. 'I thought it was a good opportunity to speak the truth,' Wang said.

He had turned over his thoughts for a moment, then begun in his stentorian voice: 'In the past century, there have been many important events that have happened: two world wars and the advance of technology. But to me those are not the most important things. The twentieth century was the century of communism. Many people pursued it – and then abandoned it.'

There was applause. But when he repeated his remarks at a later rehearsal, someone had come prepared. This time they would not need a confession: it was all on tape. They cancelled the concert. The conductor was ill, they said.

'No one came to me. No one invited me to concerts. There was no performance of my works. I became *persona non grata*,' he said. 'They simply ignored me. They froze me out. I was very anxious and depressed. I couldn't work at the conservatory or publish anything. I was furious. But I couldn't express my anger.' The methods were different, the punishment incomparably milder, but to Wang the impetus was identical: instantly recognisable from the Cultural Revolution.

The new cultural realm, high and low, was at once transformed and familiar. I had been struck by a postcard tucked into one of Wang's shelves: Audrey Hepburn in white Courrèges helmet and shades, in *How to Steal a Million*. The film was released in 1966, as Maoism soared to new heights. In the West, a universe away, it was the year of Twiggy and *Blow-Up*; of *Revolver*, *Pet Sounds* and *Blonde on Blonde*; of acid, Andy Warhol and Haight-Ashbury. In China, even three years after Mao's death, a magazine sparked a national controversy by printing a picture of Richard Chamberlain chastely kissing a co-star in a version of *Cinderella*: it was 'decadent, capitalist, an act meant to poison our youths,' one correspondent raged.

In the subsequent decades these worlds had collided and partially converged. Now cinemas could show a slick popcorn movie in which a young woman tried to figure out who had got her pregnant. The skyrocketing prices of Chinese contemporary art – and the vacuous, repetitive nature of much of it – suggested rampant commercialisation might be as great a threat as political constraint. Edgy novels tackled sex work and addiction. Armed police squads filmed themselves dancing in formation to trashy summer hits. But then a thirty-episode drama series was commissioned to celebrate

Jiao Yulu, a tireless official once lauded by Mao who had died of liver cancer and overwork. The Party interfered at the pettiest level. One director urged me to buy the bootleg version of his movie, since he had been required to make four hundred changes for the official release. Foreign film-makers were ordered to show China's skyscrapers, not its poverty. Domestic dramas were told to shun time-travel themes, a 'frivolous' approach to history. Adultery in shows was acceptable, but not if mistresses seemed happy. These edicts were a kind of muscle memory as much as a political decision. The good ended happily, and the bad unhappily: that was what art meant. But the orders were proliferating. Television stations were told to devote two months of prime time to 'patriotic' and 'anti-fascist' content around National Day. Revolution-themed shows were warned to draw a clear line between friend and foe. Little by little, the edges of the creative space were crumbling.

Wang's unplayed symphony had, in the end, received its premiere in Taiwan. The performance of the quartet I had seen was the first of his works that the Central Conservatory had hosted, more than thirteen years after his fall from grace. While his music had been performed around the world, in Rome, Rotterdam, Tokyo and Geneva, it was barely heard in China.

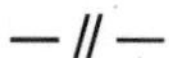

Most Cultural Revolution survivors had learned to bend with the will of the time; not only to do as they were told but to imply that doing so was their own idea. It was better – safer – to stay silent or lie. Wang still insisted on the truth in matters large and small. I brought him a strawberry tart from a new French patisserie one day, thinking that it might appeal to his cosmopolitan side. 'You bring me these things, but I don't like to eat them,' he told me, not unkindly. His honesty seemed an instinct rather than an ethos – a compulsion, not a decision.

Towards the end of that afternoon, his daughter stuck her head around the door. She was a composer too, the winner of awards he had already detailed, and lived in Germany; she had sent the Audrey Hepburn postcard. She had Wang's warmth, but a little more reserve, and when her father left the room she eyed me for a moment. She was my age; we lived thousands of miles from our parents, and worried for them; and perhaps because of all this I was waiting for her to say it. At last she did: 'I hope you'll . . . be careful with what he says.'

But it wasn't her story. Nor mine.

That morning I had read a fresh warning from a top official that culture should not only uphold socialist values but 'send constructive and positive messages' to the audience. Communism is utopian, a vote for the future: to see things darkly was subversive. Mao's vision of egalitarian chaos had been supplanted by Xi's Chinese dream: stable material prosperity and expansive national pride. But it was still about looking forward, never back, and focusing on the sunlight, not the shadows. China's art should still be red, bright and shining. Wang's was not, could not be. It lived in the shadow of the era that had made him. 'No one demands or asks that I do it, but I must tell the truth. The subject isn't finished.'

And yet Wang himself forged ahead. When he was angry or amused, it flashed across his features, chased away by another mood before it could settle. He was always looking for the next idea and adventure, something to learn or explore. He sought out new music and films. He enunciated the latest phrases gleaned from his English textbook. He would like a lady friend, he told me. But when it came to politics he could not or would not learn his lesson. His desire to be heard – to have his concertos and symphonies played; to have critics discuss his work; to teach the next generation – was subverted by his wish to express his real meanings. There was no way to say everything he needed to and still win the audience he wanted. He had found a voice, but he could not really use it. He could occupy the place he still hankered for, and enjoy prestige at home as a composer, but probably not if he made the music he really wanted to make, and certainly not if he said the things he really wanted to say. He was indignant, and perhaps a little baffled – how could he be good and not be heard? But he was not exactly surprised.

He seemed unusually buoyant at our last meeting. It was a while since I had seen him; he and his daughter had been travelling in Europe, around Austria and Poland. A musical tour, I surmised. What had he seen?

'Auschwitz!' he boomed, a wide smile on his face. I was startled into silence. But – Of course, I thought, after our goodbyes, as I shoved the steel door of his apartment block so that light spilled into the murky hall. How incredible, how remarkable it was to remember everything.

THREE

> Without the right to remember, there can be no freedom to forget.
>
> **Chang Ping**

On a rare blue-sky day, when the smog had receded past the Western Hills so that the whole city was crisp with promise, I climbed the steps of the National Museum. High overhead, the red flags blazed in the sun. The museum stands in Tiananmen Square, directly opposite the Great Hall of the People, where grand political ceremonies are held; across the way hangs the portrait of Mao, stretching 4.5 by 6 metres and reputedly 1.5 tonnes in weight. When his successors leave their red-walled compound and drive along the Avenue of Eternal Peace, they pass beneath his vigilant eye. He gazes over the soldiers and selfie-taking tourists, just as he oversaw the massed Red Guards, towards the mausoleum where his body now lies in a crystal sarcophagus.

The picture morphed through a few incarnations before Mao approved its final template at the height of the Cultural Revolution. Now it is replaced with an identical version each year, just before October's National Day celebrations. At least one spare is kept at the ready in case it is damaged, as in 1989, when dissidents pelted it with eggs (and paid with years in prison). Come what may, Mao continues to surveil his successors and his country. Most assume that the picture will hang there as long as the Party hangs on to power, so symbolic that the leadership would never dare remove it, though a friend once claimed to me that it shrank by an inch or so at each replacement. I was charmed by his confidence that Mao might be diminished slowly and steadily, until one day only a postage stamp would remain on the fortress wall. It seemed more than unlikely. Each time I passed, the mighty scale of the image startled me anew.

For centuries, this part of the city has been the political heart of the nation. The square lies in front of the Forbidden City, home of the emperors, on Beijing's north–south central axis. Mao both took up and transformed this geography. In imperial times the square had been a restricted space; now it became a public theatre, expressing as well as embodying power. Its size was quadrupled to 400,000 square metres, making it the world's largest city square, if still disappointingly modest to Mao – he had mooted a site that could hold a billion, far in excess of China's population at the time. The Great Hall of the People and what were then the twin Museums of the Chinese Revolution and Chinese History were completed in the same year, 1959, as part of a monumental building programme marking the Party's tenth year in power. It had established already that its rule depended not only on the promise of a better future, but also on a shared understanding of that pledge's contrast with former misery. So the grand museums were erected, and workers and peasants were encouraged to dwell on long-gone injustices in rituals of 'recalling past bitterness and cherishing present happiness'. The people were still developing their political consciousness. Sometimes they included the terrible famine just past in their list of miseries, but officials would quickly set them straight, reminding them that Past Bitterness meant the years before the Party came to power.

The vast columns of the museum thrust into the sky. When China rebuilt it, in the late 2000s, the architects were instructed to ensure it was larger than any other in the world. At almost 200,000 square metres, it has outgrown the Hermitage and boasts almost four times the floorspace of the Louvre when storage areas are included. It is an austere and imposing construction, asserting the builders' dominance and the visitors' insignificance. Much of modern Beijing is on this scale: six lanes of traffic circling huge featureless blocks that look still more brutal, as well as incongruous, when fake Chinese eaves perch on top. Nothing about the museum is human-sized. The ceilings are so high, the spaces so expansive, that weekend crowds look like model railway passengers clustering at a real station.

For Chinese people, Tiananmen Square is their history. It saw the nationalist student protests of the May Fourth Movement in 1919, Mao's proclamation of the founding of the People's Republic thirty years later, the mass rallies by Red Guards. Foreigners mainly associate it with the bloody crackdown on the protests which erupted here in 1989, attacking corruption and demanding reform and even democracy. When Chinese troops launched the final assault to clear the square, hundreds of soldiers poured in from behind the museum building. Turning its guns against its citizens finally demolished the Party's mandate: its claim to serve the people, already fatally undermined by the Cultural Revolution. Its rule now rests upon its promise of economic well-being and its restoration of national pride. The more conflicted and uncertain the former, with China's years of double-digit growth rates well behind it and the effects of rapacious capitalism glaring, the more essential the latter. Since 1989 the Party has redoubled its commitment to patriotic education, portraying the Communist triumph over foreign aggression. It has rewritten textbooks and opened a swathe of red history sites. Officials and schoolchildren are bussed to places such as Shaoshan, Mao's birthplace, and the former revolutionary base at Yan'an, where red tourism bolsters the local economy and fosters the national tale – business marching in step with the Communist

Party. I had become a connoisseur of such attractions, moving and heroically dull and plain bizarre, with their mixture of genuine historical drama, sloganeering, Mao souvenirs and features like the Irrigation Canal of Happiness.

Xi Jinping, born of the revolution, has embraced his party's heritage. His first Politburo Standing Committee, the top political body, was dominated by fellow 'princelings' born to famed revolutionary leaders. Their ascendancy echoed the 'bloodline theory' of the early Red Guards: that the children of the revolution's founders were uniquely placed to uphold their parents' legacy. 'If the father's a hero, the son is brave . . .'

Xi's first public act on assuming power was to escort the Standing Committee to the National Museum's landmark exhibition: *The Road to Rejuvenation*, conceived a few years earlier but now promoted from its more modest home in the Museum of Military Affairs. A photograph blazoned across state media showed the seven men posed with such exquisite awkwardness that they could have been on show themselves, as he acclaimed 'a retrospective on the Chinese nation, a celebration of its present and a declaration on its future'. At the heart of the narrative was China's Hundred Years of Humiliation at the hands of foreign bullies and its liberation by the Party. It was the story of the country's suffering through the Opium Wars and subsequent imperialist aggressions; of how China had been brought to its knees; and how, through the sacrifices of heroic Party members, it had thrown off its shackles and returned to glory. It set the theme of Xi's leadership: the Chinese dream of wealth and power. The last room portrayed both the glories and the comforts of modern China, from a space capsule for its taikonauts to a glass case of mobile phones. These were the rewards of socialism with Chinese characteristics, that splendid euphemism invented by Mao's successors, otherwise known as capitalism within a Leninist cage.

'History has proven that without the Communist Party of China, the People's Republic of China would never have come into being, nor would socialism with Chinese characteristics,' the exhibition concluded. 'Socialism is the only way to save China, and reform and opening up is the only way to develop China, develop socialism and develop Marxism.' Only communism, it seemed, could bring these consumer comforts. The last six decades had been blurred into one broad advance, the sharp and deadly political clashes reshaped into a gentler, happier tale of historical inevitability under the Party's benign leadership. It was not the historical inevitability of Marx, with the triumph of the proletariat; rather, the notion that authoritarian power had brought greatness to the Chinese nation again. It was no coincidence that the Museums of the Chinese Revolution and of Chinese History had been fused into a single National Museum. I advanced through the galleries: The Invasion of China by Imperialist Powers; The Struggle and the Awakening of the Chinese People; Searching for a New Path for the Chinese Revolution. A little girl in a Sunday-best frock fidgeted with an empty juice bottle as her mother lectured her on China's inability to fight off Japan: 'Why did it fail? Because of the Kuomintang . . .'

The exhibition spanned four giant halls, but there was one small – very small – section that I especially wanted to see: Setbacks and Progress in the Exploration of Socialist Construction. It daintily posed the question of how the Chinese people, under CCP leadership, 'overcame hardships', without, of course, elucidating those hardships, still less exploring the causes. It did not educate; it confirmed, discreetly, and to a very limited degree. Only if you already knew your history could you see what it deigned to acknowledge. A glass case held three documents dated 1961, including one captioned: *Liu Shaoqi's notes from a meeting held during his investigations in Changsha and Ningxiang, Hunan.* This was part of his research into the Great Famine, and it helped to end the disaster, but it paved the way to his own death in the Cultural Revolution, thanks to a vengeful Mao.

There was little more on this second great catastrophe of the era. An exhibition which made space for two dozen different mobile phones could find only a dingy corner for the Cultural Revolution; and it dared not show the catastrophe itself, only its aftermath. High on the wall was a photo of Mao's heir, Hua Guofeng, and other leaders, following the Gang of Four's fall, and another of joyful youths massing in the square to celebrate the purge.

— // —

The cumulative forgetting had become an artefact: something to be inspected in the cold light of day. But it's quite a thing to watch this rewriting in action. At times it happened in the margins of official pronouncements – blink and you missed it. At other times the erasures and recompositions were unignorable. Occasionally they were genuinely shocking. Not long after my arrival in China a terrible earthquake struck Sichuan, in the country's south-west; ninety thousand people died. Too many of them were children entombed in schools. In the first town I reached, I took those deaths for a unique tragedy. That was naive; they were everywhere. The pupils lay upon concrete ping-pong tables in a playground, or upon the street, where parents eased them tenderly into body bags. At one school the earth was still choked with corpses, their little faces thick with dust; one boy's hand was aloft in the rubble, as if raised in a question. The force of the quake had uprooted that town, but in other places schools had crumbled while the buildings around them – the police stations, the Party offices – stood firm. Seven thousand classrooms had collapsed across the province. The parents believed that corrupt and negligent local officials had cut corners, signing their children's death warrants. Their bitter questions resonated throughout China, even in state newspapers. Experts came forward to condemn poor construction. The injustice was so palpable that the government took the rare step of promising an inquiry.

But within weeks, the censors had ordered the media to stop reporting on the subject. Within a month, police were dragging parents from protests and officials had bulldozed the wreckage; there was nothing left to examine. Within a year, at least three activists who tried to help families had been detained or jailed, and the artist Ai Weiwei, who had tried to compile a list of the dead, had emergency brain surgery shortly after he was punched in the head by police. By then his researchers, despite repeated detentions, had amassed over 5,200 names. But when I returned to one of the towns, the parents who had been so anxious to talk were now too scared; plain-clothes police were watching the site and their homes. Those who did agree to speak met me in secret.

The only memories allowed of the earthquake were of heroism. I had watched firefighters risk their own lives to rescue people from sagging buildings; I had seen soldiers march into treacherous valleys; I had heard dazed and hungry survivors turn down food in case those further into the quake zone needed it more. But there was something sickening and almost hysterical in state television's constant invocation of glory in the midst of despair. The endless parade of glossy images – the rescue teams wiping sweat from their brows, the officials donating wages on stage – all this, presented over and over, denied the suffering that saturated the land.

The cruelty with which the parents were treated was flagrant. It was only afterwards that the sheer committed bureaucratic effort really struck me. The drudgery. The months spent monitoring traumatised families, mostly too numb and despairing to cause any kind of trouble. The censorship which stamped out even muted comment. The effort which could have driven an investigation to prevent future tragedy had been invested instead in erasing discussion. Remembering, when officials didn't want you to, was hard. It demanded guts and persistence. But forgetting was hard work as well, and there was so much of it to do. Every year the list got longer. Beijing's watchword was maintaining stability, and its generally good support from the public did not ease its watchfulness. It constantly assessed the mood of the people and granted some of what they wished for or needed – electricity in villages or clean air in cities – albeit usually belatedly, and without acknowledging such demands as legitimate. It could be unexpectedly flexible, as in its adoption of market economics. Yet politically it remained entirely rigid. Even when it judged it could tolerate changes, it made clear that it was bestowing them as gifts, and it regarded many apparently innocuous matters as threatening to its bottom line.

Though its repertoire extended beyond repression and propaganda, it depended upon them. Amnesia was the bedrock, and maintaining it took exertion, thoroughness and discipline. If tens of millions had starved in a famine, you shuttered the archives for decades. If your smart new trains crashed, you warned off your reporters. If you imprisoned a dissident, you pressured his wife so she would not talk; and then you harassed the relatives who spoke out about their treatment. You scrubbed web pages and blocked foreign broadcasts. You kept watch every minute of every hour of every day. You did it for one person, or a family, or a village. And then, as in 1989, you had to do it for millions: erase a city-full, a country-full of memory. You had to battle not just stray thoughts, the angles and caches of each mind, but a collective experience. You had to isolate it; fence it; zero in, eradicate and replace it. For the most part, it worked. Only a fringe of a fringe, among friends, discussed 1989 and the killings. And yet you could never relax. Bao Tong, the most senior official jailed for sympathy to the protestors, once told me that six undercover cops still followed him each time he left his apartment: 'Two on foot; two in a car, in case I catch a taxi; two on motorbikes, in case their car gets caught at traffic lights.' By this time he was an octogenarian and any trace of liberal instincts in the leadership had long since been eradicated. But you couldn't take any chances. When the anniversary rolled around, you had to redouble your efforts. Your police escorted pensioners away lest they try to mourn their children in public. Your security agents interrupted private dinners and barred the doors of academics. Your censors went into overdrive, deleting and blocking sensitive words from websites or social media: 'tank' and 'massacre' and 'turmoil', then 'mourn' and 'candle' and 'memory', then even 'sensitive word', and 'person', and finally 'yesterday', 'today' and 'tomorrow' – scissoring until there seemed nothing but holes, holes which swallowed people and time and the very words 'never forget'. It meant persuading people that all of these things were their own omissions, of their own volition; that there was nothing to see. It meant finding something else to fill the gaps. It meant doing all of this again and again. Liberty is not the only thing you pay for in eternal vigilance.

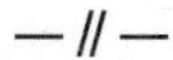

History, in China, sometimes feels like a war. Its use is woven deeply into the culture. Each dynasty chronicled the one it had supplanted, and these annals functioned as a moral primer rather than merely an archive: the eleventh-century history of China compiled by the scholar-official Sima Guang, at the emperor's command, is titled *A Comprehensive Mirror in Aid of Governance*. 'For Chinese people, history is our religion,' the intellectual Hu Ping has argued. 'We don't have a supernatural standard of right and wrong, good and bad, so we view History as the ultimate judge.'

The Party has finessed this tradition. It sees history not as a record, still less a debate, but a tool. It can be adjusted as necessary yet appears solid and immutable: today's imperatives seem graven in stone, today's facts the outcome of a logical, inexorable process. Life is as it is meant to be. China's five thousand years of civilisation brought us here, to a prosperous country, under the Party, reasserting its rightful place in the world. The bronze vessels in the National Museum's basement paved the way for the Communist pamphlets and flags shown a couple of floors above them, and the Audis and iPads in the world outside. The contingencies and contradictions of the actual past are irrelevant. The truth is what the Party says, it is what the Party chooses to remember, and the less plausible the thesis, in fact, the more clearly it asserts the Party's omnipotence. Brazenness is its own reward. (The Party is not the first to realise this: the *Records of the Grand Historian*, from the first century BC, describe an ambitious Qin dynasty eunuch presenting a deer and calling it a horse, to find out which officials would obey without question. Some were quick to agree with him; he had the others executed.) When China bid for the 2022 Winter Olympics it described an opening ceremony inspired by the Great Wall: a place 'where different cultures of China met and integrated . . . a symbol of the Chinese people's pursuit of peace'. The world's longest and most famous defensive structure, built to keep out the barbarians, had been reinvented, without embarrassment, as the emblem of international friendship. Thus history made China the rightful host; and hosting the Games would burnish this history, showing its citizens a glorious nation respected by the world.

To the outsider, the ceaseless, almost neurotic repetition of China's five millennia of history only betrays its ruptures and discontinuities. ('The empire, long divided, must unite,' begins one of its greatest novels, *Romance of the Three Kingdoms*. 'Long united, must divide. Thus it has ever been.') But the Party has erased the disasters that Mao brought on the nation and emphasised those wrought by foreigners. When protests broke out at the Japanese embassy in 2012, over contested islands in the East China Sea, police marshalled demonstrators instead of arresting them – a tactic they had also employed in previous nationalist unrest. I watched the marchers arrive on buses, complete a circuit or two past the building and reboard their vehicles. Some waved placards of Mao. Soon each day brought a news story on wartime atrocities, with archives releasing thousands of documents and state media reinterviewing survivors. Xi instituted Nanjing Massacre Remembrance Day, commemorating the hundreds of thousands of civilians who died in the brutal invasion of the city. There was no doubt that anti-Japanese sentiment was real, built upon horrific war crimes and stoked by the hawkishness of right-wing Japanese politicians and the denials, evasions and provocations of its nationalists. But Chinese authorities fed it. Critics pointed to the hypocrisy of expanding upon foreign crimes while ignoring China's often deadlier domestic catastrophes. It was evidently convenient for the Party. But perhaps the people needed it too – to have a trauma, if not always their trauma, recognised. In some way, these externally imposed disasters and humiliations also represented deeper shames.

No country faces its past honestly, and some in China have asked why the West was transfixed by the Maoist trauma recorded in *Wild Swans* when it appeared uninterested in slave narratives. America's self-image as a beacon of democracy is undimmed by its cosying up to dictators, plots to oust or kill elected leaders, and backing of murderous anti-communist purges. The 'shining city on a hill' prefers not to inspect the bedrock of its modern wealth and freedom:

the extermination of Native Americans and enslavement of Africans. More Britons believe the empire was a source of pride than shame; a benevolent institution, not created at gunpoint to enrich ourselves but rolled out to bring railways, cricket and Shakespeare to the globe's four corners. My years of schooling taught me all but nothing about the forces that created modern Britain, and our island nation's destructive impact, including the crippling Opium Wars waged on China over our right to peddle drugs. As children we learned more about the abolition of slavery than about the trade which we had dominated, and nothing of the lavish compensation paid to owners. We weren't told that, by then, our country's wealth and fortune had already been built on the bones of slaves. When we looked at London's broad stone facades and glassy skyscrapers and expensive restaurants, we didn't see that the city was built on empire, built on blood, built on the exploitation of nations that had never called the shots.

The West didn't consciously conceal as China did; in its arrogance, it rarely noticed there was something to forget. We had often preferred to export our greatest sadism, and to allow others to enrich us by means we never questioned or recognised. Most of us didn't participate in cruelty – but we didn't need to do so. That was a luxury the Chinese never enjoyed. The Cultural Revolution happened *here*, not *there*. The victims were not strangers in a far-off land but friends who died in front of you. We had chosen not to look, but the Chinese had to pretend they had not seen, a far harder task. In Britain, convenience, implicit bias and power differentials were enough to produce the distortions and erasures. In China, explicit orders and self-censorship did the work. In Britain, universities and the state broadcaster would pay you to dissect imperialism's inequities. In China, challenging the party-state's version of affairs could end your career or freedom.

The Cultural Revolution was not a totally forbidden subject, as discussion of the 1989 crackdown was. People found spaces in which they could operate by picking their times, shunning the spotlight, bending the rules and having the right connections. Octogenarians retired from state media had created *Annals of the Yellow Emperor*, a quaint, antique-sounding title for a magazine which painstakingly investigated some of China's most sensitive episodes. The haziness of the line between forbidden and permitted was partly a by-product of China's size and the multiple levels of bureaucracy. But it was also deliberate. While some were adept at exploiting grey areas, many shrank back further. It was simply easier and more efficient to make people censor themselves; after a while they often forgot they were doing so. 'It's not like foreigners think – we can talk about anything,' young people sometimes assured me. And if you asked them whether that was really true – could you talk about the 1989 crackdown on the radio? Print an article on princeling corruption? Criticise Mao on a TV show? – they stared at your stupidity. Obviously, you could not talk about *that*.

Blur the boundaries and you could also move them without acknowledging the shift. In some ways the Cultural Revolution had become less risky territory. Online discussion proliferated. One professor, though barred from launching a course called 'The Cultural Revolution', won approval by simply retitling it 'Chinese Culture, 1966–1976'. But in most ways it had become harder to talk about. The amnesia about the Cultural Revolution is more recent than it seems. In its immediate aftermath, a flood of memoirs and novels had laid bare trauma and oppression, handily confirming the wisdom of the Party's turn from Mao to market under Deng Xiaoping. Then, in the early eighties, a campaign against bourgeois liberalism began to target such 'scar literature'. In 1988 a regulation warned that, 'from now on and for quite some time, publishing firms should not plan the publication of dictionaries or other handbooks about the "Great Cultural Revolution".' In 1996 researchers held a symposium on the anniversary; ten years later they were warned off. In 2000 Song Yongyi, a repentant Red Guard turned historian, was held for more than five months due to his work, despite his American citizenship. And in 2013 Xi Jinping would issue his warning against 'historical nihilism'.

'How fortunate we are that history is decided by the people,' Liu Shaoqi told his wife as the Red Guards parted them forever. (Four years later, when the couple's children dared at last to ask if they could see their parents, Mao would respond: 'Their father is dead. They can see their mother.' Liu had died in squalor in his cell, of untreated pneumonia.) In fact, the public have never had their say, though the Party rehabilitated Liu, years after his death and Mao's; later still, Xi Jinping would hail him as a 'glorious model' of 'high morality'. It is The People's History, not the people's history, just as it is The People's Republic. This is not exactly disingenuity or deceit on the part of China's rulers. The Party and the People must exist in spiritual unity; the Party is of and for the People. Its duty is to lead them to correct understanding: how the country should be run, how to make sense of the past. If it is to serve them, it must shape them first.

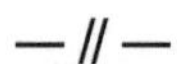

The official Party verdict on the Cultural Revolution called it a catastrophe, which isn't surprising. By the time it was formulated, Deng Xiaoping was in charge, having supplanted Hua Guofeng, who in turn had seen off the Gang of Four – Mao's widow Jiang Qing and her leftist cronies. Deng had been purged not once but twice, and his son has used a wheelchair since 'falling' from a third-floor window while imprisoned by Red Guards. But Deng didn't want to brood on what had happened; he aimed to put it in the past. The Party's conclusion is not included in the National Museum's exhibition, and does not appear in textbooks. It was designed not just to show the worst was over but to draw a line under the subject for good: 'The aim of summarising the past is to lead people to unite and look ahead,' Deng instructed those drafting the judgement. Remembering correctly would allow them to forget.

The verdict, redrafted multiple times and toned down heavily in the process, was one small passage in a much longer narrative of China's triumph under the Communist Party. It acknowledged that the events had caused 'the most severe setback and the heaviest losses suffered by the Party, the country and the people since the founding of the People's Republic'. Mao had led it, yet its principles were 'obviously inconsistent' with Mao Zedong Thought, which still guided the country. It was 'initiated by a leader labouring under a misapprehension and capitalised on by counter-revolutionary cliques'. *Labouring under a misapprehension.* It was worse than a crime, then; it was a mistake. His errors were acknowledged but could not be dwelled upon. Conventional wisdom has it that the Party had no other way to square this circle: Mao was both Lenin and Stalin. Chinese communism's triumphs and disasters cannot be separated; he stands for both and still commands love and respect from many. To cut him off would saw away the roots which anchor the Party's power, as well as raising dangerous questions about other leaders' failure to stop him.

Cloaking the Party in Mao's aura veiled its rejection of its past and its adoption of the things it once sought to destroy. Instead of acknowledging its turn to the market, the Party proceeded as though nothing had happened. Deng said his reforms were upholding Mao Zedong Thought, and he borrowed words from Mao himself:

seeking truth from facts. But his use of the maxim, unremarkable as it sounded to outsiders, was heroically un-Maoist: it was the promise of pragmatism, a rejection of the idea that ideas themselves could change the world. The Party pulled a similar trick in putting Mao on the banknotes circulating in a system he would have despised, and in leaving his portrait at Tiananmen. It appeared to hold him close as it backed away – or perhaps so that it could. He was kept in place first by Deng, one of the many who suffered at his hands, and now by the children of his victims: most obviously, Xi. Mao's preservation, psychically and even physically, made sense in terms of the Party's own past: the Lenin/Stalin dilemma. But it addressed a larger problem too. Allowing people to judge their history acknowledges their right to judge things in general. Permit them to repudiate Mao, and they may repudiate you. Let them write history and they will write the story that they know best: their own.

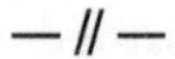

A few months after my visit to the National Museum, on an early morning in Shantou, a quiet port in the southern province of Guangdong, I hailed a cab and set off for the still quieter district of Chenghai. It lay on the very fringes of the city, almost an hour away: through the sprawl of billboards and across a wide river; past the chaos of shopfronts jammed with pipes, joints and drills. The traffic had already thinned when the taxi turned off the main road by a jumble of warehouses, heading towards Tayuan, Pagoda Park. I knew my destination stood towards the very top of the hill, but there was no sign of it on the map at the entrance. Buttoning my coat against the drizzle, I began the steep climb up the winding path, past palm and glossy banana trees. Birds fluted and twittered down in the ravine, where morning glory tangled over the bushes; the throaty curdle of a rooster sounded from somewhere up the slope. At the rebuilt Ancient Temple, a man chatted loudly on his mobile over chanting monks. The rest of the park was deserted. The pedalos on the lake were chained up, eating places and amusement stalls shuttered. At a shooting booth, toys suffocated in sagging plastic bags. Finally, only partially obscured by a white plastic sign for one of the restaurants, I found a monument. Three slender stone pillars read:

It is fortunate that Tayuan could bury these long bones here to inspire and teach descendants about the ruthless history.

During chaotic times, heroes shed tears and blood and suffered here.

The blood turned this area red.

Close by, a handful of headstones poked out, topped by scarlet stars. Dozens more were scattered across the hillside, a few almost entirely overgrown. Yet someone remembered. Wilted bouquets, flattened by rain, lay in front of one stone. A rusting can holding skeletal joss sticks sat before another. These mass graves held the victims of factional fighting, and Peng Qi'an should have lain in one. Peng, an official, was placed on a death list for reasons he never fully understood, then spared for reasons which remained as obscure. Friends had died; his brother was killed. Years later, walking on Pagoda Mountain, haunted by the bodies beneath the soil, he asked himself what could – what must – be done to prevent another catastrophe.

Across the shattered nation the question tormented survivors. The writer Ba Jin was the first to call for a Cultural Revolution museum, in the 1980s. He had been persecuted for years, and his wife was beaten by Red Guards, then denied the cancer treatment which might have saved her. He believed a museum would force everyone to remember, to confront their own behaviour and to search their conscience. To build one, he added, 'is not the business of any one person in particular: it is the responsibility of all . . . so our descendants, generation after generation, will learn the painful lessons of these ten years. "Let history not be repeated" must not be an empty phrase.'

Others soon echoed his demand. It was symbolic as much as literal; authorities were never likely to comply. People were permitted to glance at the subject, but not to focus upon it. Once made, the official verdict was rarely recalled. Like many of the boldest initiatives in China, the Shantou museum required the connections born of years on the inside of the system, the sympathy of some in authority, and luck.

By the late 1980s, Peng had risen to become the city's deputy mayor, and had found other veterans who supported his plans. Guangdong was known for its relative open-mindedness; it was where Deng launched economic reforms. But Peng's ambitions for a museum had run into problems from the first. The district government rejected his proposal; then city and provincial governments stalled, too wary to either support or refuse. In the end, the province's former top leader gave Peng his tacit backing. Shantou's mayor had granted some funds and among the donors was Li Ka-shing, a Hong Kong tycoon with close ties to Beijing. Almost four decades after the disaster unfolded, Peng finally opened his museum. Beijing, as both the country's capital and the birthplace of the Cultural Revolution, would have been the obvious site for the institution Ba Jin had demanded. Yet the city, which had museums dedicated to socks, eunuchs, tap water and goldfish, had no space for it. Only 1,000 kilometres away, far from attention or passing traffic, could it set down roots.

The museum itself was just a small part of Peng's memorial park. Statues and stone tablets interspersed the graves. Plaques listed counter-revolutionary offences – mostly thoughtcrimes such as False Marxism – and the names of thousands of victims. Halfway up the hillside the land flattened out into a giant square. On the long wall ahead of me, calligraphed characters read: *Using history as a mirror, never let the tragedy of the Cultural Revolution happen again.* Beneath them, images of Deng and Mao flanked the official verdict on the decade: *History has clearly decided. The Great Cultural Revolution was a mistake, put in motion by leaders, used by counter-revolutionary groups for their interests, causing turmoil that brought a serious disaster to the Party, the country and the people.* At each end stood a little statue – one black, one white – of a painted Persian cat playing with a ball, as stone lions might have guarded a gate. It was an oddly playful reference to the maxim often attributed to Deng: that he didn't care about the colour of a cat, as long as it caught mice.

I didn't have time to study the wall any further. As I crossed the square, a man bolted from his chair beside a snack booth and snatched up his phone. I increased my pace, heading straight for the path up the hill, but there were too many stairs. By the time I reached the museum, breathless, the screen door was locked and a sign outside apologised for its closure for safety maintenance. Pass a building site in a third-tier city or drive upon a provincial road and China's commitment to such concerns might look casual. But try to visit an activist or report on a sensitive event or place and its anxiety for your well-being was humbling.

It was too dim to see much through the windows, but I glimpsed a few images engraved in black granite: jeering crowds and desperate victims, heads bowed. The museum didn't have much of a collection anyway; its existence was what mattered. As I circled the building, two more polo-shirted men appeared. Undercover cops in

China often came dressed for the golf course, and these men began photographing me without even perfunctory attempts to conceal it. They hustled behind me down the hillside, halting each time I paused to inspect a statue or a plaque. I took pictures of the memorials. They took pictures of me. I smiled and held up my phone to reciprocate, then thought better; I wanted to hang on to my shots of the graves. They scowled and kept snapping.

When I had finally retraced my steps, all the way to the car park at the entrance, I clocked the larger group of men now clustered by the ticket booth. They watched me climb into the taxi, and one leaned into a car as we drove away, honking the horn to tell colleagues up the hill that they had seen me off. It had a jaunty rhythm and he grinned at me, not maliciously, but with the frank pleasure of an opponent who had triumphed in a fair fight.

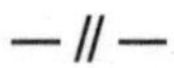

My failure to visit the museum shouldn't have surprised me. Today's 'maintenance' had been hastily scheduled; the outer door was still open when I arrived. But despite the museum's dearth of visitors, it was perfectly possible, even probable, that authorities watched it round the clock. I knew that it was often closed on the sensitive dates in China's calendar, such as the big annual political meetings, or anniversaries of unwelcome events. The museum's memorial service each August attracted a phalanx of plain-clothes police as well as survivors, the grieving and sympathisers.

The Party had seen off all challenges. It had cajoled or coerced the vast majority into at least tolerating its rule, and often actively supporting it; people joked that if it allowed real elections, it would win by a landslide. Yet its paranoia was astonishing. The lesson it had drawn from 1989 was to stamp out any sign of trouble at root, or, better still, pre-empt it entirely. When the museum in Shantou first opened, in 2005, it attracted up to a thousand people a day, an intriguing hint at a public appetite for examining the past. So Chinese media were ordered to stop reporting on it. Visitors slowed to a trickle. The museum was now unsignposted, unknown and unloved, but they still couldn't be too careful.

Peng, its founder, had appeared undaunted by all the restrictions, telling a reporter that he did not need to care if he was punished. It sounded less like bravado from a man who had outlived his death sentence by four decades. But by the time I visited, the museum was under increased scrutiny again. The introduction I had arranged fell through at the last minute, and he demurred when I called to ask for an interview. I braved a downpour to try him in person, water pooling in my shoes as I crossed the brimming gutters and dashed into his apartment block. Peng was at home, but declined to speak to me; an elderly lady shuttled between us, carrying my requests and his refusals. At last the door closed. My earlier call to him might have alerted security services to my museum visit; equally, his refusal now might have been sparked by the visit, and a resulting warning. He had reason to be cautious. If the museum raised its profile, as some volunteers had urged, it was certain to be shut down. Yet if no one knew of the museum, its existence was pointless; it had no way to prevent another disaster. All he could do was hope that one day, years or decades down the line, the mood might relax again.

But a few months after Xi's visit to the National Museum, details of a new internal communiqué were leaked. Document Number Nine urged cadres to guard against seven perils that had 'seriously eroded' the Party. They became known unofficially as the 'Seven Nos'. Enumerating policies went back a long way in Chinese history, but the Party seemed to have a particular attachment to the practice. Numbers gave an air of scientific exactitude to conclusions and cloaked the Party's zig-zag course with an air of continuity, even certainty: the Two Whatevers (a personal favourite), the Three Represents, the Four Comprehensives or the Eight Honours And Eight Shames. Many of the Seven Nos were predictable: old foes of the Party such as civil society, constitutionalism and promoting the West's idea of journalism. The most singular was the promotion of 'historical nihilism', a phrase that had come into favour after the Party crushed the Tiananmen protests but was then used more sparingly until Xi adopted it.

'Historical nihilism seeks to fundamentally undermine the CCP's historical purpose, which is tantamount to denying the legitimacy of the CCP's long-term dominance,' warned the document. Nihilism meant, for example, suggesting that China need not have taken the socialist path, or repudiating the 'accepted conclusions' on events and figures from the past. More remarkably, it included arguing that the periods before and after reform and opening were distinct. There was no difference between Maoist totalitarianism and the embrace of individualism and the market. There were no mistakes, no diversions, no distractions – only seamless progress towards the future. Like China's attachment to its boast of five thousand years of history, it betrayed the underlying anxiety. Only a nation that had seen such fractures could be so anxious to assert that there had been, in fact, no change at all.

The Party was never complacent. Its own triumph had been so unlikely that it kept a jealous watch for rivals. The fall of the Berlin Wall – and ensuing collapse of the Soviet Union – came just a few months after the Tiananmen protests had shaken the party-state to its core. The Party had spent years poring over the death of its patron and brother: an epidemiologist anxious to establish both symptoms and cure. It concluded that the ideological thaw had proved fatal. But now Xi went further, in an echo of Mao's anger at Khrushchev's denunciation of Stalin. Historical nihilism meant dismissing the history of the Soviet Union, of not only Lenin but also Stalin 'and everything else', the document said helpfully. It 'confuses our thought and undermines the Party's organisations on all levels'.

Soon afterwards, researchers noticed that archives were imposing new restrictions on access or shuttering large sections. A year or two later, in a single sweep, more than a hundred social media accounts were closed for spreading distorted views of history. A commentary in the official Party mouthpiece, the *People's Daily*, warned of the serious consequences of 'the haphazard assembling of historical facts in a far-fetched manner, or their presentation in a one-sided or slanted manner . . . With time, falsehood became truth.' The Party's discipline inspectors accused its own history office of 'a weak sense of responsibility' in opposing nihilism.

In Shantou, Peng cancelled the commemoration service. When I rang, months later, asking for an interview again, he was polite but firm. I was welcome to visit Pagoda Mountain, but he rarely went there these days. He was too old, and not interested in discussing it any more. I had come too late.

FOUR

> So our memory is the only help that is left to them . . . If every deceased person is like someone who was murdered by the living, so he is also like someone whose life they must save, without knowing whether the effort will survive.
>
> **Theodor Adorno**

Long before Ba Jin conceived of a museum, Wang Jingyao prepared for one. He saved everything. His wife's bloody clothes were folded in a suitcase, hidden beneath the bed. Her futile plea for help from officials was cached in a cavity behind the bricks. He hoped that one day she would be vindicated, that these things might be displayed, that the public would see the evidence. When everyone else was busy forgetting, Wang had persisted in remembering – secretly, carefully, stubbornly.

Yu Xiangzhen had told me of Wang. When I mentioned the painter's show, before I could ask her about the picture of herself as a teenager, she said: 'The first painting was of Wang Jingyao and Bian Zhongyun. You walked in and saw them, straight ahead of you. To tell the truth, the exhibition shocked me, especially when I saw that portrait. The death of Teacher Bian is a marker in history; the marker of our generation's cruelty.'

Teacher Bian was Beijing's first victim, battered to death by her pupils in the early days of Red August. Her husband, Wang, was a historian, and though he could not protest her death he documented it. He bought a camera the next morning, a little black and aluminium Shanghai 202. Here's a family portrait. The four children are smart enough for a studio, with faces scrubbed, the elder girls in plaits and bunches. Their father has arranged them: they're lined up by size, Von Trapp style, behind the battered body of the woman who once fed and soothed them. Here are Bian's daughters again, with a basin, washing her corpse: its swollen face, its bruises, the holes torn by nails. Here are the posters hounding Bian, pinned up around their rooms. The Red Guards broke in days before they killed her – ransacked the place, even pulled up the floorboards, burned books and smashed up the family's things. They hung the place with hatred; Wang captured every slur. There are caricatures of Bian as a sweaty, fearful pig. The angry scrawls of big-character posters, attacking her as a demon and bitch, boasting of the torment forced on her already:

> **Behave! Or we'll teach you how to!**
>
> **At the struggle meeting you trembled like a leaf . . . doused in water, mud in your mouth . . .**
>
> **Carry on running roughshod over the workers and we'll whip your dog hide, rip out your dog heart, lop off your dog head.**

Wang's rage didn't burn. It was hard, like a diamond. It had rigour: he captured everything. He photographed the smoke from the crematorium chimney. He rigged up a secret shrine for her ashes. Closed, it looked like an ordinary bookcase. When he and the children were alone, they left it open, keeping watch over her.

She had seen it all coming. The violence did not explode. It built. It had begun with that first big-character poster and its broadcast on Mao's orders. The next day, pupils at the girls' school attached to Beijing Normal University scrawled their own attack on the management. The prestigious institution was packed with the children of senior leaders. Bian was vice-principal, handling discipline – a tough, even formidable figure. Though a party veteran, her position, reputation and background as the daughter of a banker marked her as a target; an acquaintance who had taken against her was quick to fan the flames. She 'opposed the Party's class road'. (She had rejected a leader's daughter who didn't meet admission criteria.) She 'opposed Chairman Mao'. (A student asked whether they should rescue his portrait before fleeing the school in an emergency, and, though prudent enough not to answer directly, she replied that they should leave quickly.) She had, it was claimed absurdly, been involved in an attempted coup of the Beijing municipal committee.

Girls dragged her onto a stage in shackles and forced her to kneel while they kicked and struck her, beating her with iron-banded wooden rifles used for drilling. When she fell they hauled her up by her hair and began again. They trashed her flat and blanketed it with the posters: 'Don't dream you are free at home!' Officials ignored Bian's plea for help, and Wang began to understand that there was no escape: nowhere to go, no one else to beg. 'Beating someone like me to death is just like killing a dog,' Bian told him. One morning, she woke earlier than usual. She shook hands with Wang, as though they were strangers; then she went to work.

Practice had perfected the rituals of abuse. The girls at the school poured ink over victims and forced them to chant as they paraded: 'I am a capitalist roader! I am a counter-revolutionary revisionist! I deserve the beatings! I am damned to death!' They hit them each time their voices dropped or broke. They drove them into the centre of the playground. They forced them to kneel in the blistering sun, and to carry large baskets laden with earth. When Bian fell they trampled her in their heavy army boots. Someone yelled for clubs. They beat one teacher till her pelvis fractured; they hit another till his shirt was soaked in blood. They were not finished with Bian. They dragged her to clean the toilets. A staff member saw her there, stained and unsteady, trying to brace herself against the wall but sliding down to the floor.

'You fake death! You did that already!' a girl screamed. Her companions tried to make Bian drink from the filthy mop. They were laughing. They ordered the man from the toilets to load her onto a rubbish cart outside. She lay, covered in blood and dirt, with traces of foam at her mouth. The heat was unbearable, too intense to linger; the teenagers drifted away. A kernel of anxiety was forming, perhaps, or simply boredom. Some of them went to buy ice lollies.

The hospital was metres away, but it was hours before students and a teacher took Bian across the street. The doctor was too frightened to help a counter-revolutionary. Treatment, when it began, was too late. Wang arrived later still. Perhaps shock cauterised his grief and rage: he took in the blood, her swollen face, the puncture wounds from nailed clubs. When he realised that Bian had soiled herself, he finally lost control.

At school the next day, a fourteen-year-old pupil, Wang Youqin, listened as a student leader claimed the loudspeaker and announced Bian's death: 'She died. It is over.' There was a short silence in the classroom and someone changed the subject, 'as if Bian had been a dream and her being beaten to death was no big deal, not even worth discussing'.

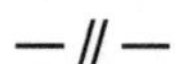

Youqin waited for someone to speak – for days, then months, then years. She wrote diaries, then burned them, frightened they might be found. When the Cultural Revolution was over she wrote it all down again. She had seen the gang forcing teachers to their knees.

She had heard one yell to another to fetch clubs. She had seen the stains and bloody handprints. 'I thought my job was to tell *my* story – what I saw. I thought other people would write the rest. China has such a long history of history. We have chronicles. I'm not a confident person. So many smart, well-educated people – why me? But even twenty years later, in 1986, they still hadn't done it.'

When the Cultural Revolution ended, some were jailed for its murderous violence. But the early Red Guards never faced trial for cases such as Teacher Bian's death, probably because of their connections. With the help of Wang Jingyao and other witnesses, Youqin began to piece together events. Her timing was both good and bad. She started her research in the flood of 'scar literature' in the Cultural Revolution's immediate aftermath. But by the time she had finished, the experiment was over. Her work was only publishable in Hong Kong. She moved to the United States to study. 'I started to write, but I never thought I'd do something on such a scale. And then I planned to finish it. I'm still doing it.'

She amassed more names: more murders, more suicides. In 2000 she started a website, Chinese Memorial, naming the dead. Few in China had access to the internet, but every few days an airmail arrived with details of another victim. Authorities blocked her site, yet the names kept coming from those still mourning and those seeking only to bear witness. The list grew to dozens, then hundreds. On official figures, more than 1,770 people died in Beijing alone in Red August; the true toll is probably far higher.

'Without the victims, the Cultural Revolution becomes just a radical idealistic young people's movement, like France in 1968,' she said. Without the victims, Mao's decision was merely an error, not a crime.

Youqin was sixty-two now, half auntie, half teenager in a shapeless cotton dress and perpetual flurry of papers and indignation. She spoke fast, as though expecting to lose my attention before the end of the sentence. She was scrabbling through creased foolscap sheets, covered in tiny print and biro annotations, looking for information and numbers to share. With fitful, earnest hospitality, she had urged coffee and a tour on me. She was a language teacher these days, back to teach a summer course for a US university. It was housed high in a gleaming new tower; the glass doors were smudgeless, the carpets immaculate. We looked down at the busy road below, only faintly hazed today. We were a long way from the Beijing she grew up in.

We made our way back to her office, sat down. She would have been an engineer without the Cultural Revolution, she thought – she spoke wistfully of equations. Maths: 'So beautiful. So logical, so reasonable, so wonderful.' But after everything that had happened, she thought about what she should have learned, and chose humanities. Still: 'Facts first. Maybe we don't need very complicated theories.'

The facts. There were, for a start, the school's other deaths. Three teachers who were hounded and leaped from buildings; another forced into heavy labour – he lay down and never got up again. A teenage waitress from a nearby restaurant, tied to a pillar and beaten to death, probably for supposed promiscuity: 'They killed a girl! Just eighteen years old! Just from a working-class family! A medic checked the girl's eyes and said: "She's dead." Then they untied the ropes.'

And there were the others across the city, and in Nanjing, and Shanghai, and Luoyang: 'This woman was an elementary school principal. All the government gave her family was 420 yuan (£50) . . . This dead man had six children. They gave the son a letter to collect the body, but that night Red Guards killed two people so he didn't dare go to get it . . . This one, he had a mental illness and said maybe Khrushchev had been correct – perhaps he couldn't control himself. They sent him to a detention house and two years later gave him the death penalty . . .'

She hunted down newspapers and documents. Harder was persuading people to talk. She hadn't understood at first – she was no one special; no threat. Some admitted they feared harassment, or missing out on promotions. A widower said he wasn't meant to talk and told her to ring his boss. Another, though living in the States like Youqin, could hardly get her off the line fast enough, certain that someone would be listening to their phone call.

'I didn't realise people would hate it so much. I found an old notebook where I said: "There are so many bad things and I can't change them. But at least I can write them." But now I realise that to write something is still a big thing! All these years later! I'm lucky because I have the chance to do this. I'm really free. It's not my job. I don't get research funding. I teach language and support myself. I don't have a family; I don't need to consider financial things. All I need to do is follow the truth. It was just obvious to me: Bian Zhongyun was killed. You have to admit that. That was my naive idea – but now I know that if they don't believe you, then they don't believe you. People didn't believe stories about the gulag.'

But with time, other pupils from her school began to talk about Bian too. They collected money for a statue of the teacher. Then they rowed about what to put on the plaque. Some wanted to say that she had died through the violence of the Cultural Revolution. Others insisted that there was nothing to write. In the end, as a compromise, they put her birth and death dates: 1916 to 5 August 1966.

'Wang Jingyao was really mad,' Youqin added. 'At least they put the date of her death.'

Wang Jingyao's grief had been private, by imposition rather than choice. Perhaps it would have stayed that way without Youqin and Hu Jie, an independent documentary-maker who had made a remarkable film of his story. Wang agreed to meet, but on the day of our appointment said suddenly that he was too busy and that we should meet in a few days; he would call to set up a date. He didn't. On the next attempt, he said that he did not feel like speaking. His second wife said their home was being redecorated. Our meeting was not convenient. Try another time, she added, and though I guessed there would not be another time, I tried again. There were polite excuses. Then his daughter called. Wang, now in his nineties, was in poor health. They had decided it was best for him to avoid emotional exertion. No, she did not want to speak about her mother. In any case, she added, just before she put the phone down, her father was older, affecting his mental state. He could not take responsibility for what he might say in an interview.

They were trying to protect him. But was it only from himself? And if not, from what, and whom?

— // —

The Cultural Revolution covers a few scant paragraphs in Chinese textbooks – there is no mention of suffering and death; certainly no mention of the victims, the teachers and artists and officials and, yes, workers and farmers. You wouldn't know, if that is how you learned of it, about the torment and torture. And even if you knew a little more, from your parents or from more obscure histories, you might not have heard about the scholars who hanged themselves and Party veterans who jumped from windows. You certainly wouldn't know about the militias who eradicated families; about children buried alive or thrown from clifftops; about the ghouls in remote, rural Guangxi who killed class enemies and ritually feasted on their livers. There isn't any mention of Teacher Bian.

To anyone who lived through the era, however, her pupil Song Binbin is famous, or notorious. When her school marked its ninetieth anniversary, it commemorated notable alumnae and staff; Bian was pictured in a commemorative book, but it was Song who was pictured on a banner outside. She was born in the year that the Party seized power. Her father was a general. She wrote that first big-character poster attacking the teachers. She was at school on the day that Bian died. Less than two weeks later, when Mao gathered a million delirious Red Guards in mid-August, it was Song who climbed the dais to present him with her armband, thanks to her school's prestige and her father's connections.

He asked her name: 'Binbin, as in "refined"?' Then he told her: 'Yaowu ma!'

Be martial!

Propaganda footage shows that encounter, that defining image of the era. Carefully, she pins the red band onto the Chairman's arm. The ringmaster of this circus is almost expressionless; there's the faintest smile as he speaks to her. Seen too close up, with the distance of years, Mao is not a radiant icon but a plump, ageing man, a little weary. Despite his height, approaching six feet, he sags in his baggy suit.

Song's in army uniform too. Its belt accentuates rather than amends its shapelessness. She wears her hair in two little knots, like bunches. Though in her late teens, she still looks like a child; there's no hint of the woman she will soon become. Even with her eyes blurry behind spectacles you can see how thrilled she is – all teeth as she pumps his hand, gripping and gripping. She jumps as he speaks to her. A photograph of their meeting appeared on the front of newspapers across the country. Alongside ran an article, supposedly by one 'Song Yaowu': 'I Put a Red Armband on Chairman Mao.' Beneath that boast came a vow to carry on the Great Proletarian Cultural Revolution to the end, and the words '*Violence is truth.*'

Admiring letters poured in. Institutions across the country renamed themselves Be Martial School. And the students followed

Mao's instruction as they had once obeyed their teachers. Beatings and deaths became commonplace, though their execution was increasingly baroque. Pupils poured boiling water over teachers, made them swallow excrement or crawl over embers, forced them to batter each other. The movement spilled off campuses and onto the streets.

'This is something that never happened in three thousand years of Beijing's history!' said Youqin. 'Of course, people were killed here. But by soldiers or armies or criminals! Never teenagers and students! I understand why Chairman Mao began the Cultural Revolution in schools. You kill teachers, you destroy schools – you can destroy much more: traditions, ideas, values. Destroy schools and you destroy civilisation.'

Scholars and the families of landlords were beaten or stoned by mobs. The violence rippled across the land. Within days, the treasures from Lhasa's temples, thousands of miles away, were burning. Meanwhile, the minister of public security – a friend of Song's father – urged police not to criticise Red Guards: 'Don't say it is wrong of them to beat up bad people. If in anger they beat someone to death, so be it.' By early September local officials had ordered the extermination of all 'bad elements' in Daxing District, just outside Beijing, on the spurious claim that class enemies planned to rise up. Party activists and local militias stabbed, clubbed and strangled 325 adults and children. The youngest was a month-old baby. No one was left to take revenge.

Two people died in Beijing before the rally; hundreds in the days that followed.

'Mao wearing the armband meant that he too was a member of the Red Guards,' said Wu Di, a historian of the era. 'The newspapers called him the Red Commander of the Red Guards, and that meant that everything the Red Guards did was good and supported by the Party and government. In that sense, the armband's significance can't be stressed enough.'

From that piece of cloth you could draw a line to the destruction of the Four Olds and the killings which swept the capital, then the country. And so, as Youqin said, one school's story reflected all that was wrong about the Cultural Revolution. One name became synonymous with Red Guards and violence: Song Binbin. When details of Bian Zhongyun's death spread, it fuelled the whispers about Song. There was no evidence that she beat her teacher. But many wrongly believed, or assumed, that she had killed Bian and others. Her moment of triumph in Tiananmen Square thus looked like a reward for violence, as well as a spur to it.

For decades, Song said little. And then, not long after Wang cancelled our meeting, the news began to bubble across the internet. She had apologised.

— // —

Like Youqin, Song Binbin had moved to the US to study and settled there, marrying a Chinese American. After retirement and her husband's death she returned to Beijing but maintained her low profile. People advised her not to discuss the past. Few Red Guards did. But as the years passed, a number came forward to confess to persecuting teachers and even to killing rival faction members. Their apologies drew some sympathy and, in Beijing, the close attention of the historian Wu Di. He was the same age as Youqin, and like most of their generation he had been exiled to the countryside in 1968, when the Party dispersed the Red Guards from the cities. Soon after he arrived in Inner Mongolia he was arrested and jailed, giving him a close-up view of one of the era's worst atrocities. Twenty-two thousand people were killed in pursuit of the secret Inner Mongolian

People's Party, a party which, officials later admitted, did not actually exist. Wu promised fellow prisoners that one day he would write their story. After his release he fulfilled the pledge, but like Youqin's work it was too sensitive to be published on the mainland. In time, he founded his own digital magazine, *Remembrance*. Each issue was emailed to just under two hundred people, which meant that – under some obscure rule – officials classed it as a private message, not a publication demanding censorship. He could not stop recipients passing it on. He did not seek to increase its reach.

He had devoted several issues of *Remembrance* to Teacher Bian's death, and had encouraged Song Binbin to apologise. Her only interventions to date had been, she said, reluctant, and they had only reinforced suspicions about her. In 2002 she threatened to sue over a book (drawn in part from Youqin's work) which suggested she had played a leading role in Bian's death, winning an apology. Soon afterwards she appeared silhouetted in a documentary, *Morning Sun*, insisting she had always shunned violence. She was not asked about Bian, though a classmate talked about her teacher's death. A few years later she participated in her school's ninetieth anniversary celebrations, where her meeting with Mao was lauded. In 2012, Wu persuaded her to write about what had happened on the day of Bian's death. Now he pressed her to say sorry to surviving teachers. Much more was at stake than one woman's reputation. Once, Song's image had sparked a conflagration; now it might extinguish the smouldering rage, prompt wider contemplation and perhaps one day – a long, long way off – reconciliation.

The very idea was potent enough to inspire other schools to plan similar events. It was January 2014; the lunar new year was approaching – a time for sweeping out the house and making space for good fortune, for settling debts and dealing with unfinished business. Twenty surviving teachers attended. The daughter of a famous writer read a poem. Song and her classmates bowed to the teachers, and to the bust of Bian which stood in the school. The teacher was their junior now, forever fifty; Song was in her sixties and grey-haired. Tears gleamed behind her glasses as she read her statement. Her failure to protect the school's leaders had caused her pain and remorse throughout her life, she said. How a nation faced its future was largely determined by how it faced its past. She hoped that all those who did wrong in the Cultural Revolution would 'face up to themselves, reflect on the Cultural Revolution, seek forgiveness and achieve reconciliation . . . That reflection must start from myself.'

— // —

I knew Song and her friends were unlikely to talk; they turned me down point-blank. I sent a letter anyway. No. It was not convenient. Then they reconsidered. They asked for questions. A few days later the phone rang: if I could get there in the next two hours, they would speak to me. Within five minutes I was in a cab, heading west across the frozen city. In the summer, despite the best efforts of Maoist industrialisation and rapacious capitalist development, the city thrummed with unexpected life. As twilight fell, bats jittered past the windows of my top-floor flat. Emerald dragonflies hovered over lakes; azure-winged magpies swooped onto lawns. Sometimes you glimpsed yellow hutong weasels scrambling through the alleys. But winter stole the colour from Beijing; the branches, the attenuated bird song, the pale skies and streets were ungenerous. The bundles of twigs in the bare trees surprised me as we sped past. How could anything have made a home in this inhospitable place?

The taxi dropped me at the gates of Beijing Normal University, so close to where it had happened. They had booked a room there and we faced each other across a long conference table, wooden but plastic-shiny. Fluorescent lights, plasterboard walls – we might have been anywhere. The pale sun struggled through the windows. The meeting felt almost surreally formal. The girls of that long, hot, bloody summer were now ladies of a certain age, piano-teacher-neat and precise, and friendly in a cautious manner: Liu Jin, a close friend of Song's since childhood, Feng Jinglan, Li Hongyun and Luo Zhi. No Song.

'We've been talking about this for a long time, but in the past environment we couldn't talk about it publicly. We kept long memories,' Liu began.

Another of them: 'Because this apology included Song Binbin, it attracted a lot of attention. She's regarded as a symbol of the Cultural Revolution.'

And that was a burden to her?

'Yes. A great one.'

They assured me that the staff had been deeply touched by the apology. The teachers had never blamed the pupils even for 'very extreme' behaviour, regarding them as children. They addressed the issues methodically, from time to time referring to a thick report before them. Through eight years of research and over a hundred interviews they had gathered scattered memories – though 'of course, sometimes memories are not absolutely accurate' – and transmuted blood and death into ink on paper. It was a kind of magic: a way of containing the chaos. A way of righting a world turned upside down – which was, after all, what I was attempting; searching for coherence in a story which could not and must not be true.

Foreigners sometimes summon *Lord of the Flies* when they talk about that summer. This carnival of violence and hate – the young girls remorselessly stalking their Piggy – is too raw, too cruel, too wrong to be real. But it was worse than the fiction. No plane crash, no desert island was required; this happened in the midst of civilisation, a civilisation founded in large part on respect for scholars, elders and authority. And it happened at the instigation of adults. The teenagers who killed Bian Zhongyun were not feral as much as well drilled. The Party had raised this generation to fear the enemies of the people. In 1966 the sense of encroaching menace had grown stronger.

'We felt our red country was about to change colour; we felt it was under threat,' said Liu. So she, Song Binbin and another classmate put up that first big-character poster. It urged students to take action and join the movement, attacking school leaders for encouraging them to focus on studies instead. It asked – ironically, in light of Song's own background – why so many pupils were leaders' children and so few from worker or peasant families.

'It didn't really mention the target,' Liu said; but she acknowledged it had sparked the school's upheaval. The government sent work teams onto campuses to denounce 'anti-Party, anti-socialist' figures such as Teacher Bian, but also to calm the mood. They had misunderstood: 'Trust the masses,' Mao ordered, and 'Allow the students to liberate themselves.' He withdrew the teams, leaving colleges and schools in turmoil.

'Jiang Qing also encouraged people,' Liu added.

Mao's wife had stepped into the storm in late July, assuring Red Guards: 'If bad people beat good people, the good people achieve glory. If good people beat good people, it is a misunderstanding. Without beatings you do not get acquainted and then you no longer need to beat them.'

Another of the friends took over: 'Ms Bian was tortured for a long time. Most of the students were confused and unclear about what happened or what they did in the 5 August incident. People said Ms Bian died because of heart attack or high blood pressure. We wanted to find out and clarify the facts.'

Song and Liu had said they learned what was happening when someone rushed to their room to say that younger girls were hitting the teachers. They dispersed the crowd and told them not to beat people, but later heard the violence had resumed and rushed back to the playground. Song urged the girls to stop again, but then returned indoors. When the pair heard the teacher was lying outside, near death, they helped rush her to hospital. Song had been scared to intervene more decisively, she said. She thought once people left it would be fine. She was responsible for Bian's death because she had 'followed those making errors'.

'Although Song Binbin and I went down to stop students, I feel deep regret I didn't try harder to control the situation,' Liu told me now.

Her friend stepped in: 'I think Song Binbin and Liu Jin did not have the ability to control the situation or stop anybody. The force of the revolution was so strong.'

It wasn't clear which one of us she was addressing.

That night, the girls had informed a top leader, friendly with Song's father, of the teacher's death. Liu recalled his silence, and then his slow reply: 'In such a big movement, anything could happen. It is inevitable that these kind of problems can appear. She already died; it is past . . . Don't worry or be scared. Go back to school. Keep this confidential. Do not expand its influence.'

The next morning, Liu had taken charge of the tannoy system and made the announcement that so shocked Youqin. It was an obedient echo of instructions: Bian was dead. It was past. 'I have thought a lot about why I stayed in the room that day. I went down twice, but why didn't I go again to save her?' she told me now. Somewhere inside her was another world: a world in which she had gone down a third time, a world in which she had acted differently. A world in which Teacher Bian had not died.

'I want to record this history truly, even if it can't be published,' she added. 'I still want to record it, so people in the future have the facts.'

There were plenty of facts. The report was full of them. What time had it all happened? Where? Were the beatings carried out by Red Guard groups, or other pupils? And yet it did not answer the most obvious question.

A nod. 'Many people wanted to know – who's the murderer? Firstly, I want to say: this event was not a murder,' said one of them.

I stopped myself. Waited her out.

'This was a mass incident in the Cultural Revolution environment. During the process some people shoved her and kicked her and beat her with a stick. And they forced her to labour and carry soil from one place to another and back. Her health was not good.'

'It was torture,' another interceded; perhaps my face had said what I had not.

'It was the hottest day and she was beaten and tortured,' the first agreed. 'And she fell downstairs because she was weak, and she fainted. No one dared to make the decision to send her to hospital. Who beat her? Who kicked her? Who delayed her being saved? Every detail created a risk of her death. We couldn't confirm who gave the fatal blow. But we know the whole process was full of human evil. All of the torture should be criticised. So far no one has had the guts to stand up. We hope that people can save themselves, by themselves.'

They would not indulge in the satisfying but inadequate business of blame. The killers were children; no one person led the way; adults had induced it all. This was true. But if you spent eight years investigating and didn't name names, what was left? Without them, it was as if no one had really beaten Teacher Bian to death. She 'was beaten to death'. Or 'she was beaten, and then she died'. A middle-aged woman, in poor health, died one afternoon. You didn't have to think about a teenage girl bringing down a spiked club on her.

'Our aim is to face history, refuse to forget, restore the facts. The purpose is not to create new problems or conflicts, but tolerance and compromise.'

And for Bian's family?

'Right now, we are trying to restore Song Binbin's reputation and remove all the smears made against her – that she killed seven or eight people, she was involved in a beating competition and involved in the death of Principal Bian,' another replied. 'But more, we aim to improve people's reflections on the history in the Cultural Revolution. To get people to reconcile and forgive each other is based on restoring reality and facts. That includes restoring Song Binbin's reputation. It has been so long and the teachers and students know what kind of person Song Binbin is and try to clean up her reputation. But there are quite a lot of rumours and we don't understand why it's happening. Her friends want to help her. But that's only one of the things we want to do. We want to restore history and facts and not let lies continue. Our aim is that the whole country will reflect on the Cultural Revolution. For us, we hope to do it ourselves as people who experienced the 5 August incident. We have a responsibility to stand up and tell the truth.'

There it was again: 'the 5 August incident'. The words were as jarring as their reluctance to discuss Teacher Bian's family (though her widower had previously rebuffed Liu after she apologised to him). 'Incident' is a term often used for serious, even tragic events in China. Perhaps to them it was a solemn phrase, giving her death its true weight: not as a personal tragedy but as a matter of historical import, an event that shaped a nation. But 'incident' was also a word that distanced, blurred and evaded. It told you something important happened – but not what, not how, not who, not why.

I thought of Youqin, and her restless hunt for the victims: 'If we don't respect their deaths, we don't respect their lives,' she had told me. And: 'The problem is not people lying but people not telling the whole truth. They tell a part of the truth.'

Yet the 'whole truth' often depended on perspective. Take Song. Sure, some said, she hadn't beaten Teacher Bian. But she had whipped up initial ill feeling, and she had failed to stop the assault or to help her teacher until it was too late. Others asked why it had taken her so long to come forward and express remorse. But it wasn't what she had or hadn't done that unsettled me as much as the tone of grievance in her initial article, in particular. The *Remembrance* essay read more like a plea bargain than a confession. It talked at such length about the pressures she was under and said so little about Teacher Bian. She explained how she had come to present the armband, and had been propelled to fame against her wishes, and how the article praising violence was not written by her at all. Each expression of responsibility distanced her further from it.

There was a consistency and rhythm to the interlocking answers, studded with all the details I might need, and a care not quite like the meticulousness with which Yu Xiangzhen had owned her mistakes when she recalled Red August. Perhaps sometimes remembering was also about not remembering. They were telling a story, a difficult story, unwelcome to authorities and many they knew, and that took courage – and yet, with this story, they displaced another. All memory is creation, not retrieval, and what we remember is partial, by intent or accident. Trauma, in particular, can shatter, distort and scramble what we remember. Song had written that it took the research to restore her own memories; classmates had helped her to recall not just what happened but her own state of mind. Yet we can fool ourselves even when we believe we are most scrupulous. Research has suggested that each time we remember we gradually make ourselves more central to the story, unconsciously structuring events around ourselves. The Cultural Revolution seemed to have the opposite effect: people shifted to the edge of the picture. In memoirs, someone else was the instigator. The author had said and done as little as possible. They were not there at all.

The women pointed out that they too had suffered in the Cultural Revolution. When Mao turned on targets inside the Party, Song's father fell from favour and was exiled to a labour camp. Song and her mother were detained. Her brother was savagely beaten. There were no clear lines between oppressor and oppressed; only Mao had been truly secure. But there were also degrees of suffering, and drawing parallels hid as much as it revealed. Song survived; her teacher did not. And as Song grew up, her connections served her well. Her father was restored to the top leadership and, like Xi Jinping's, became one of the Party's Eight Immortals: founders who survived to steer it into the eighties and nineties.

Her friends had told me that the apology was more important than forgiveness. Exposing ourselves and risking rejection takes courage. But apologising is also a request for the generosity of others and they seemed tired, understandably perhaps, of shouldering this debt. They had spoken of truth and reconciliation, but not once of justice. Every remark brought them towards closure, not accountability.

— // —

'How are they still so powerful that they can control people's memories?' Wang Youqin poked at a polystyrene box of rice and vegetables with her chopsticks. It was a Sunday, and I had invited her to a restaurant to talk; she'd said we could save time by eating in her office.

'It's the Cultural Revolution's Rashomon: everyone just says something for themselves. Years ago they didn't want to say anything.

Now they become aggressive and blame me. Apologies are a good thing. We need to know what went wrong. But when Song Binbin started, I felt it wasn't serious. She has really destroyed the atmosphere. Forty-eight years later and we're still arguing?'

Song's apology was too late, too little, too contrived, too superficial, raged her critics. It was an attempt to exculpate the children of the elite. A cartoon circulated online of a weeping crocodile in a Red Guard uniform. *Remembrance* too was attacked fiercely, accused of taking Song's side. The other schools which had planned apologies aborted their arrangements – for, as Wu, the historian, asked, who would dare to say sorry after that?

'Given that this is still a taboo, any apology is a good start, even if it's just trying to get past the subject,' he maintained. 'Be they thorough, shallow or even just a muddled attempt, as long as they mention the Cultural Revolution, the beatings by the Red Guards and their regrets, they are good enough.' Not one of those who killed the hundreds of victims in Beijing that month had confessed. They were his age; they should still be alive. Not one had been held to account or punished. But the flood of condemnation was directed at those with the guts to stand up and say sorry. Song was the easiest target of all. The perpetrators needed her to take the blame, shouldering the moral and psychological pressure. The intellectuals needed a symbol: so many atrocities had been committed that someone should be condemned.

Song herself had been an irrelevance since the age of sixteen, I realised. She was not a woman but an abstraction – what everyone thought they knew about the Cultural Revolution. That she appeared only fleetingly, preferred the shadows, seemed apt. Even as a youth, with the chaos still unfolding around her, 'It was said that Song Yaowu had done murder, arson, rape, nothing but evil,' she had written. After all the lies and rumours, she could not talk about what had happened without clarifying what hadn't – but that clarification implied that she was seeking to excuse herself, to focus on what she had not done and circumvent what she had. Even taking Bian to hospital was interpreted as evidence of guilt and not an attempt – however late and inadequate – to help. 'No matter what I said it was misunderstood,' she had written.

A more convincing apology might have acknowledged her fear more fully, and whether she suspected that the beatings would continue in her absence. It might acknowledge, too, the heady sense of power and importance thrust upon a teenager, the tearing away of constraint, the exhilaration of that meeting with Mao and of being at the centre of the world. But an account like that would be wildly insensitive, implying to some that she still revelled in her prominence. It would force one to ask how she could have taken pleasure in any part of such a brutal movement. There was nothing she could say to satisfy people; there was no way to make amends. Whatever she said would fall far short of what needed to be said, regardless of what she herself had done, because no words, no guilt, no repentance could match the horror of what happened.

'In the Cultural Revolution, different factions fought each other despite the fact they all claimed to fight for Mao,' said Wu. 'They all thought they were fighting for the truth, and yet they were just fighting for individual interests. Many intellectuals in this debate tend towards a similar mindset – as long as I can beat our opposition, I don't mind fabricating a few facts; as long as I can make people condemn the Cultural Revolution, I don't mind twisting a few truths. Though some might appear to advocate freedom, democracy and liberalism, they still can't escape the influence of the Cultural Revolution.'

Wang saw the start of the struggle session. Yet, he noted, she had not identified perpetrators either. (Wang had made this point herself, saying it was the victims who mattered.) He saw her work as sloppy, 'and she didn't take corrections well'. He feared that emotions and subjective experience were prevailing over rigorous study.

But experience tells us something that no facts and statistics can. Youqin knew that people had a choice because she hadn't denounced the teachers, or gloried in the violence. She'd spent years pursuing the subject when no one else wanted to talk about it. She'd submersed herself in traumatic case histories, accepting rebuffs and some risk. She didn't see why showing up late and half-heartedly merited praise. Still, her righteousness didn't leave room for mercy, or even, perhaps, understanding. It seemed to me both were partially right, or rather, if I was true to the spirit of the argument, both were wrong. I remembered, now, that Youqin had quizzed me about which historians I had met, and what they had said to me, and whether they had talked about the violence at their own schools, questions I hadn't entirely understood.

'Of course people have a reason to hate me, because I've been trying to tell these facts since 1986,' she'd said. I'd assumed that 'people' meant former Red Guards or perhaps the authorities. China's security apparatus took a close interest in this kind of work; though Youqin's American citizenship helped her, it did not guarantee her safety. But instead she spoke mostly of rows with other researchers. One had recently said she was unbalanced because she was single and childless. I was surprised – I'd met the scholar a few times and liked him; he seemed a gentle man – and I wasn't, because it was the kind of casual misogyny you heard so often here, and because I was beginning to realise that this subject could push everyone, even the wise and kind, to unwise and unkind places. To focus on something so sensitive was at best eccentric, inherently unreasonable.

'He told everyone I was trying to kill him,' Youqin added.

'Kill him?' Perhaps it was a metaphor.

'Yes! I called to complain about what he said! And then he said I was trying to kill him, because I was calling on his mobile phone during a thunderstorm! He told everyone!'

I had thought that these people were on the same side. I had thought that there were two sides, for remembering and forgetting. Three at most, if you distinguished those who brandished it as a warning from those who glorified it as a fairer, more egalitarian age. But the fissures were endless and multiplying. Those who cared most about remembering the worst were pitted against each other. There were too many sides, or none at all – just an endless, ugly, shape-shifting row. What was the nature of the evil, and where did it spring from, and who was to blame? Could a fourteen-year-old be held to account, or only Chairman Mao? Was forgiveness possible without justice? And who had the right to judge?

The Chinese leadership's mantra was 'harmony': not multiple voices woven together but everyone singing the same note, never straying from the melody. (Bloggers joked that they 'had been harmonised' when censors erased their work.) Explorations of the Cultural Revolution were the antithesis: cacophony. Everyone was crying out and no one listened – no one would even let you hear the other. These were not academic arguments. They were bitter and fierce and ad hominem, as if there could not be anything in life that didn't touch upon your basic worth as a person. You could not make mistakes; you could only be wrong – wrong as a thinker, wrong as a person. These survivors had defended themselves for so long, from the political winds of Maoism, from the idea that the self itself was a trivial bourgeois snare. Why would they consider anyone else's ideas of who they were or could be?

— // —

Far from achieving reconciliation, Song's apology had unsettled those who suffered the greatest loss and sparked vicious rows over memory, guilt and repentance. As the storm grew, the censors stepped in. Propaganda officials banned further reporting; online censors removed posts discussing the row.

'We want people to reflect, but the process is not very easy and has had a lot of ups and downs,' one of Song's friends had said.

She'd hesitated for a moment, then continued: 'The country hasn't given time to reflecting on this. In 1981, at the Eleventh Party Congress, they defined the Cultural Revolution as a historical catastrophe. But the question of who should be responsible – what we learned from this experience, and how we could prevent it happening again – they didn't really have conclusions about that.'

Acknowledging the horrors made it harder to justify the Party's benevolent rule. The victims' families knew there was no prospect of seeing the killers punished; the law is the Party's tool, like every other part of the system. That some of those culpable came from the elite increased leaders' reluctance. But I'd begun to see that there were many reasons to shy away from the discussion. The broadest brushstrokes – blaming the Gang of Four, acknowledging the errors of Mao – covered an uglier and more fractious picture. Honesty about the past wasn't just a danger for the Party and the state; it was a danger for the nation. Song's friends had talked of South Africa's Truth and Reconciliation Commission as a dear but impossible aspiration. I wondered if they understood how painful they had been: how it must have felt for families to watch the killers of their sons and mothers walk free in amnesties. People talk vaguely of truth, justice and reconciliation as if they are almost synonymous, each blending into the next. But seen close up they are quite different things, even contradictory. Justice is a sharp instrument; it must draw fine distinctions. Conciliation depends on finding commonalities. It might require a little blurriness. There was never a time when people were going to sit down for a temperate, rational discussion of abuse and torture and murder. The psychological damage cut too deep; the events were too horrific. So the leaders had tried to conceal the worst. But these were deep wounds – and left dirty, they had festered.

A furious statement in Wang Jingyao's name surfaced on Chinese websites. Was it accurate? His anger spurred him to pick up the phone: 'I don't believe their apology, because I don't dare to believe them. They don't keep their word. Red Guards cannot be trusted,' he spat.

Song had said she had not invited the widower to witness her apology for fear of upsetting him, and perhaps that was true. But Wang believed the worst and why wouldn't he? His wife was traduced, and those lies killed her; her murder was dismissed as an accident; he was forced to hide the facts and conceal her ashes and remember her in secret, like a man ashamed. Deceit and deceit upon deceit: the only truth, indeed, was violence. Wang, who had spent half a lifetime remembering, was too old and too tired, while others who had tried to forget now wanted to remember. Was the Cultural Revolution receding or coming closer?

FIVE

> There are some who ask, isn't this too left? Isn't this returning to the Cultural Revolution? They obviously don't understand. If you could experience it yourself, you would know that is not the case.
>
> **Bo Xilai**

A man, small and thickset, not quite seventy perhaps, trudged up the path towards us. From each hand swung a navy-shrouded cylinder. He stopped by a tree near the top of the slope and reached up to hang one from a branch. He pulled away the thick cloth to expose the wicker cage, suspended the next one and unveiled that too. The birds inside darted their heads about, startled by the light, and in a moment their songs spilled into the mist.

I knew the ritual well from Beijing. A couple of pensioners came early each morning to the entrance of my compound, to air their larks and thrushes on spindly trees beside the busy road. The charm of this echo of ancient China, and of the bearers' solicitude, was shaded by its cruelty. People said that songbirds confined within walls, without the company of their own kind, would fall silent and begin to moult, solitary and desolate. Outdoors, hung alongside others, they chirruped and hopped and preened. Their owners saw nothing wrong in tantalising them with this wider, freer, unreachable world; and what was sad in the shadow of tower blocks felt harsher still in this sprawling park, where the far edge of the lake blurred into the haze and a wild bird could take wing over the treetops and up, up to the clouds. The larks' gain was to see the space denied them.

My companion crushed his cigarette on the stone seat and nodded at the bird owner. 'He's my age. Maybe he was involved,' he said. Han Pingzhao could have been the son of the man he had indicated. His hair was cropped and glossy, with only a fine line at the temples revealing the white beneath, and he wore a khaki Timberland shirt over jeans and laced tan boots. But he had already retired from his job in state media, and now he researched a subject that the Party preferred to avoid: the movement that had consumed this city, and Han himself.

He had voiced the thought that had hovered in these past few days, as I watched men sipping from chipped teahouse cups, women jollying peevish grandchildren. I could not connect what I saw with what I knew – that among them were the warriors who had bludgeoned classmates and colleagues. Chongqing saw some of the era's fiercest fighting, with the rift between Red Guards descending into warfare. The Kuomintang had made it their capital while battling the Japanese occupation, and it was home to multiple munitions plants; when armed struggles broke out in 1967, the military backed one side and helped its fighters seize what they needed. The factions battled with grenades, machine guns, napalm, tanks and ships upon the river; everything except planes, a resident recalled. They executed in cold blood too: even the injured, even the pregnant. Tens of thousands fled the city and at least twelve hundred people died, though the true toll was probably much higher. Some were caught in the violence by chance, like the eight-year-old killed by a ricocheting bullet as he played on the street. The others were not so much older, and you could blame chance there too, even if they saw themselves as soldiers. They never thought it would be so serious, that people would die, that so many would die. By the time they saw their friends fall they'd been battling for hours. They were numb; none of it seemed possible. Had it really happened at all?

Shapingba Park held the proof. More than five hundred of the victims, mostly teenagers, were buried here, at a Red Guard cemetery hidden on one edge of the site, behind a grove of trees. Officials had wanted to bulldoze it, as they had razed other such graveyards. They planned a theme park, with cable cars and replicas of international landmarks; a shabby scale model of Mount Rushmore stood testament to those vain ambitions. After the scheme fell through, Shapingba became the only Cultural Revolution site in the country to be recognised as a national heritage spot. But a mossy wall surrounded the plot and the public were not allowed in any more. I had come before, and stared through the chained gates. Though the cemetery was only half a century old, it reminded me of the Civil War graveyards I had seen in the American South, crumbling and overgrown. Luxuriant greenery crawled over marble monuments, immense and once stark white but now lichened and grey. Stone torches topped great pillars and obelisks, carved with red stars and Maoist slogans and the number 815. It was the rebel faction the dead had belonged to, named for a critical date in its inception in 1966.

Han had been an 815 member and then fought against it in a breakaway group called Fandaodi, 'Rebel to the End'. His precise recounting of the split left me no closer to grasping its real causes than the hollered, verbose stories I had heard from his peers since arriving in the city. He took pity: the detail didn't matter so much. Mostly, I knew, it was circumstance, and pinning your hopes to someone who knew what was right or wrong, or seemed to. However clear it had seemed back then, and however you explained it now, which side you ended up on had really been the product of an unholy mixture of ideological disputes, social standing, personal grudges, old friendships, misread signals and luck, or lack of it. He unpicked as much of the mess for me as anyone could manage and explained the history of the cemetery. To learn more about its earliest days, I would need to talk to an old comrade and foe. He ran a chemicals business in the city and his name was Zheng Zhisheng, but back then he had been a student, and they called him the Corpse Master.

— // —

'People began to die on 1 July 1967. On the tenth, I was put in charge of the bodies,' Zheng recalled. He was peering through thick tortoiseshell glasses that still bore the maker's sticker. Two more dusty pairs lay on his desk, jumbled with books, newspapers, a giant magnifying glass and two lidded porcelain cups.

He delved for a photograph. 'This is October 1967. Twenty-seven people – twenty-seven corpses.' Most of the faces were turned away from the camera. One mouth gaped so wide it could swallow the viewer.

'I had seen dead bodies when I was young. But I'd never had to handle them. I was a model student, and the faction leader thought I was a helpful person and not afraid of hard work. And also,' he added, after a moment's thought, 'I'd opposed him at the beginning. So he thought of me and put me in charge. I was forced to do it. I put make-up, and an armband, and a Mao badge, on each one. At the start I was afraid of the dirty work. I had to wash the dead bodies and I used soap to wash my hands all the time. Afterwards I didn't mind about that. The second thing was the smell. The dead bodies stank and I wanted to throw up. The third thing was ghosts – I thought ghosts were terrifying. Although I was an atheist, China had these traditional ideas, and so I was afraid.'

He foraged for another handful of photographs and showed me a bobbed, full-cheeked young girl. 'She was the first I dealt with. We used formaldehyde. She went to help the injured on the battlefield and when she stood up she was shot dead. She was sixteen.' He reached for another. 'This one is from the university – people were buried there too, but the monument was destroyed later. Now it's all flower beds.' He replaced the pictures amid the clutter.

'I felt they were martyrs and it was a waste for them to die so young. After people in our faction died we treated the others as enemies and hated them. So when we captured them, some of them were stoned until they were unconscious. Then they were sent to hospital. Afterwards we moved them to another hospital – but that was just an excuse. On the way we beat them to death; that's why we ended up in prison. Back then we hated the Fandaodi faction but now I think both factions were cheated. They were all innocent. They were all victims.'

The Fandaodi prisoners, already injured, had been battered with rifle stocks. By him? 'No, no.' He shook his head. 'It was two other people.'

You ordered them to do it, I'd heard?

'Yes.' He was concise, not curt. 'I didn't feel any sadness: I just wanted to take revenge. The other faction had killed our martyrs. I didn't know them – it was factional.'

Zheng and others had been jailed for years for their role in the armed conflict. After release he wanted to search for the victims' families and make amends, or try to. But someone warned him that the parents might sue, and he gave the idea up. 'It's a lifelong nightmare. It's very traumatic. I have nightmares that I'm still in prison. Afterwards I tried to work hard and to reconcile myself with what I had done. I tried to do good things, and when I stumbled I stood up and carried on. I cried many times.'

But the lessons he had learned were priceless, he insisted, though he struggled to define them. A slight sigh escaped him, as if he was hoping I might abandon the subject. 'It can't be described in a few words. For foreigners, looking at the Cultural Revolution is like reading a difficult book. It's really hard to understand. Even young people don't have an interest.'

He was afraid of what might happen if people did not face up to the past and that later generations might echo the mistakes his had made. It was not a repeat of the Cultural Revolution itself he feared – history had progressed, he said. So what was it?

'Turmoil.' He stopped there, considering.

'For example, with the Tiananmen Square incident – I actually wrote to my son, because he was at university. Because I had that turbulent past, I didn't let him join them. The students were patriotic. They wanted to fight against corruption. But they were being used by bad guys.' It took me a moment to understand. He spelled it out: 'They were manipulated by people like Fang Lizhi, Wu'er Kaixi and Wang Dan, who were pursuing Western large-scale democracy. We can only be led by the Communist Party. We can't have big democracy like the Americans. It can only bring turbulence and chaos. We had more than two thousand years of feudalism; America started with two parties and democracy. Foreigners can't understand China; they can't understand China's past. Corruption is caused not by one-party rule but by who has checks on the leadership. We can't get rid of the Party's rule – impossible. We don't need any turbulence and chaos.'

It was a common view in China, even among relative liberals. The country was not ready to be free; though how it might ever become so, if not allowed to evolve, was never explained. For Zheng, individual caprice and disobedience, pride and egotism had produced this disaster. Stability and the common good were all.

Zheng was punished when the movement ended. Han had been a target as it raged on, one of millions of victims of the hunt for the supposed May 16 conspirators. A tiny student group was swiftly suppressed after attacking the premier, Zhou Enlai, for conservatism. But military and Party officials seized the opportunity to turn upon rebel Red Guards, labelling almost anything they'd done as part of the conspiracy, and what had begun with no more than fifty students led to perhaps a hundred thousand deaths. It was Cultural Revolution paranoia at its most absurd and intense.

Han was held for months in a black jail and forced to write endless confessions about his supposed sins. The movement puzzled him as it puzzles historians today. But, lying in the darkness each night, what nagged at him was a different question: Why had he once been so quick to oppress people as he was now oppressed? A year or so before, a friend who worked in a pulping plant, destroying dangerous books, had begun to smuggle volumes out: one was a Bible, so poorly translated that Han could barely decipher it. Now those awkward passages floated back, and he began trying to make sense of them, and of his own experience. By the time he was released he had turned his back on vengeance and embraced the New Testament's command 'Love thy enemy'. What had sounded in my own childhood like gentle, almost banal advice was a radical choice on Han's part, I realised: the very antithesis of Maoism.

'"Love" is very simple,' he added. 'Accepting guilt – that's hard. God is justice and honesty. If you believe in God, there's a conscience in your heart. But the influence of the environment is huge. It's very hard to go against the tide and it's very lonely and painful.'

For Han, Christianity was not so much a story of redemption as of personal struggle and individual conscience. He believed that only by rousing these voices, and listening to them, could China safeguard against catastrophes. When Zheng had put his faith in the Party, Han had turned to God, and to those who might hear his word. Their lives had constructed their stories, convincing them of what their country needed: discipline, Zheng was certain. The courage to trust oneself, Han knew. One was wedded to the status quo. The other wanted reform.

Those at the top, such as Deng and Xi's father, had been forced into a reckoning too. They had suffered, and watched the torment of loved ones. They had lost their oldest friends and their glorious dream of a better, happier China. When they reclaimed power, they did all they could to prevent another disaster. For their own sake, and that of the masses, they committed themselves to stability. They determined that never again would a strongman ride roughshod over his peers, his country and the people. Though Deng would dominate until his death, they did their best to institutionalise and, especially, collectivise rule. After the protests of 1989, which were fuelled by obvious divides in the leadership, the determination to avoid public splits was absolute. It is not hard to imagine the emotions engendered by millions of young people massing in Tiananmen Square again: the cold instinct for survival, the ruthlessness born of the revolution, for which they had already sacrificed so much – but, too, the visceral fear of where it could all lead.

The Party adopted unwritten rules to ensure that no one outstayed their welcome, limiting top leaders to two five-year terms and setting a retirement age. Even misdemeanours were handled in line with an unofficial code: members of the politburo might be purged for corruption, but the most senior figures of all – the Politburo Standing Committee – were untouchable, as were their families. You survived and thrived by cultivating patrons and your wider networks. The Party became safer, stabler, calmer and duller.

For years, it worked. China prospered. People who might have eaten meat once a year dropped unctuous pork into their bowls each week. People who might never have left their county journeyed to Shanghai, Bangkok or Paris for shopping and sightseeing. They got their hair permed, wore bright sweaters and Nikes, tried red wine and McDonald's, took up hobbies. It was attractive enough for foreigners to speak of the 'Beijing model'. But there was a price. Corruption was endemic. To get your child into a decent school, or pass your driving test, or push through a business deal, or dodge prosecution, took cash: a few thousand yuan to a teacher, tens of millions to a senior leader. In cities such as Chongqing, gangs flourished, sheltered by officials they had bought off. Inequality was soaring. The more the economy grew and mutated, the more static politics seemed.

Everyone understood the problems. President Hu Jintao and his premier Wen Jiabao, who led the country when I arrived, had rolled out a skeletal welfare state at remarkable speed. But it was not enough, and people don't stay grateful for long. The mantra was stability maintenance – an idea that would have horrified Mao, and in truth not much of an idea at all, since it meant More Of The Same. Everyone knew that big reforms were needed, yet they were deferred again and again. China was busy getting richer, getting bigger. A hundred new airports within a dozen years; a hundred new museums. The Beijing subway grew more in a decade than the London Underground had expanded in a century and a half. More bridges and blocks, theme parks and highways, shopping malls and factories, cinemas and stations. When the financial crisis hit in 2008, the government poured in 4 trillion yuan and was hailed as saving the world. It propped up the hyper-speed development without addressing its consequences: the hopelessly imbalanced economy, the poisoning of soil and rivers and people, the bribery and embezzlement, the growing gulf between rich and poor, city and village. But the unhappiness grew as wealth did. The Party stopped publishing the key indicator for inequality, and the number of 'mass incidents', or unrest. By 2011 the domestic security budget had soared past military spending; it would later rise still more steeply.

In part this was because the bar for intervention was set so low. There was a logic. The Party understood that it could never again allow the protests of 1989. It had to step in before trouble brewed. When important political meetings approached, or international events like the Olympics, or awkward anniversaries, the security services and censorship apparatus went into overdrive. With each fresh challenge to the Party – bloody ethnic riots in Tibet and Xinjiang; the awarding of the Nobel Peace Prize to a dissident – the difficult dates proliferated and the resulting measures grew more numerous and onerous, as well as more absurd. Beijingers were banned from flying kites or pigeons; on one occasion taxi firms removed interior window cranks lest passengers wind the windows down and fling out seditious messages. Activists and dissidents were held under house arrest, detained illegally, and sometimes, bizarrely, 'holidayed' – forcibly taken to a tourist destination by state agents who, like uncles indulging graceless children, might chide them for refusing to relax and enjoy the facilities. It was oppression with a civilised veneer and the offer of spa treatments: better than the fists and cattle prods meted out elsewhere, but only some recipients saw it as progress.

It didn't answer the underlying problem. The years of double-digit growth were what happens when an economy has been held back, and a demographic bump offers cheap labour, and hundreds of millions take their chance to claw their way out of poverty. It was not a secret Beijing had discovered, an immutable law of Chinese development. And the hole at the Middle Kingdom's heart could not be filled by villas or abalone or any number of Ferraris; there was always someone with more, and whatever you got never really satisfied. It was a hunger for justice, for community, for values, for meaning – for all the things that could not be met by the determined blandness of the men at the top. Without personal prestige or charisma, Hu could only hold the ring. A young man in Mao's red age, he had become grey by choice: this was the cult of non-personality.

— // —

Enter Bo Xilai. Bo, like Xi, was tall and assured. He was charming and handsome, and looked as though he knew it. He too was the son of a Communist 'immortal': Bo Yibo had been purged and tortured for belonging to a supposed clique of traitors. His wife died in the custody of Red Guards. Bo Xilai, when released from the brutal prison camp where he had been held for several years, told schoolfriends that his mother had been beaten to death.

Bo the elder, rehabilitated after Mao's death, made the most of his connections to help his son rise quickly. As leader of the north-eastern city of Dalian, Bo Xilai charmed overseas investors and won over residents too, moving factories to its edges and beautifying the centre. He had ideas, and he got things done, and made sure others saw it. He kept climbing. Promoted to minister of commerce, he proved as adept at doing business with foreigners as he was at wooing ordinary workers.

The Party wasn't so sure. The problem was not just his vaulting ambition but its conspicuousness. Xi built connections steadily; and even when marked out for the highest office, he avoided ostentation. His wife, an army singer, was far better known than he was. Bo was too obviously a man in a hurry, and he made too many enemies. He didn't quite make it to the very top body, the Politburo Standing Committee, in 2007 – his keenest champion, his father, was dead by then. His next post, running Chongqing, was a sideways shuffle. There, he adopted the same business-friendly policies and courted foreigners, inviting Henry Kissinger and others to the city. Yet he also recognised the growing frustrations of ordinary people with the soaring gap between the haves and have-nots, responding with measures such as taxing private home ownership (not, as it happened, very effectively). Wang Hui, one of the left's most influential thinkers – though by no means a neo-Maoist – described the overall effect as a clear shift away from neoliberalism, with 'more emphasis than in some other places on redistribution, justice and equality'.

Bo also turned to something that seemed distinctly new in the way it drew upon the old: the Sing Red – Strike Black campaign. The first part was self-explanatory: mass performances of revolutionary songs such as 'The East Is Red', the tribute to Mao which had replaced the national anthem in the Cultural Revolution. The campaign was 'voluntary', and there was real enthusiasm, but equally, few were naive enough to opt out of the tens of thousands of events. Officials arranged grand public concerts. Newspapers printed scores. Radio stations broadcast tunes non-stop. Bo's sentiments were self-consciously Mao-esque: 'There's no need to be artsy-fartsy . . . Only dilettantes prefer enigmatic works,' he declared. (Perhaps so, but when local television dropped soap operas for red song shows, its ratings plummeted.) Singing red was 'spiritual medicine' to cure China's ailing soul. He texted Mao quotes to residents' phones, ordered students to labour in the countryside and shipped cadres off to tour revolutionary sites. Alongside came a crackdown on the 'black' gangs who made life a misery for many in the city. Thousands of arrests culminated in dramatic trials and a handful of executions.

Chongqing loved it. China loved it. Everyone was talking about Bo. Almost every member of the Politburo Standing Committee – including Xi Jinping, soon to be the country's leader – visited Chongqing and stood alongside him. (Hu Jintao and Wen Jiabao were notable exceptions.) In the city itself, spirits were high. Shopkeepers were freed from the gangs which had terrorised them. A middle-aged local recorded a tribute song to the leader's piercing stare and 'spring-like smile'. Academics wrote about the 'Chongqing model', though it was hard to know what rules could really be observed in its heterodox mixture of low-cost public housing, high foreign investment, singing red and striking black. Where admirers welcomed Bo as a burst of colour in the monochrome world of Communist politics, or of principle in a market-driven country, detractors judged him flashy, superficial and malign. Foreigners compared him to Silvio Berlusconi, Huey Long and even JFK. But of course he was quintessentially Chinese, and in China they saw a more obvious comparison. Bo wrapped himself in Mao's mantle – and then, unblushing, professed shock when anyone remarked on the resemblance. When he sensed he might have gone too far he reglossed his efforts as a vaguer feel-good attempt to promote public spirit. 'The East Is Red' made way for modern patriotic songs, and officials explained that 'red' did not just stand for revolution but also happiness, health and positivity.

The material had never been the real issue. Those who had lived through the Cultural Revolution had recognised the danger: Bo's tactics. Propaganda was knit into the texture of Chinese life, but the brazen narcissism of Bo's self-promotion was something else. Torturing suspects to extract confessions was a widespread practice, and Chinese courts were not independent but under Party leadership. Yet the blatancy with which those who had run afoul of Bo and his friends were targeted, their assets seized and redistributed, was eyebrow-raising even in China. When a defence lawyer was jailed for falsifying evidence, people started paying attention: the exploitation of grand spectacle; the manipulation of mass emotion, and channelling of hostility to the rich; the overt use of personal power to knock out opponents, abandoning the law; the terror. Above all, the mobilisation of the public to overthrow the will of political institutions.

'He actually used the methods of the Cultural Revolution,' Han said. 'He had massive support from the population because so many people still think the Cultural Revolution was correct.'

It began to dawn on observers, long after it had struck his peers, that Bo was a powerful, charismatic leader leveraging the masses to take on – or take out – opponents. He wanted to force his way into the Politburo Standing Committee – and, after all, if one got there, why not climb further still? Until now, each heir had been picked out by one of the founders of modern China. Xi was the first prospective leader too young for such an anointment. His ascendancy was the product of a backroom deal between leaders. He was due to take power in November 2012. Some began to wonder if that was so certain. And then, as spectacularly as he had soared, Bo imploded.

— // —

As strange as Bo's exploitation of the Cultural Revolution was the enthusiasm it met in Chongqing. He had lost his mother to the movement; the city had lost so many of its youth. But the appetite for Maoism had never been wholly extinguished. People were not just bullied into it: they chose it. And when it died, they mourned it. They missed belonging to a shared endeavour. They missed an age where officials had been poor, and had struggled to serve the people. The millions thrown out of work by reforms to state-owned enterprises missed their jobs, and money, and sense of certainty. The middle classes missed the confidence that they had no less than their neighbours. They missed public spaces, replaced by shopping malls.

They missed not having to make decisions. They missed security. They missed the clarity of right and wrong. They missed the brief shining moment when the world had seemed new and everything possible.

For most, grief was balanced by the pleasures of their new life. They leaned towards Zheng Zhisheng's view: that Communist moderates had saved China, offering wealth and stability. But others believed that thieves had stolen their future. In a world without trust, many lived in permanent terror of cheats. Maoists saw Deng and other reformers as the biggest conmen of all: snatching the people's birthright from them and dishing it out to their own families and cronies. The Cultural Revolution was not a perversion of the Communist cause but its zenith, and, like their late but eternal leader, the Maoists saw it as unfinished business. Some of them remembered the glory days when they were in the vanguard. To others it was a gleaming legend. A group of them founded a bookshop and website called Utopia. If the name implied that their destination might never be attained, they nonetheless garnered a growing band of travellers. Some organised trips to North Korea, to admire society as it should be. Another set up a rural commune for students. Many of them saw Bo's Chongqing – or at least its leftist elements – as a beacon.

Maoism is inherently an ideology of struggle, and the Maoists were true to the cause. They complained that the media, dominated by reformists – what they called the right – was blinkered and intolerant, ignoring the problems and voices of the poor. They believed they were a persecuted minority, though they did not suffer as democrats did: no one was jailed for urging a return to the good old days, as they might be for demanding multiparty elections. Maoists berated critics of the Cultural Revolution. They harangued reformists at lectures. Ten thousand people signed a petition demanding the arrest of Mao Yushi, a softly spoken octogenarian economist, for describing Chairman Mao as 'the backstage boss who wrecked the country and ruined the people'. Others threatened him with violence. One Utopia co-founder, a professor, made headlines for slapping an eighty-year-old 'traitor' who had dared to scoff at young Maoists.

Han, one of those who hoped for reforms, shook his head at their behaviour, but told me I should speak to leftists: 'I can introduce you. Talk to Zhou Jiayu,' he said. 'We agree about the problems today, and totally disagree about the solutions. There are very few who think like me, a lot more people who think like him. We were friends in the past – we all fought in the Cultural Revolution. That's why we can still get on. That, and because I believe that everyone has the right to be different and disagree. For me, I oppose your thinking, but I support your right to say it.'

Then he laughed. 'If Zhou and the others were in power they wouldn't be so compassionate.'

— // —

Han wasn't the first to mention Zhou. 'No one could call him a scapegoat,' Zheng had said.

'He always had this petty mentality. Even now he denies it all,' another Red Guard complained.

And then there was the historian who had told me, with a bleak smile: 'There are people who are willing to talk. There are people who are not willing. And there are many people who are willing to talk but not to tell the truth – like Zhou Jiayu.'

It was April: Tomb-Sweeping Day, when the Shapingba graveyard was unlocked at last for Red Guard veterans and families. The annual gathering was an unlikely blend of feudal ritual and Maoist remembrance. Zhou had taken a large white wreath with green-and-orange trim. Last year he had stood on a bench there and declaimed to leftist veterans, urging them to honour the sacrifices of their fallen comrades. This year he delivered his speech in the confines of a tea-house; after Bo's fall, officials were anxious. White tape fluttered at the entrance to the cemetery and damp officials, encased in plastic raincoats, sat in line at a folding table. Only those with proven links to the dead could enter – certainly no foreigners. I didn't press the point, already anxious that my interviews might be interrupted. 'The police want to know whether you're working or on holiday?' the receptionist had called out as I left the hotel that morning.

Perhaps the cops had tombs of their own to sweep, for no one came to call, and Han and I met Zhou at a restaurant near his home the next day. After all I had heard, Zhou seemed small and unassuming, in a patterned acrylic sweater and slacks. I was unprepared too for his opening gambit: 'Oh, you're British. Thatcher, eh? Thatcher was like an iron lady but also had that womanly kindness.'

I'd grown up in the north in the eighties; this wasn't my take, still less the one I expected from an unrepentant Maoist.

'Yes,' he swept on as I demurred, 'she was great. Yet when the time called her, she acted tough. Like with the war in the Falklands. That was great! Chinese leaders should learn from her. They should learn from her in every regard.'

The opening bars of 'The Internationale' erupted, and he broke off to take the call. When he hung up he got straight down to business: 'For the past thirty years the Great Cultural Revolution has been marginalised and demonised. When ordinary people hear about it they naturally associate it with something bad and evil. And people attribute the improvements in society to reform and opening. That's because they don't know the truth. Very unfortunately, the Great Cultural Revolution failed. What we feared most back then is now at its height.'

Everyone else used a two-syllable abbreviation for the movement, wenge. Zhou spelled it out in full each time – wenhua da geming – to give the Cultural Revolution its full due of Greatness.

'What we wanted was not to let China enter capitalism. We had major problems like corrupt officials. The purpose was not to make myself a great man. It was not for any fame or fortune or personal benefit. The purpose was simple – for the country and the nation. To save the country and defend Chairman Mao.'

Zhou's commitment was a matter of simple gratitude: he owed everything to Mao and the Party. His father had been killed in the war of resistance against Japanese aggression; six of his siblings died in childhood, as his mother struggled to feed them. In desperation she sent her four remaining children to an orphanage. When the Communists took power, his older sisters joined the Party, found good positions and reunited them.

'From primary school to university, my family didn't spend a penny on tuition fees. If you went to hospital, it was free. Housing was free. We even got an eight-yuan stipend monthly – back then that was a lot. Chairman Mao gave a bright future to the poor. Back then we said that the contrast between the old and new society – Chiang Kai-shek's and Mao's – was like heaven and hell. But contrast the present with the Mao era and it's the same: today is like the old society. China is the world's second-largest economy. But eighty-five per cent of ordinary people can't afford to buy a home or get medical care or education. It's a joke. Officials don't treat people as the owners of the country. They treat themselves as the owners. They're corrupt. They don't care about morality or humanity. What they want is money. People call officials "boss" – it's the same as capitalism!'

Han leaned back in his chair and closed his eyes, hands behind his head. He had heard this monologue before.

'The boss can fire you any day. If you want to increase your wages, they'll fire you. Workers live in a miserable state, like lambs to the slaughter. In culture, what's propagated is money and power. It's not traditional culture – it's the worst part of traditional culture. They also use Western culture in place of the best wisdom: Mao's Thought.'

The first part of Zhou's lecture was almost concluded. He began to calm down.

'There are the oppressors and then there are the people who are oppressed. In Mao's era it was totally different.'

I judged it best not to mention the old joke – under capitalism man exploits man, under communism it's the other way round – and took advantage of Zhou's temporary pause to order. The restaurant was a chilly place that approximated indulgence with fake marble walls, a plastic chandelier and polyester brocade on the tables, while dispelling it with curt signs warning that gambling was forbidden. The mixture of gaudy and austere was a microcosm of Bo's Chongqing. Like everywhere else I'd seen in Chayuan New Zone, it appeared abandoned. There were few signs of life around the soaring grey-and-white tower blocks. Chayuan stood on the edges of the city, with the unsettled, ragged feel of land only recently reclaimed from the countryside. Zhou believed political persecution had forced him out here, far from his old friends – 'like sending me to Siberia'. He had lived in the centre until he was abruptly evicted, and not long afterwards was allocated this housing. Though it might have sounded paranoid, officials often put pressure on the landlords of activists, and Zhou, as I had already gathered, was not the kind to keep his head down.

He had been nearing the end of his studies at Chongqing University when the Great Cultural Revolution began.

'We knew there were corrupt officials and bureaucratism, but we didn't know at first who their representatives were. Then, when the Great Cultural Revolution started, we knew who the biggest capitalists were and we fought against them,' he said. 'I stood up and wanted to defend Chairman Mao, and that was why I dared to oppose what was happening. They turned leadership of the workers into the leadership of capitalist running dogs.'

When Han spoke of 'capitalist running dogs', I heard the inverted commas. For Zhou it was simply a definition, an unadorned statement of fact. Chongqing leaders, he complained, had turned on lower-level officials to divert attention from themselves. One of their first targets was the university's president – a veteran revolutionary loved for his humility and devotion to students as well as for his learning. He was the kind of model cadre often hymned by the Party. But Chongqing's Party secretary, the city's boss, had clashed with him and wanted him to go. The work group sent into the university forced students to denounce him, then detained him. He killed himself.

Zhou led the protests which followed. Thousands of students paraded in anger, joining Mao's battle for the people against inhuman officialdom. The sports group drove twelve motorbikes; the entertainment group brought flags and drums. Back then, he said, you had the freedom to march. You could write big-character posters. You could debate.

'I wasn't afraid. Why be afraid? So many people supported me. Because of the Great Cultural Revolution, we realised democracy and human rights. It provided a stage and platform for the lowest class: ordinary students like me became leaders – all because of the Great Cultural Revolution.'

Unexpectedly, Han agreed: 'It was splendid. We were pursuing the ideal society. You could choose what you believed in very freely and they told us, "Believe in the people and rely on them", "Let the people set themselves free." I was very much in favour of all that.'

For the dispossessed and marginalised – for poorer students, for casual workers struggling to get by, for anyone who had suffered an injustice at the hands of the bureaucracy – this was a chance to claim status and dictate the terms of their own lives, and simply be heard. Forcing scholars and officials to clean latrines was a calculated humiliation. But to those who usually did the job it also felt something like justice. For the first time they dared to rage about their daily battle to feed their families, about their unfair treatment. They believed in the 'great democracy' in which leaders (leaders, of course, below Mao) would at last be answerable to them. This flourishing of radical possibilities was always marginal, and would soon be cut short. They had made the mistake of taking Mao at his word.

Zhou, Zheng, Han and others formed the 815 brigade. Its influence quickly spread from the campus to the city's factories; the military would back the brigade against the municipal government and work groups – and the portion of its members, like Han, who would split.

Zhou was deft in blaming the right for even those things that most regarded as unquestionably the work of leftists. The burning of the British embassy in Beijing? 'That was done by the fake Communist Party. Chairman Mao wasn't behind that.' Armed fighting in Chongqing? 'It was the capitalists. They tried to incite tensions between people – they supported them into different factions. At the beginning it was only arguments. Then it became fighting with sticks and that sort of thing. Then it was fighting with arms and guns and tanks.'

A Fandaodi fighter had told me about the worst of the battles. Faced with defeat by 815, those who could swam away across the river. He was among the injured left behind, beaten again as they were captured, until the trucks which carried them were awash with blood. In detention they were beaten again, and he demanded to see Zhou, his old comrade. But Zhou had ignored his plea for help and walked away, he said.

'I don't have any recollection of that,' Zhou retorted when I asked him. 'It's all just rumour.'

You were involved in the armed struggle, though.

'No. I didn't beat anyone.'

A lot of people say you were involved. Besides, you were jailed for it.

'It's all hearsay. Someone else wrote a book saying I was in charge of the armed struggle. That's not true either. It was just an old grudge. I'm not scared of taking responsibility. I'm not shifting blame to others. I have been in jail for fifteen years – I'm not scared of anything. But we need to respect the truth.'

Zhou said the military command had liked him and had kept him on the army base to stop him being dragged into violence as it peaked. Besides, he had been in charge of the cultural defence section, not the fighting group, he added. 'I went to the scenes of the armed struggle, and moreover I promoted armed struggle in propaganda. But that was inevitable in that climate, if you were part of the Great Cultural Revolution. I went to encourage people not to be afraid and to carry on the fighting. And they called me "Three-Highs Zhou", because in a central government meeting I had a speech, and Zhou Enlai said: "Comrade Zhou Jiayu is high level, high style and has high credentials."'

He looked suddenly taller, more confident. I pressed him once more on the fighting.

'From the first, I felt it was wrong!' He was shouting again. 'I was sick of it. But I was forced to react. The other faction were fighting. If people strike you, what are you going to do? There was no other way. Of course there are things I regret in the Great Cultural Revolution. I was very young, only twenty-one; of course I was not sophisticated enough. The armed struggle was a mistake, and I didn't carefully study the people in power before I turned against them. But it was an honour to be in the Great Cultural Revolution. It means I didn't waste my life. I was a child from a very poor background and I was able to discuss things that really mattered to the country.' *They* had been the idealists. They didn't have children in foreign countries; they didn't have bank accounts abroad; they didn't have passports from other places, like officials now. They never looked for personal gain. They fought for the people. Their souls were pure.

And the cost – was that necessary?

'You can't say it was necessary. Thirty per cent of the Cultural Revolution was wrong. Because of that thirty per cent we had this suffering and death. But any kind of social revolution will have necessary sacrifices. From that viewpoint, it was necessary. The American Civil War killed how many people? Was it necessary or not? Liberation, here, killed how many people? Necessary or not?' A crescendo: 'The Second World War against the fascists – how many did that kill? *Necessary? Or not?*'

He sat back. 'It's not "necessary" or "not necessary",' he scolded. 'Some things are inevitable. It's a process of history.'

— // —

Zhou's star had crashed to earth after Mao's death and the fall of the Gang of Four. 'Liu Shaoqi and Deng Xiaoping's power was bigger. So they won,' he said.

Liu, of course, had died a few years into the Cultural Revolution, in agony on the floor of his cell, denied medical treatment. But to Zhou, ideology trumped all. Death was no impediment to victory, and no reason to forgive: what was one life, or a thousand, in the struggle to conquer history? Besides, the reformers had celebrated their return to power by seizing millions of Red Guards.

Millions? 'Tens of thousands,' he snapped. 'It was a horrible, miserable time.'

Jiang Qing and the rest of the Gang of Four faced a televised trial; leftists across the country were put in the dock. Zhou was charged with being a counter-revolutionary, and killing people, and plotting against the government: all unfair, he said. Most of the cadres arranging the trials had joined the Cultural Revolution too – where were their charges? And where was the evidence against him? No victims were named, no specific battles cited. The trials – like the reform and opening which followed – were nothing but victor's justice: 'All the law and the courts were just fake,' he complained.

The elite Red Guards – like Teacher Bian's killers – never had to face judges. Plenty of people had done worse than Zhou, whatever precisely it was that he did, and never paid the price. Yet there was, at least, a legal process. Jiang's case is known as the birth of defence in China, though she insisted she did not want a lawyer. (Her bitter interjections and testimony put the show into show trial: 'I was Chairman Mao's dog,' she famously declared. 'I bit what he told me to bite.') Televising it – at least in a censored version – was a way of showing that times had changed in more ways than one. In the Cultural Revolution the accused had no right to defend themselves, or be defended, and they faced purely political bodies. Now the state was reasserting its monopoly on violence. The lawyers were not permitted to plead not guilty for their clients, nor to address Mao's role. They were haunted by the very real fear that they might pay for defending these people: who knew when the political winds might shift again? But victims of the Cultural Revolution – purged leaders, purged lawyers, purged judges – ensured defendants the rights that those people had denied them.

Like Jiang, Zhou had put up a fight, dismissing his lawyers and defying the court. He crowed about besting the judges on legal points and winning applause from observers. At the trial's close he cried out: 'Long live the Communist Party! Long live the Great Cultural Revolution! Long live the spirit of swimming against the tide! Socialism will triumph over capitalism! History will judge me as innocent!'

'When I said this,' he added, 'there were three images in my mind. The first was the chairman of international communism when he was put on trial by Hitler. The second was Che Guevara. The third was Castro.'

His satisfaction didn't last long. In jail he was kept underground, in darkness, for three and a half years. There were three of them, but one went mad and the man on the other side died. Zhou had no contact with the outside world: no letters, or phone calls, or meetings; no chance even to see the sky. The loneliness devoured him as hunger did. He recited poems from the Tang and Song dynasties, and more recent works by Mao, of course, and sang songs – 'and I believed I was not guilty,' he added. 'That's how I persisted.'

He was sent to a labour camp; at last he could see the sun, breathe fresh air and speak to other prisoners. They dug out clay from deep pits, allowed food only when each had amassed enough to make 200 bricks. Then, barefoot through the winter, they stamped down the clay, the grey turning red with blood. Later he was promoted to the technical department of the camp factory, and, after fifteen years, freed. But liberty proved harder than he had imagined. His feet were still scarred and even now, when the wind changed, he felt the pain deep in his bones. Long-term malnutrition had weakened him and caused him chronic stomach aches. His marriage had broken up after his arrest and he had no contact with his son, now living in Canada. 'You don't have kids? Good. A household is a burden.'

The greater shock had been the new world he faced. He had managed to master the practical changes, but the death of the country he loved had thrown him off balance. He believed the movement's briefest tendencies – the flowering of truly radical ideals of control by the people, so quickly suppressed – were the real Cultural Revolution. Anything else he discounted as a distraction or distortion. On his balance sheet, all credit was to Maoism. Even China's economic growth owed nothing to reform and opening; it was just the natural progress brought by technological advance.

'There are three huge mountains in China: education, housing, medical care. These are problems caused by corrupt interest groups. These problems were eradicated before the Great Cultural Revolution. They say we're living a better life now but only a few people are better off. Politically, economically and culturally they're oppressed. China's reform and opening is actually increasing the process of transferring wealth from the public to the super-rich. The main class struggle now is between vested interest groups and the people oppressed and exploited by those vested interests. As a representative of the very lowest class – today is very bad.'

He sealed his lips. He was done.

— // —

He insisted on escorting us to our taxi, though the winds blew high and the rain pulsed across the square in bands. Han tried to slip him cash for his medicine as they said goodbye, but Zhou rebuffed him. He stood politely as he waited for the car to pull away, gripping his insubordinate umbrella with one hand and tapping his chest with the other to distract himself from the pain.

Han shook his head, both anxious about and exasperated by his not-friend. Liberals had once believed that economic reforms would bring political progress. But they too acknowledged that wealth and power had formed an apparently unbreakable alliance. Billionaires were multiplying and so were the assets of officials and their families. Meanwhile the reforms needed desperately by the poorest and most vulnerable never gained traction. Either they threatened someone's profits, or any alteration to the status quo seemed too risky. Yet Zhou's desire to return to the past seemed to Han regressive in every sense: naive and essentially biographical, reading the world entirely through his personal experience.

'Even though it was less corrupt, it was really just a different type of corruption. Many people criticised during the Cultural Revolution didn't even have any experience of capitalism. They were from poor families, workers, farmers. We were fighting a fake enemy,' he said. 'For the leftists it's not an idealistic position, it's personal. If they had a better life they would agree with the current government. Zhou's fate has been miserable. He doesn't have anything.'

The Cultural Revolution had been the zenith of Zhou's life. He had been a force in the world: vital, admired, praised and feared. Now he lived in poverty, his health wrecked by his years in prison, reliant on the charity of old foes. But Han and Zheng, who preferred the present, had after all done pretty well out of it. They could afford to be magnanimous, even if Zhou would not have been, and if they felt he had deserved his punishment, they agreed that he deserved better now. Together with other Red Guard veterans, they gave money to Zhou regularly. These three men had been friends and comrades once, then bitter enemies who might have killed each other. In some ways they had less in common these days. They didn't like each other's views; they didn't seem to like each other much. But they had found an accommodation, even if the relationship was shaded by need, a hint of condescension, prudent suspicion and mutual disrespect for the other's choices and beliefs.

Individuals could reach these tacit arrangements. Institutions could not. And the Party could not rely on the Zhengs, not least because the Cultural Revolution effect – the promise of the Party as the guarantor of stability – was largely generational. It had decreasing potency; many had not lived through the torment and, since the Party preferred not to mention it, knew little of it. Prosperity, too, was a diminishing asset. People needed a better rationale for the Party's rule. Something had to be done.

— // —

Bo had looked as though he was doing something, however superficial his response. He had run up huge debts, squandered public money on whims (spending $1.5 billion to plant ginkgo trees unsuited to the climate) and handed his associates cushy deals. He was the wrong – the terrible – answer to the right question: what next? But he had shown the Party that there had to be a next; that the status quo could not last. He demonstrated it so successfully, in fact, that it spelled his own defeat.

His fall was as remarkable as his rise. In February 2012 his right-hand man, the police chief, tried to defect at a nearby US consulate. He was taken away, not by Bo's men but Beijing's. Two weeks later the annual political gathering began in the capital. It was normally an event of calculated dullness, but Bo turned it into a spectacle. He attacked critics for 'pouring filth' over his family. He vowed to 'fight for the high ground with these devils', a quote from a Cultural Revolution poem. He portrayed himself as the standard-bearer for the Chinese masses: 'If only a few people are rich, then we'll slide into capitalism. We've failed,' he said.

Wen Jiabao was bowing out too, for his term as premier had come to an end. A known enemy of Bo, and seen by some as a liberal, he used his last press conference to criticise the Chongqing boss and call for political reforms. Without them, economic changes would stall, and the new problems society faced would go unresolved, 'and such historical tragedies as the Cultural Revolution may happen again'. It was a very rare public reference to the era by the leadership.

Bo was sacked the next day, to an instant outcry. Neo-Maoist websites were shut down before they could share their outrage too widely. They had held Bo up as a lodestar for the masses, though others – including Zhou Jiayu – saw him as an opportunist. A couple of weeks later came a bigger shock: Bo's wife, Gu Kailai, was detained on suspicion of killing a British man, Neil Heywood, over business dealings that went awry. This was the secret that the police chief had carried to the US consulate. Gu would be convicted and imprisoned, and Bo – after a fresh act of defiance at his trial, reminiscent of Jiang Qing's – would be jailed for taking huge bribes and abusing his power. But the explosive nature of the scandal disguised its systemic roots. Bo had already been a target. Investigators from Beijing had begun their work, focusing on the police chief; their strategy is always to take down subordinates, building the case against the man at the centre. The chief had tried to force Bo into protecting him by threatening to expose Gu. Bo had cut him loose. It might have been another overreach: he thought his ally disposable. Or he might have gambled that he could not survive any other way.

We cannot know what investigators sought as they circled Bo and his police chief. Bo, we learned later, had been spying on top leaders. Some believe that, with his future imperilled, he contemplated a coup. The country's mighty security chief, Zhou Yongkang, was rumoured to have plotted with him. In the days after Bo's disappearance all sorts of rumours flourished. But one proved particularly enduring: that, in the early days of the Cultural Revolution, he had won the Red Guards' favour by slapping his own father's face. Former classmates of Bo, no admirers of his, told me it wasn't true. That didn't matter. Many children had turned on their parents in those brutal times, when survival was all. His brother had been a Red Guard leader, and students at his school had tortured their teachers; *Long Live the Red Terror* had been scrawled on a wall in blood. More importantly, the slap felt like *the sort of thing* he would do. It rang of truth, even if it was a lie, so convincing that it might not even have been consciously invented. As an adult, after all, he had drawn inspiration from the movement that killed his mother. It was one small detail in the great morass of murder and corruption and abuse and ambition that brought him down – and yet it stuck. The Cultural Revolution was a potent way to tar him, and its grip on the imagination owed much to its vagueness as well as to its horrors. On the rare occasions it was mentioned by the state, it was brandished as proof that any deviation from the current paradigm must end in disaster. Quasi-Maoist Bo was as much its product as the 'rightist' student protestors of 1989 had been, or as pro-democracy demonstrators in Hong Kong would be in turn. 'If China imitates the West's multiparty parliamentary democratic system . . . it could repeat the chaotic and turbulent history of the "Cultural Revolution" when factions sprang up everywhere,' warned the state news agency, Xinhua. It was a bogeyman, drawing its power from its place in the shadows. It was whatever you wanted or feared it to be.

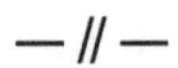

One morning, as I left our block in Beijing, I noticed that the lion outside had shed its abundant coat of plastic ivy. From a distance the foliage had lent a distinguished air to the fibreglass model, redolent of an English stately home. Now the beast wore a red ribbon round its neck, and I thought of the recent pictures of Xi, surrounded by the Party's Young Pioneers – he had worn, as the children all did, a scarlet kerchief at his throat. A week or so earlier he had visited France, where he had cited a quote often attributed to Napoleon: 'China is a sleeping lion. Let her sleep, for when she wakes she will shake the world.' The lion had woken, Xi told his audience, 'but it is a peaceful, amicable and civilised lion'. His vision for China was broad and expansive: a theme of national rejuvenation, wealth and power. Deng Xiaoping had told the country to hide its light and bide its time, a formulation his successors stuck by. But Xi had grander ambitions in the world. China was to lead again, to broaden its sway. And to do this it would narrow its vision, be more focused in its ideology, and more strongly led from the centre; would reject still more decisively Western values, and reassert its political commitments at home. China would establish a new place for itself only by strengthening Chinese Leninism.

Xi did not initiate the turn towards repression; it predated him, probably prompted by the Arab Spring as well as by domestic discontent and Bo's machinations. The Communist Party never handed power to its citizens, any more than it lifted them out of poverty. They had earned their growing prosperity, paying for it in sweat, in fractured family relationships, and sometimes in mangled limbs. Little by little they had hacked out a space to argue, debate, assert themselves. People had learned that they had to look after themselves. They were tougher, more individualistic, freer-thinking. The Party found this helpful in some ways, but it tolerated the growth of civil society and the appetite for increased rights rather than encouraging it. And as people gained confidence it grew more anxious. The pact between party-state and society was eroding, generation by generation. Using the Cultural Revolution as proof that the Party was a bulwark against turmoil became less effective when much of the population could not remember it. Experience is always more potent than advice, and in any case people don't stay grateful. Just as the approval which greeted improvements in health insurance or pensions was soon supplanted by grumblings about their inadequacies, so the more general increase in prosperity was taken for granted and people wondered why they weren't doing better, and why other people were.

Some in the Party were already pushing for stronger leadership, capable of forcing through reforms. Bo's case suggested it was not a matter of whether things should change, only whether such change could be controlled. Perhaps it was enough to tip the balance. History had taught the Party's leadership that power must be caged. Yet they handed Xi the key. They allowed him to break with precedent, by taking down Bo's patron, Zhou Yongkang, the security tsar – the first member of the Politburo Standing Committee to be expelled from the Party since the fall of the Gang of Four. Xi claimed Party and military leadership at once, though his predecessor had waited years to take control of the gun. Within a few years Xi's ideology would be enshrined in the Party's constitution under his name: he was the first living leader to have the honour since Mao himself. Soon he would abolish the presidential term limit, in a statement of intent. In time he would embark upon indefinite rule as general secretary, too: the party position was the true source of his supremacy. It seems unlikely that his elders foresaw that he would gather quite so much power, so fast. But they had given him the opportunity.

Xi was no Bo. He was not so flashy, not so short-term. But there were uncanny echoes of what had happened in Chongqing. Each day his power was asserted more boldly and celebrated more loudly. He was lauded in the media for his humility, his charisma and his strength. He turned to modernised versions of techniques that Mao had once employed. There were videoed confessions by tycoons known for their outspoken social criticism; long televised rectification meetings where cadres were called to account for their faults. The state media became increasingly doctrinaire. These demands for ideological purity; the call for China to play a leading role in the world; his personal, emotional appeal to the people – all were familiar, though he was seeking the masses' tacit support, not their active intervention. This was not real Maoism, even in purely political terms: he sought dominance without the disruption. He did not want to upend China, but to rein it in. Yet he had set about dismantling the changes designed to safeguard his party and country against such disasters. He believed, it appeared, that stabilising China required not the dilution or containment of power but its concentration, enabling decisive action. And these lessons were drawn not despite the scars of Maoism but precisely, it seemed, because of his family's suffering and his long years in internal exile in the countryside.

SIX

> The world is yours – ours, too, but in the final analysis it is yours. You young people, in the prime of your youthful vigour, are like the morning sun. Our hopes rest with you.
>
> **Mao Zedong**

No one had thought a revolution could be boring. But by late 1968 the Red Guards' excesses had come to an end: no more burning and smashing of feudal relics, or raids on bourgeois homes. Travelling the country in the Great Link-Up was just a memory. Idling in alleyways wasn't such fun any more. After two years of study sessions and struggle sessions and nothing much to do at all, even the keenest felt their fervour ebbing. They hadn't expected to miss education, but with their adventures on the railways long behind them Yu Xiangzhen and her friends pined for books and studies. The one class her school restored was English: an especially odd choice when Red Guards had besieged and burned the British embassy only a year before. 'But all we learned to say,' she added, by way of explanation, 'was "Long live Chairman Mao! Long live Chairman Mao!"'

What most people think of as the Cultural Revolution – the reign of the Red Guards – was a relatively short stage. The Chairman had planned a three-year movement, but after two and a bit even he was irked by the chaos. He had ordered the military to curb the Red Guards, who were no longer useful. Thwarted teenagers, with no outlet for their energies, fed the pool of disenchanted urban youth. Education had expanded under the Communists, but better opportunities hadn't grown with it. A fifth of the Chinese population lived in cities, without the jobs to match. The atmosphere was combustible, a toxic mix of frustration, grudges, fanaticism, adolescent posturing and sheer idleness. Young people had little to do but look for trouble: hooliganism and, one newspaper fretted, things that 'do not lead to socialism'.

And so, on another long, dull day, Yu was summoned by a leader and handed a batch of papers. Her job was to deliver them to friends and schoolmates.

'There was no choice. It happened overnight,' she said. 'There were four possibilities for young people. You could join the army, which was considered glorious – but the criteria were so strict; you had to come from a revolutionary family, or your father and grandfather and even great-grandfather all had to be from very poor families. For girls, there were two hundred applicants for one place; for boys, I'd guess maybe one out of a couple of dozen would get in. You could work in a factory, as I did – that was thought very lucky, because you got to stay in the city close to your parents, and if you could get into a state-level factory you were very, very lucky. You could go with the construction corps' – the big state farming schemes – 'to Heilongjiang, Inner Mongolia or Xining. That was not such a bad option. The worst was that you would go to the villages.'

But that was where almost all of them ended up. Yu's schoolmates were the first wave in the great tide of urban adolescence that swept towards impoverished rural China: 17 million boys and girls, enough to people a nation of their own. They are known, now, as the Lost Generation. But the Party called it going up to the mountains and down to the countryside, capturing its lofty justifications and the humble soil in which these students were planted. Some were as young as fourteen. Many had never spent a night away from home. They were sent hundreds or thousands of miles away, and back a century: to places with no electricity or running water, perhaps not even reachable by road.

As Yu walked from door to door, handing out notices, every family wept. In the days and weeks that followed, train and bus stations filled with sobbing teenagers and parents gulping back cries of fear. The Great Link-Up had been an adventure. This was real life, and it was for life: you were to 'set down your roots' in your new home. Since most had relatives in the countryside, they knew how harsh life there could be. Many had lost family members in the Great Famine.

'They were still kids. And of course people knew that life would be tough, so they were also afraid. The ones who had been so active in the Cultural Revolution's early stages began to realise their good times had come to an end,' Yu said.

Mao's ideological compulsions drove this pragmatic solution. Marxist theory dismissed the peasantry as a relic of feudalism. Mao – bullied for his farming background as a teenager – had overturned that, seizing on the rural poor as the engine of revolution. Now the urban youth were to harness their skills, knowledge and acuity to the welfare of the countryside. They would drag forward villages mired in poverty and ignorance: improving hygiene, spreading literacy, eradicating superstitions. But the peasantry's task was to uproot a more profound form of ignorance: the urban elite's indifference to the masses. Mao had always warned of victory's dangers. Now he had his proof. The sugar-coated bullets of the bourgeoisie had pierced the souls of Communists. Cadres who had worked and fought and risked everything facing down the Kuomintang had been seduced by city living and white-collar work. Their children had sunk further. Their instinct for comfort over struggle, their selfish concern for family and desire for personal accomplishment, would all destroy his legacy. A decade of revisionist education had poisoned them. The peasantry would reforge this generation: teach them to live with nothing; to endure, even love, the dirtiest labour; to not merely sacrifice but efface themselves for the greater good. They would bear his revolution to its ultimate triumph, a country whose economy, society and culture were as communist as its political system.

— // —

The propaganda posters show them marching to the fields for another day of labour. They have often paused to address a cheery, wrinkled peasant; are pink-cheeked, always; guileless, hearty. These handsome children in cotton jackets have sickles or hoes slung over their shoulders and in their free hands they hold, of course, *Quotations from Chairman Mao Zedong.*

Here they were before me upon the stage. They were uniformed, Mao-capped and armbanded, clutching Little Red Books to their hearts as they sang. The slightest of the trio called himself Zhong Sheng, or Voice-of-China; he didn't think I should use his real name, though nothing he said could possibly have bothered even the most neurotic official. Being an Educated Youth – a city kid sent down to the country – had made him braver and stronger, he said, when he stepped off the platform. It had taught him how to value life and to take satisfaction in quite ordinary, modest things. He was proud of the strides that his country had made, and the little part he had played in that, and was grateful to China's leaders. The cluster around him nodded and smiled and whispered to each other. They were the Chongqing Educated Youth Friendship Group and I had met them, quite by chance, in a park the previous day. They'd been dancing in a square by the gates, moving back and forth in a complicated piece of choreography, with some waving of scarves and much calling of instructions. I didn't want to interrupt, but they saw me watching and halted, urging me to attend their gala. They were not youths any more, of course, but in late middle age. Still, from a distance, you might have mistaken them for teenagers. It wasn't just the miniskirts and heels on their slim frames, or the ponytails and flaming lipstick, but the girlish way in which the women held hands, stroked arms, massaged shoulders, smoothed sleeves and straightened bag straps. They were giddy with affection, teasing each other and posing for photograph after photograph, crooking their fingers into rabbit ears. A woman in pleather over-the-knee boots playfully twisted the ear of a man, who yelped but tried to look game. Close up, their clothing was a fiesta of colour and pattern and flourishes. A sequinned collar topped a lace dress; ruching and roses enlivened bright stripes. Their make-up was heavy, with boldly pencilled brows, and their long hair tinted back to startling black or dyed brassy blonde.

They met up two or three times a week to climb mountains, eat hotpot, play mah-jong and sing. Things were more fun when you shared them. Once a year, after months of preparation, they staged their extravaganza. They had rented a hall and courtyard this time, for a long, elaborate programme which I gave up trying to understand. I surrendered to the waves of activity – group photos, plates of peanuts and cucumber, songs, photos, dances, photos, mouth-numbing chicken, more songs, more food and of course more photos, requiring multiple costume changes and endless reorganisation and fussing, including over me. The celebrity treatment had begun with a hush, an announcement and a standing ovation as I arrived. Now I was photographed with ladies in frocks and ladies waving fans, men both beaming and serious, next to friends and between them, seated and standing, with arms around my shoulders, cheek to cheek. A hand eased into mine; I looked down into a sweet smile and crinkling eyes. Auntie Gu was underdressed beside her peers, in a pink-and-black tracksuit, with a bare face and long, unstyled hair; and calmer, too, though she talked in a stream of reminiscences and questions and suggestions and remarks, interspersed with comments to passing friends and brief forays to rescue her grandson, a chubby, placid three-month-old being passed around the tables. These were her people. There were twenty-six registered Educated Youth groups in Chongqing alone, they told me, and many more unofficial ones; together their members numbered in the thousands. Some specialised in particular pastimes, such as photography or dancing. This group were generalists who prided themselves on diffuse interests and a cosy, informal tone. I had assumed they had reunited after decades spent apart, but in fact they had met in a chatroom six years ago; the experience of rural life, common but not shared, was enough. They spoke the same language. It was their spiritual wealth, Auntie Gu said: 'We're proud of being Educated Youth; it was something unprecedented. We know that nothing like it will happen in future.'

Voice-of-China lingered as I chatted with the others, interjecting every now and then, reminding us how pleased they all were that China was developing so well and how much they respected the country's founders. Despite his age, something about him – his uniform, the unstinting obedience of his answers – made me think of a Boy Scout. My attention drifted as he spoke, and snagged on the Little Red Book he was still gripping. It had the scarlet plastic cover, Mao's avuncular face, the gold characters spelling out the title, but no pages.

— // —

There's a story – as implausible as it sounds – of Deng Xiaoping meeting Shirley MacLaine when he visited the United States in

1979. The actor was seated close to him at a White House banquet, and expounded about a Chinese scientist she'd met, who said that he'd been happier and more productive when sent to labour on a farm. Deng cut her short: 'He lied.'

Deng, of course, had been purged twice in the Cultural Revolution. He had spent three years working in the provinces, in a tractor factory. It was better than dying, or sweating in the fields, but he saw no reason to romanticise it. His bluntness was echoed in the first wave of Educated Youth memoirs, which attacked the pointlessness and hopelessness of rustication; they formed part of the 'scar literature' struggling to find meaning in the Cultural Revolution. But just as the squalor of a run-down hamlet can appear picturesque from a distance, so rural exile began to look wholesome, even life-affirming, as it receded. In the early nineties, an exhibition of photos, reminiscences and mementos of daily life from the Educated Youth drew 150,000 visitors in a fortnight, sparking similar shows and a fashion for reminiscence. Groups organised sentimental returns to villages. Tourist agencies cashed in. It is not coincidence, perhaps, that the turn to the past came just after the massacre of 1989 had destroyed a compelling vision of China's future and as mass lay-offs caused by the restructuring of state-owned enterprises threw into doubt many of this generation's sense of identity. The nostalgia industry boomed and the Party began to discern its potency. Despite Voice-of-China's anxiety, it was – is – the only part of the Cultural Revolution that is widely discussed and celebrated, albeit subject to the usual policing. Rustication was severed from its roots in fanaticism and repackaged as fresh air, comradeship and honest toil. Nostalgia for the hard times is not unique to China. But this was akin to toasting the 'Blitz spirit' on the basis of Tube station camp-outs, without mentioning bombs and mass civilian deaths.

Xi Jinping and fellow leaders were among the 17 million. He left Beijing for a little village in north-western Shaanxi province, where he lived for seven years in a narrow, musty cave house built into the yellow-earth hillside. He grew into manhood in Liangjiahe, hauling coal carts, carrying manure, building dykes, farming corn and potatoes. He endured the fleas, the biting cold, the monotonous diet and still more monotonous labour. He read books while herding sheep or late into the night, cutting short his sleep. When he returned as president, in 2015, he described it as the place where he had embarked on his life.

His ascension turned Liangjiahe into an attraction. Thousands of visitors – mostly officials – came to inspect his old home and admire a well he had dug. But Xi had begun to highlight those years of hardship in interviews and articles as early as the nineties. When he took the top job, his book *The Governance of China* – more than 13 million copies distributed in thirty-three languages, and counting – hymned his grace in austerity, his selfless dedication to the peasants and the humility with which he had learned from them (*like Mao*, was the unstated implication). He helped the farmers to develop the place, reinforcing the riverbank to stop erosion. His exemplary dedication earned him the title of a Model Youth, but he exchanged his prize for farming equipment to help the villagers. Even the local Party secretary turned to him for advice. Xi, who had arrived as a naive teenager, left as a man set on serving the people. 'When I arrived at the Yellow Earth, at fifteen, I was anxious and confused. When I left the Yellow Earth, at twenty-two, my life goals were firm and I was filled with confidence,' he wrote later.

It was quite a creation myth. The story testified to his grit, his discipline, his humility. His service emphasised his impeccable heritage, echoing his father's revolutionary labours; it also proved that he was one of the masses. He had suffered, and he had risen above it. In early interviews he was surprisingly candid. But over time the official version lost awkward details, such as his bullying by Red Guards in Beijing ('On the whole special train there was no one who was not crying, except for me, who was laughing,' he recalled. 'If I did not go I don't even know if I would live or die here, so isn't leaving a good thing?'). One English-language state media report spoke of 'the city boy who went to the countryside', which had the ring of an ancient fable or perhaps a reality show. It didn't mention that he left Liangjiahe after only a few months, returning because there was nowhere else to go. It wasn't chance that Xi found himself in an area where people remembered his father fondly and were inclined to look out for him. Nor was it so surprising that they called upon him with their problems; he was more likely to know someone who could help. Educated Youth sometimes enjoyed better rations than regular villagers. State media described how he could carry almost a hundred kilograms of wheat, earning him respect as a tough lad, both hard-working and capable; villagers recalled the future leader of the country sliding downhill on his bottom as he struggled to carry the pails that they shouldered easily.

But however you told it, the story was potent in an age where the gulfs between town and country, rulers and ruled, had expanded so fast, and where corruption was treated as a matter of course by both those benefiting from it and those paying for it. It had echoes of the Long March, turning rural adversity into a triumph of Communist spirit and discipline, in striking contrast to the lavish lifestyles now enjoyed by the Party elite. It emphasised that the leader understood what it was to struggle. It was also true. Xi had worked and studied hard; people seem to have liked and respected him. Long after he had left, and had climbed to an important post, he sent back money so an old friend could have an operation. His experiences had taught him the harshness of life at the bottom of society, giving him a visceral understanding that few young people – or Western leaders – could appreciate. Important as his privileges were, they could only temper the draining conditions and relentless graft. He remembered the shock of manure in the face as he cleared a blocked pipe. The food was bad and there was never enough of it, rest was scarce yet boredom rife, and the little luxuries he would once have taken for granted – meat, fruit, clean clothes, companionship – had vanished. In the first few months, he and the villagers struggled to even understand each other's speech. It was a lonely life.

— // —

The next time I saw Auntie Gu – after she had hugged me and shown me the latest pictures of her grandson, but before I had a chance to ask her any questions – she began to tell me about a girl she had known in the villages.

'There was a talented schoolteacher who fell in love with her – he was really able. He got caught at her house one night and was so scared he hid underneath her bed. They dragged him out and sentenced him to eight years in prison. He had a family; it was adulterous. It was common practice: if local guys slept with Educated Youth, they could be executed. The girl denied they had a relationship, so that he could walk free, but he ended up admitting it.'

It wasn't hard to imagine the treatment required to extract that confession.

'She only just got in touch with him last year,' Auntie Gu continued. 'I knew them both – she had been married, but her husband was dead by then – and they met again, for the first time. They got each other's numbers and were on the phone for hours. She was crying all the time. They decided the guy would leave the countryside and move to Chongqing. They live next door to each other.

She takes care of him – he's disabled now – even though they're in separate apartments. The guy's wife is still living in the village.'

Auntie Huang chipped in: 'The wife was quite understanding. At the same time, his pension is three thousand yuan a month, and she has no income. So she had to put up with it.'

'They were basically all arranged marriages back then. You didn't get love matches,' Auntie Gu said, scrolling through her phone. She pulled up a picture of the girl and the teacher to show me. There was nothing remarkable about this grey-haired pair; nor did they look especially happy to be standing alongside each other. It wasn't clear what Auntie Gu thought of their affair – a grand folly? A true romance? – and I wasn't sure why she had broached it. The story lingered as we walked and talked.

Carts of pineapple along the street sweetened the warm spring air. Women scooped cherries and inky mulberries from woven panniers. Migrants from the countryside, in torn plimsolls and old army jackets, squatted at the kerb with their thick bamboo poles: they were the city's famous bang-bang men, who would bear your loads, balanced at each end of their sticks, up Chongqing's hills for ten yuan a time. A more extravagant generation might have hired one there and then, for we were laden with plastic boxes of food, sunshades, hats, hand-me-downs for the grandson, more dancing costumes, a portable CD player and other sundries – today was an outing, but with so much baggage and so many participants, it felt like an expedition. Voice-of-China, despite his job in logistics, had abandoned attempts to marshal the troops. He and the handful of other men were an afterthought anyhow. The energy pulsed from this band of sisters, scattering and regrouping as we made our way along the streets to Chongqing University.

We turned in at the gates. It was a public holiday; families picnicked on the campus amid palm trees and willows and great thickets of bamboo. We straggled down the long slope, all chatter and distraction, eventually converging on a little pavilion set upon the lake. Voice-of-China made a speech which I tuned out as I spoke to Auntie Gu. Another woman switched on the CD player, selected an old song and began to dance. I recognised her now: she was wearing the over-the-knee boots again, this time with a short, frou-frou black net skirt.

Student couples played cards and badminton around us; young men sweaty from the basketball courts pulled off their vests to mop their necks as they strolled.

'Sometimes I envy them a bit,' said Auntie Huang. We were watching a couple of teenage girls, in jeans and pastel T-shirts, heads bent towards each other as they sauntered.

'We didn't have all these kinds of outfits. We only had blue or grey clothes. When I see this – well, that's why we all dress up in such a fashionable way. There's a huge generation gap caused by that particular historical period. It was made by society – nothing to do with us. Just like today's young people, I wanted to do many things, like go to university, but I couldn't realise them. I was eighteen. I felt there was no hope. We had no hope at all. One person would cry and then everyone would start. I missed my mum and dad. People were desperate. We thought we'd spend our whole lives there. It was dejection. Despair. I was in the countryside for four years, and Older Sister over there away for eight. There was a lot of bitterness.'

The woman she had nodded at, who bore an elaborate, gravity-defying puff of raven hair, shot her a strychnine glare and moved away. Whatever she'd confided was not for outsiders. Auntie Huang was oblivious. Having met online, the Chongqing Educated Youth Friendship Group knew nothing and everything about each other. They rarely met up with the people they had actually worked with – they lived too far apart, or never quite got the timing right; there were too many practical obstacles, and perhaps others too. This group offered distance as well as intimacy. It was Educated Youths Anonymous. You could talk about whatever you wanted, open up about the things that you couldn't tell your husband, or which your children wouldn't quite understand. But it was up to you whether you chose to reveal or keep your secrets. These friends were only part of your wider life if you wanted them to be – an unimaginable freedom for people who had spent most of their lives in production brigades and work units which determined their housing, their right to travel, and whether they could marry or divorce, as late as the 1990s. The closeness of this group reassured them. It mimicked the tiny, tightly knit communities they remembered, but there was no risk of contradiction here. No one could say that it wasn't this way or that you had not been that way. You were what you said you were. The stories you brought were yours alone, however they resonated. Everything was as you remembered it – and they remembered everything: those days were becoming more vivid, and more enticing, and more bewildering.

One of the men began to sing, and Auntie Gu joined him, her slight voice a wistful contrast with his hefty baritone. They all knew this one, from those long dark evenings: its evocation of a kerosene lamp in the dimness of a little cottage and of bitter tears dampening their clothes.

Auntie Gu's lamp had rested on the coffin in her room, and its dim light had eased her terror a little. In the countryside, people liked to prepare for their death well in advance, but that big wooden box frightened a city girl sent to live and die far from her friends and family. She hadn't had it easy before that. Her father was a factory worker, but her mother had died when she was little and she'd taken on most of the chores. She was young – so young – and had somehow thought this new life might be exciting: living and working and playing together in the countryside. Yet the moment the truck set off from Chongqing, nerves overcame them all. Auntie Gu and her schoolmates vomited and wept their way through the three-day drive.

'At the very beginning we were all idealistic. We wanted to make a difference to the countryside,' Auntie Huang recalled. But the villages were filthy and desolate, and the bone-thin peasants were unimpressed by their theories for grand improvements. They had been urged to remake the world; they began to wonder if they could change anything. The differences were too great. In villages composed of a single clan, where everyone was a Meng or a Li, the city kids stood out in every way. In the first few days the village children crept up to stroke Auntie Gu's soft, pale hands, touch her long hair and feel her simple cotton clothes, which bore an air of glamour there.

Auntie Gu really wanted to learn from the farmers, but the work left her bruised and blistered. Loads were so heavy that she cried as she carried them. Water had to be heaved from the well and borne all the way home in wooden pails. Drought brought a swift end to their extra rations and left them surviving on corn husks as the peasants did. Salt and oil became luxuries.

I was grateful that Voice-of-China had been drawn into another chat. This wasn't his kind of reminiscing. Auntie Huang was talking of a friend now, a young girl who died when a serious illness was dismissed as just a cold. Weakened by overwork and malnutrition, many had succumbed to malaria, pneumonia and other diseases. Thousands more died 'unnatural' deaths, killed by peasants or cadres or, usually, in work accidents: crushed by trees they were felling or carts that overturned. Propaganda revelled in these pointless sacrifices, spurring children on to fresh acts of futility. Jin Xunhua, a Shanghai teenager, was commemorated as a martyr for dying as he tried to save wooden poles from a flood. Postage stamps show him amid the waves, head high and arm raised like a synchronised swimmer's as he shouts a final exhortation back to watching comrades.

Amid these dangers, the Educated Youths grew closer than families. They defended their comrades, they nursed them through illnesses, they offered company and sympathy. But exhaustion and hunger frayed their ties too. They grew shorter-tempered with indiscreet friends and housemates who vanished when firewood was needed. They judged each other for the choices they made as they navigated this new world: they identified the sycophants, the manipulators, the ones whose parents could afford to send gifts for cadres, smoothing their path.

Auntie Gu's tender nature won over both classmates and neighbours. She helped to harvest crops for an old widow neglected by her children. She and her friends taught village kids, organised musical shows for the farmers, caught frogs in the fields to sate their hunger for meat. But even kindlier farmers grew exasperated with them. The rural population was too high, and productivity low. They didn't need the extra hands and didn't want extra mouths to feed. These kids, for all their books and ideas, were slow and clumsy, had no feel for tools or land, wasted seed and couldn't seem to manage quite moderate loads or uncomplicated tasks.

The teenagers struggled to earn the work points they needed to feed themselves. They had no hope of keeping up with more experienced workers. Children and women received fewer points than men for their labour anyway, and fewer still when relegated to the unskilled tasks farmers didn't care to do and thought the newcomers might manage. Their inability to scratch a living increased their despondency. And when allowances were made for them, peasants resented the special treatment – no one indulged a village family's laziness or inefficiency. Educated Youth stole chickens when they got too hungry; peasants pilfered objects from their homes. Cultures clashed. Farmers were shocked to see girls and boys out for walks together, however innocently, and disturbed as their influence rubbed off on village youths. Maoist puritanism, dismissing romance as a bourgeois snare, looked liberal beside the deep conservatism in parts of the countryside: 'If country boys and girls were in relationships, they wouldn't dare to look in each other's eyes,' said Auntie Huang.

But the city girls, naive and far from their families, were easy prey for peasants and especially cadres. Though fright and shame deterred many from reporting abuses, thousands of cases were recorded in a single year. The problem was pronounced enough that the centre kept threatening punishment for rapes. Often the victims took the blame, since they had worse class backgrounds than officials.

Malicious or obstructive cadres had so many ways to make you suffer: refusing rations, assigning the worst jobs or accusing you of political crimes. One of Auntie Huang's classmates, sent down at fourteen, died in jail after he was accused of joining an anti-Party organisation. You could be punished for a single remark, Auntie Gu murmured. The boy who wrote 'The Educated Youth Song', the best-known of the tunes circulating amongst them, received a suspended death sentence for its dangerously reactionary sentiments: its lyrics evoked his longing for his mother, his hometown and his schooldays. As I listened I began to regret my irritation at Voice-of-China's aggressive caution.

The Educated Youth group mourned the hardship, the bitterness, the missing friends, but they also saw the suffering as the real point of it all. They spoke of the era as veterans might talk of a war to younger men born too late to fight: with regret and sometimes scorn or anger, and disbelief that they had gone through it, but also with the unmistakable tinge of superiority. It had made them braver, stronger, more capable. They understood something no one else could, that no one ever would again.

When Bo Xilai still ran Chongqing, he had ordered college students to labour in the countryside, though only for a few months. Intellectuals had mocked or feared the edict, with its echoes of Maoist attacks on culture. Auntie Gu and her friends had rather liked the idea. The chasm between urban and rural life was growing larger by the day. Incomes were three times higher in the cities, and many young people had never set foot beyond their borders, except to sightsee. In an age of mobile phones and asphalt roads, a stint in the villages didn't sound so tough. Auntie Gu thought it would teach them self-reliance: so many depended on their parents for everything from flat purchases to childcare. But she didn't want her own stylish daughter to find spiritual wealth in the fields.

I was still thinking of the couple she had talked about, of the layered unhappinesses. I imagined the young, clever, isolated man, who had met a girl and fallen in love. Someone with whom he could talk at last, share his ideas and dreams – someone educated, interested, not yet worn down by years of labour or preoccupied by the need to feed their children. And the girl: lonely, far from home, a workhorse only toiling and sleeping, until he made her a person again, desirable, valuable, with thoughts and hopes and someone to confide them in. They had thought they were escaping from their lives, for a moment, and instead they had built a cage. He'd suffered for a short-lived passion, and left his family to suffer too. She must have lived with guilt and shame and judgement: she had helped to send a man to prison, leaving his children fatherless. I wondered if love had really lasted all those years apart, or if something stronger had pulled them back, to their strange propriety of separate homes: guilt or complicity, their debt to each other, a kind of revenge on the people who had thwarted them.

And then there was the man's wife, living with his distraction. Jealousy can thrive where love doesn't. His jailing might have brought her relief, or simply rage – after everything else, she was left to raise the children on her own. And then, when it was decades behind them, she found she could not compete with a memory, and was abandoned again. It was a little world of perfect miseries.

Auntie Gu didn't seem to have a moral in mind. It was just how it was. Perhaps the three pensioners were happy enough, or perhaps they just lived out the consequences of hopes and whims half a century old, and their memories of those instincts. It was shocking enough that she felt the need to tell me; at the same time, it struck me, it was all their stories. She understood it as something both extraordinary and familiar. None of the Educated Youth could leave their pasts. They had carried their long rural exile home with them to the cities, and their happy endings only looked that way when viewed in a certain light.

— // —

It took luck, ingenuity and unyielding drive to escape the countryside. Xi Jinping returned to Beijing in 1975, later than many of his peers, but to a plum position. Universities had resumed teaching, though with a heavily political curriculum, and to students distinguished by political credentials, not academic ability. His family connections were presumably key, and he had managed to join the Party after multiple rejections. Others found more complicated routes.

'There was a man who had been a soldier for fifteen years in my production brigade, and the policy allowed such men to take their spouses and settle in the cities,' Auntie Gu recalled. 'He had three children and a wife, but my classmate seduced him, he divorced his wife and they went to the city. And then, not long after that, all the Educated Youth could go back. So she regretted it.'

Auntie Huang had faced a dilemma of her own. Marriage in the villages drastically reduced your odds of finding a route home, but she and her prospective husband concluded they had little to lose – both had such bad class backgrounds that they would never get out anyway. They wed, and their son arrived soon after. When her hometown needed workers a year or so later, she and her son had to go alone. It would be four more years before her husband could join them.

Auntie Gu's chance came in 1977: 'My schoolmate's father was at a coal mining company – it wasn't a good job, but even that kind of chance was very rare – and gave that place to me,' she explained. For once, she wasn't smiling. 'I thought the leaders of the commune would agree to let me go, because I had behaved very well and both my parents were dead, but they hid from me and my friend's father, and when he had left they told me: "You're still young; another guy came here earlier than you, and his mother is still alive, in town." They were giving it to him. I ran off. It was raining heavily, there was thunder and lightning – people were worried and everyone came out to search for me. But a friend among the leaders told me, yes, my place was still going to the other guy. I was so sad, but there was nothing I could do. I couldn't care too much about it.'

At first there were only a few ways to return to the cities. Young people stole back illegally only to find themselves trapped in petty crime, or even injured themselves to win medical approval to go home. Extreme family hardship might also qualify you. Solidarity fractured as youths competed for rare chances to escape the villages, such as jobs and university places. Political virtue was one method, though it meant, among other things, voicing their commitment to settling in the countryside. The hypocrisy further disenchanted them, as did the willingness of cadres to help their own children and take bribes from others: so much for serving the people. Scruples began to seem expendable. Slander and blackmail to sink a rival's chances offered better odds than diligence alone. Girls were pressured to pay for their route home with sex.

From 1975 the rate of returns picked up, though more than 2 million teenagers arrived in the countryside that year. Rural desperation gradually coalesced into mass resistance and, by 1978, open protest: Educated Youth began striking, demonstrating, writing pamphlets and occupying premises, demanding a return. Their experience had toughened them; they knew they had to fight to get anywhere. Some simply fled. The government still wanted to send down more teens, but the pressure was too great. Auntie Gu finally made it home in 1979. One year later officials axed the rustication scheme, leaving almost a million mired in the countryside.

'It wasn't easy when we came back, to fight our way back into city life,' said Auntie Huang. 'We were not so young any more. We hadn't had much education. Some of us had family and had to feed them at the same time as trying to learn the skills, working skills, to survive.'

The injustice accumulated. They had suffered in the countryside for years; now they found they had little to offer the cities either. They had lost not only their ideals and purpose but their opportunities. The competition for academic places was so fierce after the years of closures that only the most brilliant and determined got their chance. There were younger, more polished potential employees emerging from the schools. Some returnees took up casual low-skilled labour. The desperate resorted to sex work and crime. Others found that the hardship had fired them up. They became entrepreneurs, seizing upon economic reforms propelled in part by the authorities' need to do something with them. (Meanwhile, former Educated Youth who had found jobs as officials would formulate the policies for developing the countryside.) Auntie Gu was one of the luckier ones, finding a job in a bike factory; now her daughter worked in an office. Her grandson would probably make it to university.

It didn't strike the group as curious that they spent so much time dwelling on the place they had fought so hard and so long to escape. Their rural misery defined them. It stood for sacrifice, community, selflessness and grit; they had earned their homes, their restaurant dinners, their lipsticks and frilled sweaters. Their story was validated by their leaders, who had struggled alongside them. While other parts of the Cultural Revolution were stamped down out of sight, deep into the mud of the past, this was elevated as part of the national story.

'Who isn't nostalgic for their youth?' Yu Xiangzhen had retorted when I mentioned the Chongqing group. She dismissed their fonder reminiscences as laughable. Her brisk reply surprised me; it was the closest she had come to anything less than impeccable politeness. I understood better later – months later – when she told me rustication had left her sister on the brink of suicide.

'It's only because the decades have passed that we think about the good things when we recall it. At the time it was all very painful,' acknowledged Auntie Huang. 'Life was so miserable – words cannot describe it. A lot of people can't even tell others how miserable their experiences were. But people feel they need to pass on the spirit.'

It had meaning to them; it wasn't, as some thought, just a waste of their best years, time stolen from them?

'Yes, I wonder that!' She seized the question. 'I can't decide. It *was* time wasted. But when I remember, it was like a treasury for me in some ways. I can't say I don't regret the experience. But I can't say I'm ungrateful either. It's something you can't do anything about.'

She thought for a moment more and brightened: 'The best part was that we went through so many hardships when we were young that hardships we met later seemed like nothing.'

It echoed Xi's conclusion: 'Nothing could be so hard as that.' But her smile undid me.

We'd been talking for so long by then that the picnickers and athletes had drifted away and the light was softening into dusk. Beside us the woman in the boots began to dance again, stepping carefully to the blaring tune. Her eyes were startled with thick mascara. The net rah-rah skirt rose higher and higher. She looked quite, quite happy as she dipped and turned, one arm held aloft, crying out intermittently: 'Long live Chairman Mao! Long live the Communist Party!'

SEVEN

> The Chinese people's great leader Chairman Mao Zedong is everywhere in general, but nowhere in particular.
>
> **Official, to a foreign visitor enquiring after Mao**

A huge mirror, set at the corner of two corridors, created a crossroads. I hesitated. The gallery was bright, light, but claustrophobic: it twisted and turned and doubled back on itself, and this confusion distorted time as well as space. Had I been here ten minutes? An hour? All around were mirrors in mirrors, reflections of reflections. There were thousands of them, hung on the walls, hung overhead, set into the ceilings. There were mirrors with Mao's face, of course, and many more with Mao's instructions and poems. They showed bridges and plum blossom, the Great Hall of the People, books and ink pots, sewing machines and shuttlecocks. Red flags and heroes from the model operas. Endless sunflowers, turning towards their sun: another Mao. Mao alone. Mao before a red sun. Mao before more red flags. Ships cutting through neatly white-crested waves: 'Sailing in the seas depends on the Great Helmsman.' Scenic views of Shaoshan, Mao's birthplace, and the Jinggang Mountains, where he set up the first peasant soviet. Mao's poetry, and indigestible instructions: 'Serious attention should be given to policy in the struggle-criticism-transformation stage of the Great Proletarian Cultural Revolution.' Several mirrors bore the words of Lin Biao, then – not for long – the coming man. The defence minister had helped to launch Mao's personality cult, and the Chairman had anointed him as heir apparent after Liu Shaoqi's fall, but it was a strange sort of acclaim, resting entirely on his servitude. All his words are incitements to devotion to his boss: 'Read Chairman Mao's books, listen to Chairman Mao's words and follow Chairman Mao's instructions!' Or 'Long live Chairman Mao! Great mentor, great leader, great commander, great helmsman!'

Long live Chairman Mao! Long live Chairman Mao! Long live Chairman Mao!

I tried to imagine combing my hair beneath these exhortations. Some of the paintings left barely an inch of surface uncovered. They existed not to reflect you as you were but to show you the person you should be: devoted, persistent, healthy, patriotic, ideologically correct. Not mirrors at all but looking glasses, for a looking-glass world where, as the Red Queen told Alice, 'It takes all the running you can do, to keep in the same place.'

— // —

Disorientated, I tried the Red Age Living Necessities Exhibition Hall. There were pillowcases and harmonicas and bellows, all marked with Mao's words. Mao quotes everywhere: sandwiched in the feet-high stacks of enamel plates and bowls. On fans for hot weather and blankets for cold. On maths books with his image at the centre of the sun, the beams radiating from him. Tea caddies. Biscuit tins. A stretch of scarlet vinyl – stacked copies of the Little Red Book. They had pulped copies in the post-Mao years, but there were plenty spare. A billion were printed during the Cultural Revolution: it remains the second-most published book in the world after the Bible. The sinologist Simon Leys visited China in 1972, when the Mao cult had supposedly been toned down, yet noted: 'Mao images are everywhere, in all possible materials and formats, from the facades of official buildings to the inside of hovels . . . Mao's Thoughts, Mao's poems are there in gigantic letters on all the walls; Mao's calligraphy adorns historical monuments, hotel rooms, street corners, waiting rooms, public gardens, post offices, zoos, railway cars, schools, hydroelectric dams, screens, fans, the frontispieces of diaries, and the entrance to army barracks. Quotations from Mao spice radio programmes, are given at the start of movie shows, plays, concerns, music-hall revues; they are on the front pages of all newspapers every day.'

It was the sheer volume of domestic memorabilia – the basins, towels, matches, cups – that really indicated his godlike status: not only omnipotent but omnipresent. He was as close to you as your spouse; you knew him as you knew your parents. He, or his words, were on your pillow as you slept and kept you warm through the night. He was there when you woke, as you washed and dried your face, as you took a gulp of tea, as you lit your cigarette. He watched over everything you did. He guided every action.

On a wall, a red-and-white rubber ring quoted Mao's encouragement to swim. His love of the water was genuine: his personal photographer told me once how she would snap him floating on his back, puffing on a cigarette – that was before she too was purged in the Cultural Revolution. But his swimming was also political, because everything was political. He used it to humiliating effect against Khrushchev, forcing the non-swimming Soviet leader to don a pair of armbands at a 'friendly' summit in his private pool. Eight years later he turned it against his colleagues. After months out of the public eye in 1966, Mao resurfaced in July to swim in the Yangtze at Wuhan. In his seventies, he could still tame the current, the wind and waves. The front page of the *People's Daily* noted that he had covered fifteen kilometres in just sixty-five minutes, a speed to astonish today's Olympians. The following month, at a similar pace, he launched the full force of the Cultural Revolution. No one could miss the symbolism, nor did they dare to. For a decade, swimmers took to the waters on the anniversary each July with red flags and giant portraits of their leader.

I moved on. Scores of identical white busts were stacked upon each other, filling four cases. Yu Xiangzhen, recounting the later stages of her Cultural Revolution, had told me of a factory colleague who married at the height of the movement. Instead of the household essentials she needed, she received only statues of Mao. When Yu visited her tiny home they were everywhere – on the table, on the bed – since it was unthinkable to give them away. You wore Mao everywhere you went: a gold face in a red enamel circle as shiny and inviting as a foiled toffee penny. The badges were generic in appearance and weirdly specific in detail; here was the 'Return My Great Wall' model, Mao's angry response to a 1967 editorial which he saw as an attack on the People's Liberation Army, in one of the many factional skirmishes. Billions of the badges were made: enough for every man, woman and child to demonstrate their loyalty four or five times over, and to exhaust China's aluminium. One collector estimated that forty thousand aircraft could have been built, and Mao himself reportedly demanded: 'Give back our planes!'

— // —

The strange thing was how normal it all became. Repetition made the bizarre routine. The routine could not, by definition, be remarkable, and since it was drummed in from morning to night it was all soon taken for granted. What ought to be became what was, and what was became what ought to be.

'It turned people into beings without thoughts or feelings. You didn't think anything. You did what you were told. There was no self-will. No ideas,' Yu said. 'At first people didn't dare to complain. Then gradually it was internalised and you didn't think too much about it.'

Even when the initial shock subsided – when the PLA had restored order, and Red Guards were sent to factories or the countryside, and only faint tremors of those terrifying clashes still reverberated – the new landscape was unrecognisable. You could, looking back, make a kind of sense of it. You could pull together all the details and say, Yes, this happened, and this is why: his jealousy, her grudges, the sheer convenience. But none of those really explained it. You could push all the pieces of your past into a heap and attempt to sort them into some order. But, really, how much did it tell you? This was an inverted world; you saw everything at an angle. These were years of suffocating control by revolutionary committees, the political bodies set up to replace the old bureaucracy but still dominated by the PLA and long-standing cadres. Yet the ground would shift beneath your feet and what had been mandated was now forbidden, or vice versa. There were things that made no sense at all, whichever way up you turned them. The confessions you penned, one after another, never knowing what you had actually done. The political orders that you pored over, no closer to knowing how you had strayed. The new rules, so plentiful and so quick to morph. For a while you had to quote the Little Red Book when you spoke to strangers, before you could get to business. You queued for your groceries: 'Serve the people! Comrade, may I buy a pound of leeks?' When that fell by the way there were new campaigns, new orders, new taboos to master.

Yu had been lucky: when her friends were sent away she became a factory worker, an 'iron girl', assembling parts for mining vehicles. (I was not entirely surprised to learn she had notched up numerous awards at the plant: Model Member of the Communist Youth League. Lei Feng-Like Youth Model. 8 March Female Model.) It was gruelling work, and the long days were extended by the political campaigns. They began at 6 a.m., when the workers gathered before Mao's portrait to chant 'Long live!' and commence their morning political lessons, studying editorials and orders from the higher levels and criticising each other. Workers with problematic backgrounds were given the heaviest work, which would be followed by more criticism sessions.

'There were endless political movements within the Cultural Revolution, so there were endless struggle and education sessions,' she said. 'And there were many different forms. Sometimes it was groups from the same production team; sometimes it was the whole factory. All these endless movements exhausted people. The most important thing was class struggle. Revolution was put before production. Personal matters were nothing at all.'

After an hour or two of politics they would finally start work. At lunch the loudspeakers spurted out news or revolutionary songs or new political articles. They would work again until 6 p.m., when another two-hour education session began. Then, at last, they might leave the factory. But, from zeal or fear for their reputation, they might instead keep working; sometimes, when they were ordered to stay late, doctors gave them pills to help them keep going. Once, Yu worked three days and two nights with only the briefest breaks. On other evenings the tannoy might crackle on: Chairman Mao had issued new instructions. Even when you'd fallen into bed after a shift, they might summon you again. You would find yourself marching in the darkness, all the way to Tiananmen to listen to political speeches, or to protest outside the Soviet embassy. When you lost your shoe you kept on walking, a resolute smile fixed on your lips, barefoot, lopsided and soon limping.

— // —

What sense did it make even now? I looked at all these artefacts, piled up across the galleries. They amounted to perhaps 1 per cent of the museum founder's hoard. Its scale was dazzling. Fan Jianchuan had ten thousand diaries from the Cultural Revolution, nearly a million letters and 3 million photographs.

'One item in a collection is like a pixel; the more you have, the higher the definition of the image. You see the picture better,' said Fan. 'Even though I have a huge amount of materials, the more I read about the Cultural Revolution, the more confused I become. Because it's still quite fresh, to understand this history I think you need to stand back from a distance.'

The Jianchuan cluster, China's largest gathering of museums, had looked more like an exclusive club as we rolled up the long driveway, with its high walls of bamboo. The galleries sprawled over thirty-three hectares, surrounded by osmanthus trees and little lakes. Two birds were bathing in a tiny brook, shrugging off the water in a fluster. Photos on a noticeboard captured visits by approving celebrity-eminences: the usual officials, a film director and Mao's grandson, Mao Xinyu, whose 'many achievements', said officials, had made him the youngest major-general in the PLA. One of the twenty-five galleries, documenting the devastating earthquake that struck Sichuan in 2008, had official backing. Some, like the Pavilion of Japanese Soldiers' Crimes in Wars of Aggression Against China, might as well have done. Others spanned foot-binding, China's Aviation Industry Corporation and the Flying Tigers, the US pilots who flew with China's air force against the Japanese. The six that I had seen were dedicated to the Red Age. They did not attempt to teach, as Peng Qi'an's museum sought to. 'We let the items speak for themselves,' Fan said.

We met in the cluster's research centre. His assistant opened a door in the huge pillar at the centre of the room and I descended the dimly lit spiral staircase inside. Fan was sitting on a leather chair at one end of a long table cut from a single tree, craggy-edged but polished on top to mirror-smoothness. A tray of espressos appeared as Fan handed me his business card. It was twice as long as normal, with his name printed in enormous letters on one side and calligraphed at equal scale on the other. In smaller type it listed his credentials: *Sichuan Jianchuan Museum Cluster/Curator. Sichuan Committee of Chinese People's Political Consultative Conference/Member of the Standing Committee. Policy Advisory Committee of CPC Sichuan Committee and Sichuan Provincial People's Government/Member. Chengdu Municipal People's Government/Counsellor.*

Like Peng, Fan had once been an official; his bosses had wanted to make him a mayor, but Fan had decided that businessmen were freer and better paid. Still, no entrepreneur could prosper without good relations with the Party, and at the height of his wealth, before he built his museums, Fan was one of China's five hundred richest men. The rich in China are nouveau riche – though some have parlayed a political birthright into wealth – and Fan's was a classic tale; when he talked of fainting from lack of food, you could see that the hunger was a memory that lived in his body, not his mind. Most of the rich I'd met revelled in such tales as proof that exceptional grit and abilities had brought them to the top, but Fan dismissed his success: 'It's not because of me, it's down to reform and opening.'

He had begun his collection in 1966, the year Mao launched the Cultural Revolution. His father was a Communist veteran who fought the Japanese for eight years, the Kuomintang for three more, then battled the United States in the Korean War. When the Red Guards turned on him, he was confused as much as distraught. Neither educated nor politically worldly, he tasked his nine-year-old son with gathering pamphlets and articles which might help him to understand what he had done wrong. There was no sense to be made of it, of course, but once Fan started collecting, he never stopped. Finding a home for his hoard was trickier. At first he had tried for the major cities, seeking space in Shanghai and Beijing, but he couldn't persuade officials to give him approval. Unlike Peng Qi'an's museum, the problem was not so much what he planned to build – it was that no one believed he would actually build it. Scams and dubious dealings were rife in China's property boom. A real-estate multimillionaire demanding a huge site for museums he would fund from his personal fortune had to be up to something. No one was likely to sign it off unless there was something substantial in it for them. In the end he found land in a small town some fifty kilometres from Sichuan's capital.

Fan had really meant it. He spent $200 million setting up the galleries, and poured in another $2 million each year to keep them running; recently, he had sold a petrol station to cover the bills. When he called himself a slave to the museums – 'which is actually being a slave to history, to cultural relics and the visitors' – he was only half-joking. He didn't plan to leave much to his daughter; she and her husband could support themselves. He didn't go to fancy restaurants or wear designer clothes. He looked, in fact, more like a student than a businessman, in dark chinos and a checked shirt under a khaki T-shirt reading *Do Something Great* in red characters. He turned around to show me the back: *Educated Youth Fan, Zuixiang Production Brigade, S-1 Production Brigade, Richeng People's Commune, Yibing County*. Despite the many titles on his card, then, he still identified with the teenager sent down to the countryside. He had been the son of a hero and the son of a Bad Element, an Educated Youth, a soldier, a teacher, an official, a tycoon. Now he was a curator and historian and philanthropist. It was a lot to fit into fifty-five years. It sounded as if he had lived a series of entirely different lives. But no, he said, it was a continuing process, like a tree growing. If you could make sense of your scattered biography that way, as rings formed around a core, I thought, perhaps China's history too – its abrupt episodes and sudden switches – could cohere in some way.

— // —

But the words I kept hearing when people spoke of China's path were 'Wuji bifan' – when something reaches an extreme, it can only go in the opposite direction. I arrived home from my trip to Sichuan in late afternoon, when residents escorted their dogs along the path that ran around the little lake in our compound. Watching them, I remembered a story that Yu had told me, from the later stages of the Cultural Revolution. Her parents had been rehabilitated, to some degree at least, and were moved from their dingy lodgings to a flat in a better building. To their dismay three rooms were unusable: each one was piled, floor to ceiling, with fishbowls seized from families in their district. Growing flowers was capitalist. Pet-keeping was bourgeois. The Red Guards had trampled the gardens and confiscated the basins. Every pleasure and joy which did not glorify Mao or further the revolution was decadent and reactionary.

Even now, Beijing had a 'one dog' rule for families, and in the centre the animals were subject to a strict height limit of thirty-five centimetres; it was designed to prevent aggressive dogs, in response to rabies deaths. In the afternoons the district was a parade of chihuahuas, terriers and Pekinese – a fashion parade, to be more precise, since many of them dressed for the occasion. What they lacked in stature they made up for in ostentation: they wore baseball boots, rah-rah skirts and college sweaters; denim dungarees and crystal-studded jackets; deely boppers and fur-trimmed hoods. One lapdog often dressed as Santa, even as springtime rolled around;

others sported camouflage gear and leopard print. There were dogs in my neighbourhood with larger and certainly more flamboyant wardrobes than mine. There were also kids a few miles away who didn't dress as well or as warmly as these pets. China was not only more unequal than the United States or Europe; the differences were juxtaposed beside you, and had emerged far more abruptly.

From one extreme to another, then. Often people meant the turn from Maoism to the market, and the way that unbridled individualism had replaced the era of totalitarianism. But increasingly I heard the words applied to what might lie at the end of these years – this gilded era; this unacceptable, unsustainable period. No one expected officials to be clean, but they talked wistfully of corruption ten years ago, when leaders might have amassed tens of millions of pounds instead of hundreds; or how life had been twenty years ago, when you chatted with neighbours every day; or how it had been forty years ago, when times were hard but you still believed in something. When one of China's former top generals was arrested in Xi's anti-corruption purge, twelve trucks were needed to carry away the loot stored at his mansion. It included over one tonne in cash, and a solid-gold statue of Mao.

EIGHT

Poverty is not socialism.

Deng Xiaoping

The day began at 6.15 a.m. in Nanjiecun, as 'The East Is Red' blasted through the speakers and echoed down the wide, empty streets, past the blazingly white statue of Mao with his arm raised in perpetual salute. I was here to write a piece on his legacy, to mark the 120th anniversary of his birth. This village in Henan, central China, was one of the country's few remaining communes. When reform and opening began, under Deng Xiaoping, land had been split into plots for each family to till individually. Farmers had leaped at the change; some had pre-empted it, forming private agreements in great secrecy and at considerable risk. Most prospered under the new rules. But in Nanjiecun incomes had fallen, and they had handed the land back.

Across the country, from cottages to penthouses, families enjoyed the fruits of capitalism: potato crisps and fake Nike T-shirts, or sports cars and Château Lafite. Nanjiecun prided itself on standing above such indulgences. Workers sang revolutionary songs before their shifts instead of fidgeting on smartphones. They received grain rations for their labour and spent food tokens in public stores on their way home to free government flats, identical down to their gilt electronic Mao clocks. Except when the loudspeakers burst into life, the whole place was eerily quiet. There were no pop songs, no traffic on the spotless streets, no one out of place. No clutter of shop signs and adverts – just billboard after billboard with Communist slogans and yet more pictures of Mao. It felt like stepping back in time. It was the antithesis of the Chinese passion for bustle and liveliness and noise and clutter, and its dullness was oddly mesmerising, like watching static on a TV screen; the order, the tidiness, the nothing-happening-ness reminded me of visits to Pyongyang. Neo-Maoists, who organised tours to North Korea, regarded Nanjiecun too as a beacon: proof that, even now, Mao Zedong Thought was the path to prosperity and happiness. If every Chinese village had followed its example, how much happier life would have been. Living standards would be high. Farmers wouldn't move to the cities to be treated as second-class citizens. The rights of proletarians would be guaranteed. The gulf between rich and poor would never have opened.

But the story of Nanjiecun wasn't quite so simple. The Mao statue went up in the nineties; the thirty-foot pictures surrounding it, of Marx, Engels, Lenin and Stalin, arrived the following decade, apparently to entice more visitors rather than inspire the residents. There were reports the village was badly in debt, though it said state banks had written off its loans. The noodle factory was co-run by a private Japanese firm. Many of the workers lived outside and got wages but nothing more. The unnerving calm was partially explained by a busy market just out of sight beyond the north gate, where residents ventured for a break from utopia. Communism seemed to be as much a promotional gambit as a political commitment. The botanical gardens just outside the town's walls had models of buildings which had hosted key moments in the Party's history, but its shabby fibreglass giraffes and pandas appeared more popular with tourists. A mass wedding shoot was under way when I visited, with dozens of brides and grooms posing in matching knitwear, pastel tuxedos and prom dresses. It was Chinese consumerism at its most cloying.

At dusk the tannoys blared with another Party classic, assuring all listeners that a communist society would surely be achieved. I strolled back through the streets, even quieter now, to eat over-cooked dumplings and sip warm beer at the hotel restaurant; choice did not feature in this arcadia. A woman let me into my room, old-style, not trusting guests with keys. I'd gone to bed and was drifting off when the phone rang. It was an unknown Chinese number, which at this time probably meant someone in trouble.

'Remember me?' It seemed rude to admit the truth; in any case, he continued at once: 'It's Gao Xiguang! It's urgent!'

That seemed unlikely despite the hour, given his joviality. I hedged for a moment.

'Gao Xiguang! Lin Biao!'

Lin Biao. Now I remembered him, of course. We'd met a year or so earlier, when I was writing a piece on Mao impersonators, who seemed almost as prevalent in China as Elvises were in the West. There were dozens, of varying girths and statures, and even a female Mao, surprisingly convincing, who complained that her husband had gone off sex since she took on the role. They acted in TV plays and graced official functions. One day they might open a restaurant, the next, attend a jail to raise staff morale and re-educate the prisoners. The one I arranged to interview had turned up in full costume, latex mole and all, and with his entourage: Zhou Enlai, his premier; the military hero Zhu De; Song Qingling, a prominent stateswoman and the widow of Sun Yat-sen, revered for leading the 1911 revolution that ended imperial rule in China. To my astonishment, they were accompanied by the notorious traitor of the era: Lin Biao. He had refused to speak until Mao had given permission. Then I learned that his name was Gao Xiguang, and that he had begun impersonating just a few years before. I'd kept in touch, hoping to see a performance, but he was so cagey that I'd given up. I wondered what, after all this time, had prompted him to call.

'It's urgent!' he repeated, naming a date almost a month away – was I free? All the others would be there: Mao, and Zhou Enlai, and maybe Chiang Kai-shek. Sure, I said, I'd be happy to come. What was the performance?

'Great! It's my grandson's hundredth-day party! Call me in the morning!'

I would be playing a role too, I realised: Gao's Foreign Friend. Just as certain expats ostentatiously name-dropped My Chinese Friend X, so some Chinese people liked not so much to befriend foreigners as to deploy them. A friend, irritated on my behalf, warned that he was trading me: 'Everything's business now. They all want something,' she said. Though I often experienced unexpected kindness, I'd heard the complaint from her, and others, so many times. Everyone was hustling. Chinese society had always depended on connections – the difference, perhaps, was that in a place and time that changed so fast the bonds were fragile and ever-shifting, and that the raw need or greed could be so naked: what can you do for me? Though some blamed China's rush to capitalism – the mass lay-offs from state industry, the disposability of workers who might be sacked for their age at thirty, the urgency to get ahead and get more – many blamed what had preceded it for stripping away all feeling, all pretences, all attachment. Professions of loyalty, however sincerely made, had proved meaningless. Gao and his peers had no reason to believe in declarations of good faith. If you are a friend, show it. If you're a straight dealer, let me see the cards. Feelings come through action: don't say it, do it. That way you might begin to establish a real relationship.

Besides, I had my own transaction in mind. If Gao trusted me, I hoped, he might take me to one of his appearances. I was still fascinated by the sheer implausibility of being Lin Biao, the country's chief sycophant turned scapegoat.

— // —

There was nothing intentionally kitsch about the impersonators. They were earnest in their work, turning down bookings they judged inappropriate, such as promoting spas. Yet what was not permissible as history in China was allowed as entertainment. The country had several Cultural Revolution restaurants, serving up tragedy as farce. At Beijing's Red Classics Restaurant, gaudily scarlet, you could have a fully themed wedding, posing for photos in matching Mao suits on the tractor parked in one corner. Even in the toilets there was no escape: red stars hung over each sink. Customers ordered Party Secretary Aubergine and Educated Youth's Fatty Meat from a menu printed to look like a Party newspaper. They eyed the waitresses in Red Guard uniforms, glossy plaits tied with red thread. They waved flags, slightly out of time, at the cacophonous stage show. It had begun with a hasty commercial precis of the *Road to Rejuvenation* exhibition – 1921, the First Party Congress! Deng Xiaoping! The Olympics! President Xi! – before lurching into battle re-enactments and a suite of Maoist songs reset to a driving synth backing. Several dancers climbed onto chairs, egging the customers into a chant: 'Long live Chairman Mao! Long live Chairman Mao!'

The guests were mainly men, a few glasses down, most too young to have lived through the era or regard this as anything other than novelty. Veteran Red Guards had spoken scathingly of the appetite for such entertainment, and there had been an outcry when students in Harbin recreated struggle sessions for their graduation photos, posing as if they were interrogating victims in dunces' hats. The anger wasn't surprising. But I wondered how the young were supposed to understand what they weren't allowed to know.

Further back, a middle-aged man nursed his glass, sweat beading his brow as he mused about the pleasures of the old days. 'After spending all day in work I really enjoy singing and dancing here. I don't think – I just relax,' he confided.

Had the real thing been enjoyable? The Cultural Revolution? He focused, with a little difficulty, and gave a short, uncomfortable laugh. 'It's not good to say. You probably know.' Before I could ask more the singer broke off to scream: 'If I find someone who knows this song but doesn't sing along, they don't respect Mao, and I'll seize them for a struggle session!'

I thought of a line I had read somewhere: our indulgence of nostalgia, or something a bit like nostalgia, only made out of polystyrene. You couldn't buy a real memory – and who would purchase this one? – but you could sell something like it. The irony of the Cultural Revolution was that its ultra-Maoism had taught people ultra-individualism: how to manoeuvre and prosper and barter with whatever one could acquire. In this world, with sufficient ingenuity, anything could be traded: even something so apparently unpromising as looking like Lin Biao.

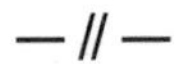

Gao had been a small boy when Lin was at the height of his power, a military hero and Mao's chosen successor. To understand the man he was impersonating, he scoured biographies and history books. He pored over pictures and footage to perfect the gestures that would bring Lin to life. He listened to recordings over and over until he had the voice just right, speeding up his pace to match the fast clip of his alter ego. He shaded his native Beijing accent with something of an old-fashioned Hubei voice like Lin's, though he could not adopt it wholesale: 'No one would understand it.' The resemblance was so striking he hadn't even had to change his hair. (Neither of them had much of it, but it didn't seem to be a joke.) Few youngsters recognised him, he conceded, but the over-fifties knew at once – he had been swarmed at a gathering of veterans. When they and Gao were boys, Lin Biao was one of China's Ten Great Marshals. Tactically brilliant, he'd survived the Civil War despite a reported bounty of $100,000 on his head, fighting bold guerrilla campaigns and leading the People's Liberation Army into Beijing in 1949.

'Without the Communist Party, there would be no new China,' Gao had told me. 'They're the people that gave us schools to attend and food to eat. Lin Biao fought for the next generation; I want to pass on these ideas. Don't forget what he contributed to our country.'

Lin was also, more significantly, a staunch supporter of Mao from early on – 'a blank sheet on which Mao could write as he pleased', as Otto Braun, the Communist International representative sent to China in the thirties, noted. When the Party took power Lin redoubled his efforts. He was 'Mao's best student', once enjoining his comrades to 'Carry out Mao's instructions, whether you understand them or not.' He did more than almost anyone, bar Mao himself, to establish the Mao cult. He led the politicisation of the army. He led the creation of the Little Red Book. To some he was a ruthless, ambitious schemer; others pitied him, seeing his illnesses or hypochondria as his chief preoccupation. Even discounting the propaganda, he seemed less a personality than a cluster of personas which emerged as required. Probably his primary thought was survival: 'Be passive, passive, and passive again,' he advised a subordinate. The strategy proved so successful that in 1969, following the fall of Liu Shaoqi, he was named as 'Mao's closest comrade-in-arms and successor'.

Obsequiousness did not help him for long. It may even have sealed his fate. Outdoing each other in slavish loyalty was the only real way for people to compete: Mao demanded but also suspected each declaration of fealty. The two men clashed when Lin kept insisting that Mao should become state chairman: some believed that Lin was hoping Mao would hand him the position instead, but it seems as likely that he thought Mao was only feigning reluctance and wanted him to press the issue. The emperor was already growing jealous of the power he had bestowed on Lin, and perhaps he guessed that Lin was critical in private despite his servility in public. Factional intrigue played a part too, with Jiang Qing – a 'long-nosed pit viper', in Lin's words – feeding her husband's suspicions.

By September 1971 it was obvious that Mao had turned decisively against the man he had so recently depended on. Lin's family panicked. He fled the country late at night with his wife and son, on a plane that crashed in Mongolia, killing all on board. Details of his departure and death remain mysterious, and probably will for ever, since key papers were destroyed. More than a thousand of his supporters were purged. 'A few days after the incident, I heard rumours,' Yu Xiangzhen had told me. 'Maybe because we lived in the Xinhua compound, people were well informed. So we knew quite quickly what had happened. It was very clear that Mao had been distancing himself from Lin. But we were really shocked.'

The public waited much longer – almost a year – to be told what had happened. Lin's disappearance made it evident something was afoot, and soon there were disparaging references to a 'Liu Shaoqi-type person'. But the announcement was astounding: Lin, at the very heart of the Party, had been a rightist traitor. He had plotted to assassinate Mao and seize power, and bolted when his plans were discovered.

The leadership did a competent job of establishing their story. There were documents and meetings and broadcasts and headlines: 'Big traitor Lin Biao will be forever cursed by the people! His stinking corpse will lie on the rubbish heap of history!' But the official verdict raised more questions, and more profound ones, than it answered. Lin Biao, celebrated for his devotion to the Cultural Revolution and to Mao, had hated and conspired against everything he praised. Nothing he had said could be relied upon; and if he had not meant it in the first place, should ordinary folk place any more faith in the movement? Worse still, it seemed their omniscient leader was shockingly fallible, having nurtured a traitor without noticing – unless he was a vengeful god unleashing his wrath.

'It was a turning point. After that, people who were politically sophisticated understood that the Cultural Revolution was going nowhere,' Yu Xiangzhen had told me. 'Even Chairman Mao knew that too. But people didn't say it openly – they just kept pretending. People watched each other and if you said anything you would be reported. No one dared talk about it.'

Those who had kept their idealism through the turmoil – and that included even victims, who had often blamed themselves for their ordeals – began to ask: what was that all about? What was it all for? It wasn't that they liked or admired Lin. It was that the Party's orders made no sense and contradicted themselves.

Mao's death and Jiang's fall did nothing to salvage Lin's reputation. Mao's first doomed heir, Liu Shaoqi, was rehabilitated. But Lin Biao had been wrong all over again. The Party held a posthumous show trial alongside the Gang of Four's: with the right of the Party back in charge, the 'ultra-rightist' was now condemned as an extreme leftist. Conveniently dead, he could be blamed for fanning the Cultural Revolution's flames and, less accurately, for plotting against Liu. He was even blamed as a 'backstage supporter' of the supposed May 16 conspiracy, though criticising him had been considered one of its major crimes. He was a perpetual villain, condemned to be forever on the wrong side of Party history. But in

2007, more than thirty-five years after his death, Lin's portrait was added to the Chinese Military Museum, hanging alongside the other founders of the armed forces. 'I wouldn't have dared to imagine being Lin Biao before that,' Gao admitted. Even then, news of the addition was muted, and the semi-tolerance had its limits: when the centenary of Lin's birth approached, officials closed off that wing of the museum 'for renovation'. Nor did it explain why Gao wanted to impersonate Lin, even if he thought it was safe. Playing the father of the nation was one thing – but acting its arch-traitor? The closest analogy I could think of was an Englishman impersonating Oswald Mosley, or a Norwegian acting Vidkun Quisling, and even they had never been vilified quite so thoroughly as Lin. The idea of officials booking him seemed even more peculiar.

'You don't know about history, so you ask these questions, but no one shows any negative attitude towards me,' Gao snapped. 'If you judge the achievements and misdeeds of Lin Biao, I think the achievements are bigger than the other part. People admire his military talents so they are very interested in him. After a performance people will shake hands with me, hug me and have their pictures taken.'

Then he retreated: 'I think the success of a person or their failure is set by the next generation. I don't think I have the authority to judge whether he was right or wrong. I can't say. It all belongs to history.'

But history is made up of thoughts and arguments, I said. You've read so much; you must have an opinion.

'History isn't what you say or what I say!' His voice rose, in outrage or panic. 'It is what the people say!' He meant, of course, The People. 'You can't write it, I can't write it; we can't tell what the truth is. There are a lot of versions. Which is correct? Which is incorrect? After the plane crashed in Inner Mongolia, I think people all felt Lin Biao was a traitor. But we are ordinary folks. I was very young at the time. So I don't really know what happened in the Cultural Revolution. History is not known by you or me, because there are all the internal materials that I don't know about. I don't know the truth about the Cultural Revolution so I don't want to judge anything.'

It was a nice recovery. It was true enough that much about Lin's life and death remained mysterious. It also allowed Gao to sidestep awkward questions: whether Lin was just a scapegoat, and why he was so keen to play a scoundrel. It was social responsibility, Gao said, promoting red culture to the next generation. He did not get paid for his charitable performances, he added, though he took 'transport fees', which usually meant rather more than expenses. His day job was as a cameraman and director for army propaganda videos, and I wondered if playing Lin had helped him forge useful contacts.

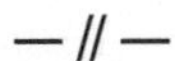

Gao seemed to be doing well for himself – or at least he was investing for the future. I'd expected the hundredth-day party to be a smallish family gathering, but when I arrived at the restaurant something grander was under way, elaborate as a wedding. A pastel backdrop stretched across the stage showed the little boy in a series of costumes. Plates of expensive cigarettes sat under the red glass chandeliers, teenage waiters piling up dishes of prawns and pigs' ears around them. There were ranks of tables: the baby had three well-wishers for each of his days in the world. But it wasn't about the infant, of course, nor even his parents, casual in jeans and clearly incidental to events. This was Gao's planning; these were Gao's guests; Gao was evidently footing the bill. It was Gao's party in everything but name. He was in one of his uniforms, buttoned to the top although it was so hot here. As he greeted me he lifted his cap, sweeping the sweat from his scalp with the other hand.

I had been allocated to a side room, along with Mao Zedong, Liu Shaoqi, Zhou Enlai and Chiang Kai-shek. Uncertain as to the lunch's status – business or pleasure? Probably both – they slipped between roles, and referred to their host interchangeably as Gao and Lin Biao. Mao was in a checked shirt but had his hair swept back like the Chairman's; Liu Shaoqi arrived in a sober Sun Yat-sen suit, subverted by his aviator sunglasses and flashy silver belt buckle. Zhou Enlai, in jovial mood, topped up all our glasses. Chiang Kai-shek projected an austere air, straight-faced as the others teased him; smiling, he confided, did not fit his persona. But every so often he slowly exhaled into a balloon, then popped it. We jumped. If you looked up quickly you could catch the satisfaction before he fashioned his features to sternness again. There was also a magician in a silver suit, collecting business cards as smoothly as he palmed the King of Hearts, and a woman clearly and systematically working her way around the most useful guests. The great events in Chinese life, from birth to marriage to death, often combined rites of passage with networking opportunities. Parents had been known to merge business launches with their children's weddings.

The impersonators were called to the main stage, smiling and waving as the inevitable 'The East Is Red' blared from the speakers. Chiang rattled through his routine: 'Those of you who applaud – come to Taiwan! Those who don't – don't bother! Lin Biao has one grandson: that's not enough. If you come to Taiwan, you can have lots of babies!'

Older people beamed and chuckled; the younger ones looked mostly bored or baffled until the magician took over. There was, I noticed, a second Mao impersonator among the guests, and when we went back to our room to finish lunch, 'The East Is Red' struck up once more and Mao 2 began his address. Clearly Gao was hedging his bets: as Beijing's only Lin Biao impersonator, he had plenty of potential bosses to work with. Mao 1 sat straighter in his chair, ears cocked, somewhat sombre. No one could afford to be complacent in their line of work. The previous years had seen bumper business: the Party's ninetieth birthday, and then the 120th anniversary of Mao's birth, had produced plenty of bookings. No such events were pending this year, and Xi's austerity and anti-corruption campaign had been implemented far more zealously, and protractedly, than anyone had predicted. Cadres no longer threw lavish events, and the State Council had cut off funding. Officials boasted that central government spending on hospitality had fallen by over a third. Even businessmen were wary of presenting too high a profile, and given Xi's focus on Party history, hiring the impersonators began to look not flattering but potentially risky.

There were still private events, of course, but as the bottles of baijiu emptied, several impersonators griped about a group of princelings who had failed to pay them for a recent performance. Only Gao, shaking the hands of departing guests, was ebullient. All reticence had vanished in the triumph of the moment and the flush of alcohol: 'I LOVE YOU!' he blurted and clasped my shoulder as I said goodbye.

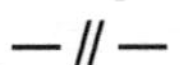

Since Gao didn't otherwise speak English, I judged his declaration to be a misunderstanding. But the next time he called he said it in Chinese too: 'Wo ai ni! I love you!' He was offering to introduce me to the sons of an important former leader. He thought it might be useful for me – red heirs still wielded a lot of influence – although he was hazy as to why he was seeing them. Somehow I was unsurprised when the venue for our meeting turned out to be a Chinese medicine clinic, where he and the manager extolled the treatments, promised me a discount and urged me to bring friends. There were no princelings in sight, and he moved the conversation on when I broached the matter then and later. But I'd grown oddly fond of Gao, frustrating as he was. It was always obvious that he had some end of his own in mind – too obvious to give offence. I invited him to dinner and he rang to say he'd bring three friends along, an announcement I politely parried. So he came alone, in full Lin Biao rig-out. 'Lingling! I can call you Lingling, can't I? It's more friendly that way.' My Chinese name is Anling, but no one called me Lingling; he didn't wait for an answer anyway. 'If you go to England, Lingling, what will I do?' He brushed away imaginary tears at the news I'd be moving home soon. I had plenty of questions and had hoped to talk, but this was another performance.

Business was looking up a bit: he'd been booked for a gala for migrant workers in a provincial city. He planned to tell them that Xi Jinping represented the masses. 'I support Xi Jinping!' he added, and raised a glass of liquor in a toast: 'We owe our good lives – good food, alcohol, the good things in our lives – to the revolutionary generation.'

I asked him if values had changed since those times. 'That's got nothing to do with what we are discussing today,' he said abruptly. I persisted: so many people felt that the values of the sixties were purer. Well, he conceded, they had all been poor; officials got little more than workers. 'Now materialism is prevalent in society. They say you should let some get rich first and they will help others, but those who got rich first are basically the families of officials – they have the resources and ordinary people don't. It's like having a cancer in the body. Xi is the doctor cutting out the tumours. We can see that in villages in remote places they have free education and medical care now. These are the improvements. Xi is caging the tigers.'

Xi's anti-corruption campaign was popular. But Gao could have been reading from an editorial in the *People's Daily*: the cancer and tiger rhetoric had been heavily used. I was resigning myself to the fact that frank conversation was unlikely, but thought the Lin Biao Incident was worth another try. 'This question is *adorable*!' He tilted his head and beamed at me, cupping his face almost coquettishly. 'I was born in 1963; I was only eight when it happened. I didn't even know who Lin Biao was, let alone what my reactions were. I'm your friend, so I don't talk nonsense.' He seemed to have forgotten that he had told me of his admiration – in fact, he denied it when reminded. I wondered what he thought of Lin these days.

'It's a sensitive question. But I think Lin Biao was sacrificed to a political struggle. Chairman Mao could not have had his achievements without Lin Biao and his brothers. When Chairman Mao was in danger, Lin Biao came to the rescue. When Lin Biao went in September' – I wondered if anyone had ever coined a more euphemistic euphemism – 'Chairman Mao was very sad and looked ten years older overnight. Zhou Enlai cried for twenty minutes. Chairman Mao said it was a great loss for the country.'

But history would bring justice and openness. Already he could dress up as Lin. People were beginning to recognise Lin's contributions and discuss the rights and wrongs, he said. Not Gao himself, of course – asked what the rights and wrongs might be, he embarked on another long non-reply. He talked a lot, almost saying something: there were jokes, pleasantries, anecdotes with no punchline, words which gestured towards my questions without answering them. He dropped his voice to a stage whisper; he declaimed across the table about world friendship. The people of the world – white-skinned, black-skinned, yellow-skinned – *we are all people*. Blonde hair, black hair, bald – he indicated his head – *we are all people*. I had stopped trying to interrupt, but he halted when 'March of the

Volunteers', the national anthem, blared from his phone. I couldn't hear the caller's side of the conversation but I recognised his: 'I love you – wo ai ni,' he told her before hanging up.

He passed me the phone to show his new home screen: a picture of him seated on an overstuffed sofa beside a woman perhaps a decade older, plainly dressed, her hair pulled into a bun: 'It's Lin Doudou.'

When Lin Biao's family had boarded the plane in such haste that September night, his daughter had refused to go with them. Lin Doudou had instead called the Party to report them, blaming her mother and her brother for forcing her father into it. Afterwards she never spoke publicly of those events. But a few weeks ago the children of revolutionary figures had gathered for one of their sporadic meetings, and she had made an unexpected call for 'more respect for historical facts'. She might have been supporting Xi's demand for adherence to the Party narrative, or requesting a reconsideration of the verdict on her father. Ambiguity was as useful as ever.

Gao said he'd been introduced by the Zhou Enlai impersonator and had hoped it would help him to understand Lin better – though he added immediately: 'Whether I meet Lin Doudou or don't meet Lin Doudou – it doesn't affect how I play Lin Biao.' They'd had dinner at a private club; she had looked at him for a full twenty seconds. 'Then – she embraced me.' He let that sink in. 'We were both very emotional. It felt like a family dinner. I wanted Lin Doudou to know it was very natural for her to miss her father.'

It was quite a vignette. Beijing was tiny in some ways, and the most lurid aspects of its past so recent – you tripped over its history when least expecting it. But I had a thought, perhaps an unworthy one: Lin was not such an uncommon surname. I asked if I could take a picture of his photograph. I was confident one of the scholars I knew could settle the question for me.

'Yes, that's her,' the historian said at once when I showed him, but he didn't pass the phone back.

'Definitely her?' – for he was still scrutinising the picture.

'Yes. But *he* doesn't look much like Lin Biao, does he? The eyebrows aren't really right.'

— // —

Shortly after my farewell to Gao, I caught a sooty narrow-gauge steam train up a steep hillside in Sichuan to a little town – very little now – called Bagou. My fellow travellers comprised a couple of residents, lugging groceries in tattered straw baskets on their backs, and a handful of visitors in sun hats. On arrival, the tourists draped themselves across the track for photographs, and posed in front of murals of Chairman Mao. The images, though original, had been freshened: the helmsman's face shone in candy-cane red and white, with a bright sunflower garnish underneath. I'd heard the town was covered in old slogans from the Cultural Revolution, and that it had attracted those who like red nostalgia, but I'd come because I liked abandoned places, caught halfway between two worlds, and because I loved Sichuan's green valleys, and because Bagou's steam train was that rarest of beasts, a good-news story. It was a working train: the locals used it to take vegetables to market, or to visit friends in the town. A few years ago they had added tourist coaches, earning enough to keep the line running for residents. Past and present worked in harmony.

Like Nanjiecun, Bagou had tried to leverage its history. But Nanjiecun was mimicking the past when it was really part of the modern world; Bagou still hadn't caught up. Its quiet was not the imposed calm of the model commune, but was born of desertion. It had never been an obvious site for an industrial town – deep in the country and high on a hillside, far past the rice terraces and bamboo groves – but the coal buried here had been too good to waste. When Mao launched the Great Leap Forward, cadres decided to find better ways of exporting the anthracite they scoured from the earth. An army of workers cut and built the railway track by hand, starting before dawn and hacking at the soil until night had fallen again. They grew thin with the labour, but the town boomed. More miners arrived, and then women to marry them; there were shops, a theatre, a hospital and schools. By the sixties, ten thousand were living here. And then, in the eighties, the coal ran out.

The great machinery was rusting. Industry had just been a phase, and so perhaps were people. Nature was reconquering. Saplings burst through gaps in the roofs and butterflies the size of my hand flashed past me along the empty streets. Giant gourds hung over garden walls, so heavy on their slender vines that they looked like an optical illusion. In a tiny noodle shop that needed a good scrub, one of the handful of businesses left here, I found a stool beside a woman in her eighties. She had come here with her husband, just before the town and its workers began their triumphant rise. No one wanted to marry a miner and live up in the hills; even today women born on mountainsides marry down them, where there are roads and schools and doctors. But the Party and the train had transformed the town. It was good to be a worker. It was right to be a worker. The wages rose, more women came, the train brought ribbons and books and blankets, pork hung for sale along the market street. Talking to her reminded me what Communism had meant to people then, not just how they lauded it today – a time when things were simpler; a time when they were winning; a way they could be winning now, if they calculated correctly. Despite the famine, lifespans almost doubled after the Party took power. Literacy rates shot up. Women won new rights and freedoms.

Now the high street's only signs of life were an indolent cat on a windowsill and a chicken scratching back and forth in the dirt. The hospital was closed. A caretaker's family camped out in a corner of the Workers' Theatre, its air musty and thick. Across the way, a grand open-air stage overlooking the square had been repainted, with Mao's portrait beaming from the back, but it was peopled only by visitors taking selfies. I asked the old woman if they had used it for model operas in her day.

'And struggling people. The struggle sessions were terrible. People boiled water to throw over them.'

So they targeted landlords and black elements—

She cut me off: 'We didn't have landlords. We were all workers. There was infighting between the workers trying to get power.'

Factional struggles, then—

'It was people being barbaric to each other,' she said. 'That was all.'

NINE

> Tragedy, he perceived, belonged to the ancient time, to a time when there was still privacy, love and friendship.
>
> **George Orwell**

'They brought my mother on a truck, across the wooden bridge. The truck stopped here' – the lawyer gestured at one side of the rutted road.

'And they shot her here.' He pointed at the other. 'Under where those boards are all stacked up, there was a dip where she was executed.'

If the contours remained, they had to be imagined. Hundreds of pallets were piled around us, loaded with wooden planks and batons, window frames and roof tiles. An excavator was parked at the roadside, wearing a *FOR HIRE* sign on its windscreen; everything else was on the go. Zhang Hongbing's precise, even fussy speech was interrupted by the clatter of construction, brusque horn blasts and splutters from the motorised tricycles that farmers used for transport. It was a cold, thin March day.

'It used to be all countryside – fields,' said Zhang. The urban sprawl had already swallowed it. The drive from his home had taken us past the long stretches of low concrete stores and dirty-white tiled houses that one saw everywhere in China. Every town and city was a work in progress. The property boom, implausibly gigantic and apparently unstoppable, had patchworked urban outskirts with building sites. Zhang summoned us into a narrow entrance and we picked our way through the dimness inside, edging round the domino-stacks of doors. Behind the house, a scrappy yard ran down to the little canal. A giant rooster scratched in the trash and rubble around an abandoned section of concrete pipe. I looked for an exit, assuming we were passing through, but Zhang had stopped to fling away empty cigarette packets and drinks cans, clearing a space around a red stone which I now saw bore a garland of plastic flowers, the name *Fang Zhongmou* and the inscription: *Martyr*. He began to prostrate himself: 'Mother! I've come! Mother! I am an unfilial son!' The screech of a bandsaw and hammering from next door punctuated his wailing.

There was only one officially recognised Cultural Revolution site across the whole of China: the Red Guard cemetery I had visited in Shapingba, Chongqing. But Zhang was appealing for his mother's grave in a small town in Anhui province, in the country's east, to be protected under heritage rules. Fang had died in the later, more orderly phase of persecution: executed as a counter-revolutionary in 1970, and exonerated a decade later, in the spate of rehabilitations which followed the Gang of Four's fall. Her son had discoursed about the need to remember, and Ba Jin's call for a museum, and confronting the public with what had happened to prevent another disaster. Now, standing amid the rubbish, I suddenly understood his campaign's urgency. A red-brick wall was already rising behind the mound of earth. Without protection the site might disappear within months. Fang had been killed as a danger; now she was merely inconvenient.

It was hard to imagine officials designating this building site a monument, even without the sensitivity of the circumstances. Fang's death was one among so many. It stood out for one reason alone: her accusers had been her husband and her teenage son – Zhang Hongbing.

— II —

The previous night we'd sat for over seven hours as Zhang laid out his story. A family friend ten or twenty years his senior – once his boss, now it seemed his acolyte – perched silently beside us. Master Wang wore a baggy, old-fashioned blue Mao suit and a toothy grin; he rearranged chairs and fetched hot water as instructed, and nodded as he listened to a tale that he evidently knew well. It began with Zhang's earliest memory: his mother washing the family's laundry in an old wooden tub one stormy night, gathering her frightened children about her, singing to bolster their spirits as rain pounded the tiles and thunder reverberated round their little home.

By the time Zhang ended, I was stiff from perching on the wooden stool in the cold of the attic room. The sky was black as he recounted how he had denounced his mother after she attacked Chairman Mao, and how he had threatened to snatch up that same yellow washtub to beat her, snarling that he would smash her head if she opposed his leader. His first memory was of family love, 'but this time it was all struggles and enemy class intentions'.

He had shown us the battered suitcase of relics – his Red Guard armband, cloth from one of her blouses, an enamel bowl she had used, now rusted through. Photos of his family in happier times, with his mother in a Mao jacket over her white shirt: broad-faced, strong-featured, serious-looking. There were stacks of paper around this room and he apologised that things were chaotic, but though he sifted through the piles for pictures and documents, his story remained in perfect order.

'What I did to my mother was worse even than to an animal,' he said, winding up. 'I dreamed recently that my mother had left and I didn't know where she had gone. Suddenly she appeared. I tried to take my mother's hand and I was so scared she would leave me. I said, "Mum, don't leave me again. I'm so sorry, I was wrong. I made a mistake." I said, "Mum, our household really can't live without you." But she didn't say a word. And she disappeared.'

His eyes had welled; now he was sobbing.

'I have this kind of dream again and again,' he added as he wiped away the tears. 'I often miss my mother and I often meet her in my dreams.' A pause. 'She never speaks to me.'

I wondered if he sought absolution or if I was meant to blame him. He had caused his mother's death, but now he kept her memory alive, his fidelity inverting past betrayal. Perhaps her silent reproach relieved him of the need to reproach himself. The horror of his story was undeniable. Still I found myself dry-eyed, awkward, and silently dissecting his confession.

— // —

Zhang's mother and father were early victims of the politics which consumed the country. They fell in love as idealistic young comrades in a military medical team. But his mother had been supposed to marry someone else, and the family of the jilted man turned upon Zhang's grandfather, using their connections to have him declared a landlord, gangster and spy for the Kuomintang – a travesty, Zhang said, rummaging for copies of his grandfather's file and dusty local histories to back him up, but a travesty that ended in execution.

Zhang grew up knowing nothing of this inauspicious beginning. His family was 'harmonious, happy and warm', he insisted, even in the famine that killed millions in Anhui alone, when the family ate leaves and sent his little brother to relatives who could feed him. But when the Cultural Revolution broke out, old fissures began to open. The family's work unit ordered that his grandmother, as the widow of a landlord, must leave the apartment it had provided. His mother hoped she could remain nearby; his father insisted she must follow orders by returning to the countryside, himself leaving the family home until Zhang's grandmother left town.

The children were largely untroubled by the drama, too excited by the unfolding of the Cultural Revolution. Zhang's parents were Party veterans; now it was the children's turn to take up the banner. They already studied Chairman Mao's essays in every spare moment and vowed to learn from Lei Feng, the model soldier whose sole wish was to be a 'rustless screw' in the great cause. In his selflessness, the propaganda told them, he seized every chance to darn socks and shovel manure. They too did their bit to build socialism in the small ways available to them. They helped construction workers to move bricks. They cleaned chairs and tables in the railway station. And when the Cultural Revolution began they redoubled their efforts. The past was dead; the feudal ways were over: 'Of course, I thought it was great.'

Zhang read of Mao's meeting with Song Binbin and changed his name too. His original given name – Tiefu, or 'Iron Man' – became Hongbing, 'Red Soldier'. The craze spread through the neighbourhood, with girls now calling themselves 'Red Youth' and boys dubbing themselves 'Protect the East' (Dong, or 'East', symbolising Mao Zedong). Zhang's sister, two years his elder, became Daihong, or 'Red Generation'. He produced her diary. It was a reminder of just how young these teenagers had been. They had found a rabbit in the street, she wrote, and – to serve the people! – had set out to find its owner. Wearying of the task, they had wanted to give up, but Chairman Mao's words had spurred them on: they should persist. And so, in the end, they had succeeded . . .

The childish writing in the notebook soon stopped, replaced by tighter, neater characters – those of their father. 'She died,' Zhang said. The sixteen-year-old had gone to a rally in Beijing, thrilling at the sight of Mao and the chance to play her part. But Daihong caught meningitis on the trip, becoming one of many to die in an outbreak fuelled by the Great Link-Up. Fang was, perhaps, angry as well as devastated. The Cultural Revolution had already taken her mother; now her daughter was gone forever. Passionate support for the movement turned to grudging suspicion, Zhang said.

Months later Zhang's father fell under attack, accused of taking the capitalist road. He was paraded in a dunce's hat, a board around his neck proclaiming his sins. Zhang had no doubt he should join the struggle against his father, attacking him in a big-character poster. His mother hesitated. When summoned, she stood beside her husband's kneeling figure and denounced him as demanded. Still, as the crowd surged forward to attack him, she tried vainly to protect him. By the time the mob had finished, Zhang Yuesheng, though then in his forties, slumped like an old man. His urine ran red; he could not walk unaided. The couple's slow journey home, arm in arm, was the first sign of physical affection their son could recall between them. Nor had he ever seen his father weep. Fang sewed her husband cotton pads to wear inside his clothing in the sessions that followed, but nothing could temper the pain of the injustice: 'I joined the revolution when I was fourteen. I took Japanese bullets in my arm and leg. I never thought it would end like this,' he told them.

The following year Fang would suffer, damned by her father's supposed history as a landlord and spy. She was held at the hospital where she worked, subjected to multiple interrogations and put to work cleaning latrines. The investigation lasted years. In late 1970 officials offered to relax her conditions and said she could sleep at home again. But she wanted a decision – anything but this endless uncertainty.

'Everything that happened to her and her family made her suspicious of the Cultural Revolution. She was disgusted by it,' said

Zhang. He still hadn't explained how he became involved in his mother's case. I asked, and for the first time he hesitated.

It was late one evening, when friends had left, and she was doing the laundry. Fang made an acerbic allusion to Chairman Mao; Zhang accused her of viciously attacking and insulting Mao Zedong Thought. As the row ignited, Fang abandoned all caution. She said she wanted Liu Shaoqi's case to be reopened. She said: 'The traitor, spy, thief – whatever they say of Liu Shaoqi – is Chairman Mao.' She said: 'The Communist Party has changed its colours. In the past the Soviet Union was friendly to us but right now, except for Albania, other countries who believed in Marxism–Leninism, we criticise them all. It's not done by the other countries – it's China.' She said: 'Why has Chairman Mao made a personality cult? His image is everywhere.'

'I warned her: "If you go against my dear Chairman Mao, I will smash your dog head . . ." There was a yellow washtub and I meant we would use that to smash my mother's head,' Zhang said.

'I felt it wasn't my mother – it wasn't a person. She suddenly became a monster. She had become a class enemy and opened her bloody mouth. My father said: "Fang Zhongmou, I'm telling you – from now on our family separates itself from you, this person who insists on taking a counter-revolutionary position. You are the enemy and we will struggle against you. The poison you just released, you should write it down." And my mother said: "It's easy. I can finish it in five minutes. I dare to say, dare to write, dare to do."'

Zhang and his father left to report her. By the time they returned she had finished her letter – effectively a suicide note. It called for Chairman Mao to be removed from all official positions and for the senior leaders he had purged to be freed and exonerated.

'My father said, "You will be buried." Mother replied: "It shows it's Mao Zedong who should be shot, not me. It's Mao Zedong who should be buried, not me."'

Zhang remembered his mother trembling, her chattering teeth, her struggle with his father as she ripped down the portrait of Mao which each family kept in their home. She barricaded herself in the bedroom and tried to burn the picture, a statue, Mao's poems.

'Beat the counter-revolutionary!' her husband cried as they forced their way in.

'I still felt I couldn't do it. She was my own mother,' Zhang said. 'I didn't smash her head, but I hit her twice on her back.'

He described the officials arriving. How one kicked out his mother's legs from under her, so that she fell. How they bound her with rope, and how he heard her shoulder crack as they hauled her to her feet. 'She walked out with her head high as if she didn't feel any shame.' He had been reading much of his account from a document – a memoir? No, he said; it was the official report his father wrote the day after the fight. His mother was executed less than two months later.

Did he have any doubts about informing on her?

'I didn't have any doubts. This was a monster, not my mother.'

Did he know what would happen?

'I knew. According to the regulations, I understood it meant death.'

There had been posters all over the walls of the town, describing the death sentences passed on people for this or that crime, 'and a brush tick on the poster in red, to show they had all been killed'.

Master Wang interjected for the first time, startling me: 'You saw it everywhere. There were a lot of death notices.' Zhang looked at him, and Wang fell silent.

Zhang resumed: 'So I knew, without doubt, she would get this treatment for what she had said at home. I knew she would be executed.'

Had he called for the death penalty?

He cleared his throat and reached for his notes. He cleared his throat again. 'I knew that in this case she would be executed. So in my report, I said, "Crack down on counter-revolutionary Fang Zhongmou! Shoot Fang Zhongmou!"'

He saw his mother one more time, at the last public meeting to denounce her, on the day she died. She was on the stage, upon her knees; around her neck hung a sign: *Fang Zhongmou, A Modern Counter-Revolutionary*. She seemed to be trying to push it away with her knees. A soldier forced her head down, ordering her to confess her crimes, but she raised it the moment he took away his hand. Then they put her on the truck. Neither Zhang nor his father attended the execution. At the site, an acquaintance later told them, her eyes swept the crowd as though looking for faces she knew.

Nor did they collect her body. They had no way to do it, Zhang said; I knew that relatives often distanced themselves in these cases. She was buried close to the execution ground, but her body was exhumed and buried elsewhere when officials decided to build a bridge there. 'Because she had white knee-length socks and a strap on her wrist, they knew it was her,' Zhang said. Perhaps because our minds have strange ways of protecting us, this inconsequential detail seemed the cruellest and most nauseating of all – that this unwanted woman should be disturbed repeatedly, and that she was identified not by loving relatives but by cadres who recognised a pair of socks.

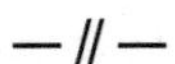

'A child criticising its parents wasn't unique to our household – the whole country was doing it,' Zhang told me.

Relatives were ordered to demonstrate their purity by 'drawing a line' between themselves and the miscreant. Spouses sought divorce to escape the taint or even led the charge against their husband or wife. Children took to the stage at struggle meetings to condemn their parents. The family relationship itself could be twisted and portrayed as inherently suspicious; the daughter of one provincial governor was coerced into accusing him not just of ideological crimes but of incest. The Soviet Union and Nazi Germany had their own child heroes, who placed their political duties above mere family ties. But in China those ties had bound people far more tightly. The Confucian ethos of filial piety had been imbued over two millennia. Children were schooled in the tales of the Exemplars: sons who strangled tigers with their bare hands to protect their parents, or sold themselves into slavery to pay for their father's funeral rites. Relations within the family – between the patriarch and his children; between male and female relatives – echoed and reinforced the bonds between ruler and ruled. The family was society in miniature, a block in the universal pattern of obedience and respect, benevolent rule and loving duty.

Maoism turned all this on its head. To Mao, who loathed his domineering father, family ties were not just a weakness – not just evidence of the decadent tendency to place personal bonds above political imperatives – but an irrelevance. He led by example. His second wife was executed by the Kuomintang for refusing to renounce him, though he had already abandoned her and remarried. Two of the babies borne by his third wife had to be left with others as they fled; the infants would never see their parents again. The ruthlessness imposed by war was succeeded by the inhumanity of power. Tiny children were sent to boarding nurseries, freeing adults to work and pursue the task of revolution. Parents were sent to labour camps, effectively orphaning their offspring. The Educated Youth were exiled to the countryside for years. But families were deliberately fractured too. It was easy to tear down the Confucian temples, harder by far to eradicate the ethos. Banning the tales of the Filial Exemplars was merely a beginning. Destroying Confucianism in China meant pounding to dust its bricks: the family units.

There was an obvious, and intended, substitute. One collection of the purported writings of model soldier Lei Feng is titled *After Liberation I Had a Home, My Mother Was the Party*. He was, admittedly, an orphan. But for many others, even those whose families remained intact, the Party shaped, nurtured, disciplined, even named them – I had met those too poor, too female, to deserve a name before the Communists arrived in their villages. They had no nostalgia for the old days: patriarchal decisions were tyrannical or whimsical as often as wise and kind. The Communists liberated others with the ban on forced marriages. Some teenagers were exhilarated by the mere act of defiance. But Mao, of course, replaced one set of restrictions with another, equally stringent. Just as he sought to tear out bureaucracy while consolidating his own power, so he sought to cut family ties and bind his people tighter to a higher loyalty: to himself.

Even now, the Chinese party-state relies upon isolating its targets: upon their intimates drawing the line. The families of dissidents are punished, their children trailed to their classrooms by goons or thrown out of primary school entirely. Parents and siblings face pressure from bosses; the brother-in-law of the late Nobel Peace Prize winner Liu Xiaobo, who supported the couple when the author was jailed, was suddenly convicted on fraud charges. It's little wonder when marriages fracture and other relationships crumble. But under Mao these tactics were commonplace and the pressure even greater. In an age of political theatre, denunciations were a grand spectacle. They showed that even family members regarded the criminal as bad beyond all reason and forgiveness, magnifying the evil of their offences. Above all, they showed the ordinary bonds of love to be trivial, even vulgar, and easily sundered in contrast to one's loyalty to the cause and its leader. Totalitarianism's reach to all parts of society, even the family, is frightening. But what's truly terrifying is that it extends to all parts of the subject, including the unseen: the soul, the psyche, the heart. It seeks to control not just your external life (what job you do, whom you marry, what you say), not just your beliefs, but even your emotions. Zhang was right: it was an age of betrayal, of political choices fuelled by fear, idolatry, adolescent rage, marital bitterness and self-preservation. What surprised me was how many had stood firm.

Around the same time that Zhang denounced his mother, Yu Xiangzhen was summoned home from her factory. Another campaign was at its peak; her parents had been under pressure for months. Her father, known for his kindness to colleagues, was somewhat shielded by younger staff. Her mother's service was exemplary, but her bluntness had annoyed other workers. Worse, she was accused of falsifying her background when she claimed to be born to revolutionary cadres. Her father had gone undercover in the Kuomintang at the order of Communist superiors. But when the Cultural Revolution began, his success in turning a high-ranking officer was forgotten, while the taint of his brief membership remained. He was sent to herd sheep in the wilderness, along the Yellow River. Yu's mother was accused of failing to 'draw a line' between them. Now her persecutors ordered her family to draw their own line, cutting her off for her refusal to turn her back on her father.

By the time Yu arrived home, the crowds had jammed her parents' flat and spilled out into the hallway. The seventeen-year-old fought her way through the chanting mob to comfort her sister, who stood shivering with fear. Her father was forced to the front of the meeting. Well versed in Party tactics, he had prepared his charges carefully. His wife had been too complacent as a revolutionary youth, he said;

because she had joined the cause so young, at just eleven, she had paid insufficient attention to ideologically remoulding herself. She had been too frank and candid in dealing with comrades and so had upset them. Besides, he added, he was to blame for her faults – he had not worked hard enough to correct her. It was a perfectly tuned performance: lamenting his shortcomings, highlighting her long commitment to the Party and reminding listeners of the personal grudges which had fuelled her case. Next came Yu. She looked at the ugly faces demanding that she cut off her mother. She weighed her words and began: 'My mother has taught us to love the Party and the country since our childhood. She is an impeccable model to us . . .'

Yu said the meeting ended in disarray, halted by this departure from the script. She somehow escaped without serious repercussions. But many paid a high price for loyalty, and some paid with their lives. (When his wife was refused cancer treatment, Ba Jin, the author, blamed himself for not forcing her away: 'She would be alive if she hadn't been [my] "stinking wife" . . . I killed her.') Yes, a Chinese historian told me, plenty of kids were forced by Red Guards to turn upon their parents. But to report their mother or father without coercion, as Zhang had done? That was really, really rare.

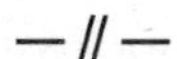

Zhang and his father had plenty of reasons to denounce Fang. Fear that a neighbour might overhear, and report them too, perhaps. Terror that their family was imperilled by Fang's recklessness. Anger at her sorrow for those she had lost and her carelessness with those she still had. Resentment over her abandonment of home, however involuntary. But Zhang didn't want to engage with the only question that mattered: why? He had a single unyielding answer to every version I essayed.

In the attic office that night, he sang to us the song that he had learned more than fifty years earlier, describing Chairman Mao as dearer even than one's own father and mother: 'All the education I accepted from society, family and schools – this song was the essence that represented it. Why I could send my mother to be shot – why I did such things – was because of the education I got. This kind of education, this thinking, could be explained or be demonstrated through red songs such as the ones Bo Xilai promoted. Especially this song.'

Zhang was lionised for his betrayal. His town held an exhibition in his honour. He showed us the cartoonish illustrations it included: pencil sketches of him denouncing his mother and – in the last frame – the blood spurting from Fang's mouth as she was shot. The grotesque images sat alongside pictures of his mother. All had been collected from acquaintances in recent years; he and his father had burned the family photographs after her disgrace. They had not just drawn a line between them: they had erased her entirely. She had vanished not only from their lives, but also from their pasts.

— // —

It was Zhang's uncle who sought to reopen Fang Zhongmou's case.

'Whenever I mention her I want to cry,' Fang Meikai began, as if apologising.

He was closer in age to his nephew than his sister, born twenty-two years before him. As a small child he had trailed after her as though she were his second mother; as a teenager he absorbed her admonitions to treat others fairly and with respect. As a young man he continued to look up to her as a woman 'who was brave enough to think, say and do things'.

He recalled no enthusiasm for the Cultural Revolution, just the derision when she saw the big-character posters denouncing this person or that, and how she had snorted that some people were always making trouble for others. Terrified, he had begged her to stay silent, warning that she was risking her life. She insisted that she was not scared.

'Zhang Hongbing and his father were very strict in their redness and wanted to crack down on her,' he added, using his nephew's full name. It was all those things together that had prompted her outburst, he thought. Her son's zealotry was a cause, not a consequence, of her attack on Mao. He was furious when Zhang and his father reported her, but impotent: 'There was nothing I could do. I wanted to see her, but I wouldn't have been allowed. I was afraid that if I went to see her I would also be involved in this case. That was the situation back then: they could kill whomever they wanted.'

But when Cultural Revolution cases began to be reversed in 1979, Fang saw a chance to partially right the injustice. He began to collect evidence that might clear his sister's name. He took her case to the local court, wrote letters to the government in Beijing and persuaded Zhang and his father to support his appeal. She was cleared soon afterwards, and the family erected her gravestone.

— // —

Brothers and sons, adults and teenagers, had different relationships and perspectives. That didn't bother me. My reservations began with Zhang's tears, and my own dry eyes, and grew when we stood by the grave and he began his prostrations as the video camera rolled.

'Mother! I am an unfilial son!' And then: 'Mother! I have brought the *Guardian* to see you!'

I wasn't sure whether he was part of his audience. Perhaps it was his work as a lawyer; perhaps it was the fact that he had written for newspapers; perhaps it was simply the way he had told the story to himself so many times, but Zhang's story had an unusual consistency and completeness. He told it, in fact, the way a journalist might have put the tale together, weaving facts into a satisfying, meaningful whole. It was polished and neat, with its perfect arc from washtub to washtub, and the poignant coda of his dream. The factual truth of it was unassailable, established in numerous documents. Was I simply uneasy that he had tried to do my work for me? He was frustratingly determined to give us what he thought we wanted ('Mother! I have brought the *Guardian* to see you!') and equally adamant in his refusal to engage with the question that mattered. He had so many facts for me, so many documents, so many tears. But however many times I asked, this was really all he had to say about the decision that defined his life: 'It was not my mother. It was a demon with a terrifying face.'

He had such a tight grasp on his dreams and memories. They permitted no confusion. Facts are – or should be – sacred, to journalists and historians at least, but facts are not the whole truth; which we select and how we understand and weave them together – that matters too. We think of remembering as retrieval, but in fact it is an act of creation. Our memories grow and change as we do, and truths can harden into something unreal if we repeat them often enough, either because we do so unthinkingly or because we are too careful with them. The consistency of a narrator reassures but can itself be a kind of lie. Zhang's memories felt stunted.

His crime could not be forgiven: it broke the law of nature. He wanted to prevent another such tragedy. He was viciously unfilial. He told me all this, and yet he had removed himself from the story. He existed in it not as a human who loved and feared and doubted, but as a Maoist algorithm: inputs, rules, outputs. I did not doubt his passion for Mao, shared by so many of those I had met, nor his desire to show it. I felt only that it was the beginning, not the end, of an explanation. He blamed himself and apologised to people who had 'kept their consciences', but he could not afford or bear to treat his actions as choices. He mentioned, without elaborating, the psychological torment he had suffered, his depression and attempted suicide. What he did not say – would not say – began to seem more important than what he did.

'My mother, father and I were all devoured by the Cultural Revolution,' he added, as though there were no difference between them. 'Society should take society's responsibility; families should take the family's responsibility; people should take their own responsibility. In particular, the responsibility also includes my mother's, because she hadn't told us that as a person you should have independent thinking. She should take responsibility too.'

Fang, exonerated from the charges of counter-revolutionary thinking, was now being held to account for the leftist excesses that killed her by the son who had denounced her.

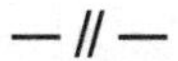

He had paused his tale for a generous dinner cooked by his quiet wife. Their neat home seemed the only clean place here; I wondered how they kept the dirt at bay. I was used to the grime of factory zones and the mud of the countryside; I had slept happily in a farmer's home where the latrine and pigsty shared a room. But this town felt like the filthiest place I had ever visited. This was not the dust and manure of villages but something man-made, unwholesome, greasing your hands and spreading black footprints over floors. Plastic bags fluttered down the streets. Everything felt contaminated. It was the dirt and waste of transition, a town aspiring to the city's glitz but not yet its standards, the fields already buried deep beneath brick and tile and plastic. My hotel was apparently the best in town, and one of the worst I had encountered: a grimy, foul, three-storey affair with few working lights, a sticky carpet and an unspeakable bathroom. Its English name was the Buckingham Palace Hotel. I was almost relieved to discover, next morning, that a plain-clothes policeman had been stationed in the next room; I lost him at the first junction as I returned to Zhang's home.

Zhang seemed a true son of this restless, ambitious place. Anhui was a province of migrants: mothers leaving behind their infants to care for the children of strangers; husbands sending home wages to wives they had not seen for months or years. Relationships were sustained by phone call and message. Perhaps it was unsurprising that so many dwindled and warped or died. Many blamed China's turn to the market for creating a generation that placed cash above family and for wrenching households apart. But most saw distant wealth as the only guarantor of their children's future. And though they were drawn across the country by the capitalist boom, they were separated from their families by a relic of Mao's planned economy: the household registration system, which denied arrivals to the cities the same services as urban-born residents. The tragedy of left-behind children epitomised the way that Chinese families are haunted by both the party-state's authoritarian impulses and the dismantling or disintegration of Maoism.

The Party has never abandoned its desire to control family life. Now it attempts to reconstruct what it once tried to grind to powder, including, to some degree, Confucian ideals. Xi talks of families as the 'cells of society', laying the foundation for national development, progress and social harmony. Early propaganda referred to him as Xi Dada: 'Uncle' or 'Big Daddy' Xi. At the Lunar New Year, broadcasters have chided children to visit their parents – over an image of Xi strolling hand in hand with his mother. China should 'promote fine family culture'. Politburo members should play an exemplary role in promoting family values. Officials are urged not to neglect their families – so much for those heroes of the revolution, sacrificing wives and children to the cause. Mao would not approve. Yet he would recognise the belief in the infinite malleability of humans and the need to judge their value by their service to a greater, grander mission.

The party-state has few weapons against the strain that an ageing population with higher expectations places on an embryonic welfare system. The coercion of the one-child policy has been replaced with pressure to bear more offspring. Pragmatic instincts lie behind the sometimes bathetic attempts to foster family feeling. (In a new list of filial exemplars, teaching your parents how to use the internet replaced tiger-strangling.) Practicality to the point of cynicism, in fact. Given a drastic shortfall in female births, and an excess of unmarried males, the state feminist organisation, the All-China Women's Federation, has been zealous in encouraging young women to wed instead of continuing their studies. Women's rights are subsumed to keep men content: filial belief is the guarantor not only of social welfare but also of social stability. Somewhere within this is the inchoate yet profound realisation of the damage caused by destroying a philosophy: a population that believes in nothing is more dangerous than a population that believes in the wrong ideals.

In a turbulent, unpredictable age, people had learned, like Zhang, to seize what they could from the wreckage and to save themselves. And he had done admirably. Unassuming Master Wang grew humbler still as the two men explained their friendship over dinner. Wang had been Zhang's boss in the factory where they had laboured in the early seventies, which made sense – his old-fashioned Mao suit was the kind you saw only on long-retired workers or ageing farmers these days. Zhang had long since left his teacher behind and abandoned such dated garb.

He had failed again and again in the ferocious college entrance exams after the Cultural Revolution, when a generation of young people had battled for a single year's places. In the end he went to a technical school to make up the classes he had missed; then, at last, to university. It was 1990 by the time he won certification as a lawyer. Fourteen years, I calculated: I understood better the stiffness of his manner, buttressing his qualifications with dignity. Against all the odds – his background of rural obscurity, his lack of connections, the chaos that engulfed the education system, his age and the competition, not to mention his traumatic past – he had become a lawyer. It had needed toughness as well as hunger. I wondered what Fang would have made of her son. In any age a certain kind of person adapts and thrives while others struggle until they go under or allow themselves to be borne away by the current. Despite Zhang's suitcase and piles of books and papers, he was afraid not of losing everything – what more could he lose? – but of getting stuck, a fear that should not really have surprised me, and which I understood better in retrospect.

For in bed each night, weeks after my visit, as the day fell away and my mind began to still, the image of his mother lying alone rose from some distant place and gripped me. The thought of her lonely body in the soil, not even able to decay in peace, was shaming every time. Even now, years later, it occasionally surprises me. It is like a memory, or a dream: a picture which I know my mind has shaped but which arrives unbidden and insistent, as if I too am guilty. It is just a story I once heard, and yet she seems more real than its teller. They did not want to remember her, yet they could not let her rest. She will not be left behind.

TEN

> This is not the end of an incident, but just the beginning. Lies written in ink cannot cover up facts written in blood. Blood debts must be repaid in kind. The longer the delay in payment, the higher the interest!
>
> **Lu Xun**

Not long after my visit to Zhang Hongbing, I met a novelist for coffee. I'd heard she was interested in the era and its parallels with more recent events; we talked of her work and how it was inflected by what happened all those years ago. She spoke a little of how she understood the Cultural Revolution, and I paused to clarify. Some used the name to refer to only the first years of Red Guard violence, and others included the full decade of hatred. When did she believe it ended?

'Last April,' she replied. I wasn't sure if she'd misunderstood my question, or I had misunderstood her answer. Seeing my confusion, she elucidated: 'We didn't escape until my father died last April, still arguing with the Red Guards. They didn't let him sleep for seventeen days – his brain became chaotic. So his thoughts stopped at the Cultural Revolution.'

Her response levelled me. I suppose I had known, from my first meeting with Yu Xiangzhen, that the past walked with all survivors. Friends edged around family secrets and tensions, glancing at the causes. I sensed it in the rage and volatility of some I met, and in the fractured recall of others: trauma punches the holes that power must drill into language, memory, families. But, really, it was everywhere, a pain that ate people up and wore them out. It corroded their stomachs, acid, relentless, or came in spasms sharp enough to paralyse. Piercing headaches reduced them to tears and rage. They shut their eyes but sleep never came, or they drifted and dozed and jerked awake, clammy, and lay cold and hot and cold. They lived in a grey world of exhaustion, worn thin. They tried Western medicine and Chinese, and tablets found online or pressed on them by friends. It wasn't an ulcer. It wasn't cancer or migraines. They went again to doctors who inspected tongues, took pulses, drew blood, ordered scans, wrote prescriptions, stuck them with needles, shrugged their shoulders, rang specialists. Eventually, sent on and on, they found themselves, resentful and wary, in another office. Their answers were terse. Suspicious. Little hard beads of fact and complaint, unstrung; it was a struggle to order them. Most just wanted the pills.

The children and grandchildren came. Sometimes their bodies had the same sicknesses, the sharp pains, the unexplained lethargies. Occasionally they spoke of other troubles, admitting that they were stressed and depressed and anxious, and did not know why. Last year there had been a student – a dutiful young man, a little quiet, but friendly enough with classmates. His grades had been high, his behaviour immaculate, until the day he posted a precise description of how he wanted to kill his teacher: how he woke up in his dorm room and seized a viciously sharp knife; how he walked into the room and saw his tutor; how he threw the man's scalding tea . . . It ran on and on, and the university authorities, when they read it, asked the mental health staff for help, who sought help from specialists, who, in turn, approached a psychoanalyst.

No one could reconcile those graphic words with this pleasant, unremarkable boy. His parents had a good relationship; they got on well with their son. They rushed to the college when they heard of his trouble and rented a flat so his mother could live with him while he underwent treatment. His father was almost silent, but supportive; over the weeks, it emerged – to the family's shock, but not entirely to the psychoanalyst's – that he had lived with deep depression for years. Throughout his son's life he had drummed in the same lessons: Keep your distance. Keep your guard up. Don't trust anyone. Never, ever let them see you are angry. He drove the message home again and again, and never told his son why. He had watched his own father murdered by Red Guards. He suppressed the pain and fear and rage for almost half a century, and still it had betrayed him, and his child.

Family after family hid their past. Some would not discuss their suffering even with the husbands or wives who had witnessed it. Others told brothers and sisters to forget the events that had scarred their childhood. Sometimes, scared by psychotic episodes or anxious at strange obsessions, adult sons and daughters brought their parents directly to psychiatrists. More often, patients came for physical ailments that had found no relief. They had seen that speech had unimaginable consequences and that a surface harmony, however tenuous, should not be broken. Silence was safety, however dearly bought. The misery stretched back fifty years and ran onwards; you could not see its end. The trauma would not die with its victims: it had already replicated itself in their children, and their children's children. Like cancer cells, it could not mature, only reproduce itself, mutating in grotesque immortality.

— // —

Few professionals were willing to speak about their work with survivors. Some published nothing, others worked anonymously with Western colleagues. Those who spoke to me did so, eventually, on the basis that they would not be identified, and some of those were so elliptical that I gave up hope of answers after several meetings. I met the man I'll call Dr Yang at an international psychotherapy conference in Shanghai. The Europeans wore expensive linen and designer spectacles: they were recognisably a caste, despite their differences. The Chinese dressed like bank clerks or PE teachers or artists. They had not coalesced into a profession. They nodded at mentions of Klein or Lacan – they had the training and the jargon. But when they spoke they told stories and joked, and used words like 'love' and 'contentment' as often as 'cathexis' and 'anaclitic'. They were unabashed and unironic about their attempts to heal themselves and others; they saw no shame in sincerity, even as they recognised the complications of their feelings and their goals.

'I saw enough of people torturing people. I didn't want to be like that. I wanted to bring happiness and joy,' said Dr Yang. He tapped a cigarette from its packet and smiled: 'This is also the outcome of the Cultural Revolution. Our parents had no time to take care of us, so we learned bad habits. These were one of the limited ways of destressing. Everyone lived in the fighting state, in a very hostile environment. The basic instincts and drives were activated.'

He inhaled, turning his head politely to blow the smoke away from me. He was a stocky man, with an easy manner at odds with his subject: struggle, hate, execution. He talked about the 'so-called' confession meetings he had watched; the public sentencings – twenty thousand people gathered in a square, waiting for the revolutionary committee to pronounce the death penalty. Beatings. Political currents and campaigns that might ensnare you at any moment. It wasn't so much the violence as the instability that defined the Cultural Revolution.

'Everyone was involved. Everyone was anxious. It was a zero-sum game – and it could flip. This group of people was successful and superior. But that could become an inferior status – it could all overturn. They were cadres and took power, and then power disappeared in one night and the family experienced a total reversal in life that they could never have imagined. People could not keep a stable, permanent and successful status.' In other catastrophes the line between victims and perpetrators was clearer. When the target was defined not by race or custom but by what was purportedly in hearts and minds; when what was right today was wrong tomorrow; when the means of destruction was mass participation – then certainty, like innocence, was an impossibility.

How had people endured these years? Some had already learned, by then, to bear unbearable abuse. ('We'll be all right as long as we keep going,' Ba Jin and his wife would tell each other. They weren't, though, in the end.) Some attempted to comfort themselves with traditional beliefs and philosophy, though only in secret because such things were forbidden. Humour, also in private. (Jokes were no joke: humour, which depends upon a sense of proportion and incongruity, was inherently a rebuff to Maoist zealotry, and in the worst instances a capital crime.) Self-recrimination, allowing themselves some illusion of potential control: they had done something to bring this disaster upon themselves. And psychosis itself was a kind of protection: when the mind could no longer bear reality, it broke before the person did. Other people, without psychoses, killed themselves.

'The second defining characteristic was what happened in the aftermath,' the psychotherapist continued. When the Second World War ended, the Japanese occupiers had been expelled – the enemy was gone. Two million people fled to Taiwan when the Communists defeated the Kuomintang. But after the Cultural Revolution everyone had to live alongside each other as if nothing had happened. They remained in place: 'In the same country, in the same workplace and even in the same families.'

Chinese culture had long existed as a web of relationships. Family hierarchies both echoed and formed part of the imperial order. To be a person was to be a link between ancestors and descendants, bound into a greater scheme that ran both vertically through time and horizontally through society: 'The path runs from the self to the family, from the family to the state, and from the state to the whole world,' wrote the sociologist Fei Xiaotong. Nothing could be more menacing than a figure unknown and untethered to society. In the eighteenth century a panic over 'soul-stealing' swept the land, with mob attacks on those suspected of sorcery, in a phenomenon in some ways analogous to the Maoist hysteria, as the historian Philip Kuhn has described. But suspicions attached themselves to 'wanderers, strangers, people without roots, people of obscure origins and uncertain purpose, people lacking social connections, people out of control'.

The Cultural Revolution showed that one thing was more terrifying than a stranger: someone close to you. To know a person was no longer the kernel of trust but of suspicion. Those around you, those who knew you best, had the greatest power to harm. In the immediate years after the turmoil, 'people might speak to strangers on trains about what they had seen – but never to their colleagues,' said Dr Yang. And morality itself was now betrayed: for traditional Confucian precepts had no ethical concepts, Fei Xiaotong wrote, which transcended specific types of human relationships. When you could not trust those beside you, trust itself was destroyed.

'Was surviving the revolution a stroke of good or ill fortune? Even now, I cannot say I know the answer to that question,' one victim wrote, decades later.

— // —

The political movements of the fifties and sixties could themselves be seen as a kind of illness, a cycle of euphoria and mania spawning open conflict, and then suppression and depression. Now the country, like its citizens, knew something was wrong without knowing what or why. It had the same torpidities and convulsions. The leading intellectual Sun Liping, who had once taught Xi Jinping, warned that the biggest threat to society was not social turmoil but social decay: the loss of morals and a sense of justice. Friends blamed the Cultural Revolution, when people had learned to survive at all costs, and indifference became a form of self-defence, and anger had been fired only to be muzzled. 'The movement destroyed human nature,' wrote Yan Jiaqi and Gao Gao in their history, *Turbulent Decade*. Others blamed the rapacious capitalism birthed unwittingly by the movement for teaching people that only money mattered. You turned the pages of a paper and counted the crises. Eighteen people walked by as a two-year-old, run down by a truck, lay dying in the street. Children died when a kindergarten owner laced yogurt with poison to smear a competitor. There was a spate of knife attacks on schools; men drove tractors loaded with gas into offices. An elderly man tried to blow up a bus with a home-made grenade from the Cultural Revolution in what was described as a revenge attack – on previous journeys the driver had halted five metres short of his stop. The device rolled down the bus but did not detonate. Its effectiveness had long expired; the rage kept burning.

'I was too rash,' the man told the court.

A psychoanalyst to whom I mentioned the case shook his head. 'It's totally a fantasy, right? The fantasy came true in the Cultural Revolution. Every soldier thinks they're killing the enemy. They want a better world. Even if they have no idea of what's at the end of a so-called better world.'

We were sitting at a table by the window – 'I like sunlight; I like warmth' – in a cafe near his workplace. Dr Chen was younger than Dr Yang, too young to remember the Cultural Revolution, and his family had been largely unscathed. He worked mostly with the children of victims, somewhat readier to seek his help – enough of them that he regarded their trauma as commonplace, nothing exceptional. But he had worked with some of their parents too, and had increasingly come to admire them simply for being alive. For enduring.

'We can't say people who survived the trauma are more healthy,' he cautioned. 'No. Think of two dogs: one strong and aggressive; another submissive. When they meet a harsh environment that wants to conquer them, the dog who goes to fight dies – and the dog who's submissive survives. Which was healthier? From a psychoanalytic point of view, maybe the dog who wanted to fight. So maybe the survivors of traumatic social movements have a lower mental health level: related not only to the trauma but also to their previous history. Everyone has their story, but they have no chance to tell others. Whether they were aggressors or the real victims, they became victims we don't know. The attitude of most people and the government is that you forget it. The page has turned; don't read it again. Life goes on. That's also the Eastern attitude to life.'

The Chinese called it eating bitterness – suffering, and enduring. It was a necessity in life, and yet a kind of virtue, demanded in job adverts and cited in the stories of magnates who had made it big from nowhere. It expressed a pride in resilience, in the power of simply persisting. Yet it embodied powerlessness, a tragic fatalism. It was all that was left when everything had been stripped from you – the choice of those who had no choice. The old used it to encapsulate hard, painful lives and losses. Younger people were naive enough to think, like Americans, that they might control their destinies, that not everything was settled. Eating bitterness sounded pointless and defeatist. They expected some sweetness – and their parents, who had fed them fruit and candy, couldn't help but worry that they had succumbed, that an easy life had softened them, and to fret that their hopes of not survival but fulfilment, and the ease with which they spent their wages and shared their dreams, left them at the mercy of whatever life might bring. China's transformation had been so profound and so abrupt that a gap of two decades seemed a gulf of a century or more. They lived different lives, spoke different languages. To many of the older generation, speech itself was dangerous.

— // —

So psychotherapy was suspect. It was essentially new to China, though some of Sigmund Freud's works were published in Chinese in his lifetime, and their translator had briefly corresponded with him. Mao banned psychology in the year the Cultural Revolution began; it was a bourgeois pseudoscience, 'nine tenths useless and one tenth distortion'. The pledge to crush the discipline meant attacking its practitioners as well as burning books. Psychiatry was permitted, but in a heavily medicalised model. Even now, there were only twenty thousand psychiatrists in a country of 1.3 billion people. Psychotherapy was not recognised by law until 2013. By then it had already become one of China's 'manias', garnering not so much followers as fans. The Shanghai conference, though garlanded by international authorities, was open to amateurs and felt more like a convention. Most of the participants were hobbyists, and several rushed up at the ends of sessions for selfies with the speakers. The country was searching for a purpose beyond wealth, unsatisfied – sometimes revolted – by modern life's materialism. Prosperity answered raw physical needs, but mentally it had proved another trauma. The inversion of values underscored the meaninglessness of the earlier suffering: all of that – for this? History was mocking its subjects. The more they gained economically, the more certain many became that they had lost something essential. Some, like the Educated Youth and Zhou Jiayu, had turned to a real or imagined socialist past. Others looked inside themselves. The country now had perhaps 100 million Christians, in both officially recognised institutions and underground house churches. Many more had turned or returned to Buddhism, often in its more flamboyant incarnations. Villages were menaced by wealthy urban well-wishers releasing snakes in pursuit of good karma. Strange and obscure religious cults seized counties; some had the anarchic, menacing aura of their nineteenth-century forebears. People hungered for meaning.

Psychotherapy promised an alternative. Like communism, it was a vote for the future. It did not claim a monopoly on truth, and where communism tried to recast the individual in the service of a larger cause, remaking was an end in itself for psychotherapists. But it too made demands. To many in the audience in Shanghai, and many of the speakers, the discipline seemed in fundamental contradiction to Chinese culture. You just didn't talk about emotions. You didn't say 'Thank you' or 'I love you' to your parents – such declarations might prompt suspicion. Love was an extra blanket on your bed, the tastiest morsels dropped into your bowl, nutritional supplements sent home to your mother. At the same time China's party-state and official culture constantly sought to define and cage meaning. Words were loaded so had to be controlled.

Yet alongside these tendencies ran an expansive, allusive tradition: 'The name that can be named is not the enduring and unchanging name,' says the Daodejing, the most famous text of the Daoist religion. What is implicit, unrecognised, unspoken may be what really matters. Look for the truth not in what is stated but in what is not:

'Clay is fashioned into vessels; but it is on their empty hollowness that their use depends.' For Chinese patients, even more than most, psychotherapy was a strained but potent love affair. The comfort it offered in initial stages might give way to anxiety and fear and loneliness as they began to understand that their wishes could not be satisfied by talking alone, without disturbing their ties to those around them. Keeping harmonious relations was the most basic principle in Chinese social life, said Dr Chen. 'Sometimes I have the feeling we have more chaos and social conflict; that's why we pay so much attention to harmony.'

What was unsettling within families might be much more so outside them. Psychotherapy looked at first like an authoritarian dream. It treated China's collective traumas as if they were individual sicknesses, to be resolved by and for patients. Disputes which might have broken out as public quarrels or political petitions were dealt with in the privacy of the treatment room. But because the experience of the Cultural Revolution remained largely taboo, mere confirmation was fraught – it was not just the patient's family but their wider community that might deny it; and linking the past and present was itself potentially sensitive. Integrating experience was a riddle: you could not understand what happened and what it meant without understanding the impetuses which drove it, and yet many of those were really irrelevant to the trauma itself. The complexity of the Red Guards' motives mattered less than the enormity of their crimes.

The scar ran through the heart of Chinese society, and through the souls of its citizens. The Cultural Revolution was a national trauma as well as a mass of personal ones: collective traumatisation demands collective meaning and a common attempt to work through all the loss and humiliation. Harsh truths can breed pain and division. But so do half-truths. Healing is impossible without an honest reckoning – without the kind of truth which is not permissible in today's China, and which many citizens would rather not hear. 'The "trauma process" is not about the truth of history in the usual sense of the word,' writes the sinologist Susanne Weigelin-Schwiedrzik. 'It is a process of social construction in which people struggle to find a way of "coping with the trauma" that can be shared by the majority of the involved collective.'

— // —

There was one session at the Shanghai conference, exploring personal anguish in the context of national stories, that I had been especially anxious to attend. Not only me – the room was crammed, the air already a little stale when the introducer announced baldly: 'Chinese history in these two hundred years means a history of traumas.'

Psychotherapists found that most survivors were already traumatised before their sufferings in the Cultural Revolution. The viciousness with which family members turned upon each other in the movement surely owed something to previously unhappy, even abusive, relations. But domestic pathologies were enmeshed with the series of disasters that had swept through China as the plagues through Egypt. Instability and violence had come to seem not aberrations but inevitabilities. In a great civilisation's unravelling, war, famine and political purges had destroyed families and minds. The wish to re-establish past glories had precipitated some of these disasters. The deadly Taiping Rebellion, invasion by foreign powers, the nation's collapse into warlordism, the Japanese invasion, the Great Leap Forward . . . Every time it seemed the nation might come to rest at last, fresh rubble piled itself upon the rubble – until China reached the culmination of the catastrophes. And even when that disaster was over, the trauma perpetuated itself in the generation which should have escaped it. Freud saw himself as an archaeologist of the mind, searching for traces from which to reconstruct what had been lost and what it might mean: uncovering 'layer after layer of the patient's psyche, before coming to the deepest, most valuable treasures'. But Freud's successors were excavating ruins built upon ruins.

In the aftermath of the Holocaust clinicians had noticed how many young patients were the children of survivors. The offspring of victims were more likely, too, to develop post-traumatic stress disorder after stressful experiences, and to be affected for longer. Experts began to develop a theory of transgenerational trauma and 'post memory' – a relationship to the suffering which was vivid and real though mediated by their parents and perhaps never even discussed. Already there is evidence of effects in a third generation. The speakers in Shanghai spoke of parents who turned aggression against themselves; of mothers barely able to relate to their children or recognise their needs, unwittingly relying on them to heal their own profound traumas; of fathers who treated their child as the mother who had been murdered, or who imposed the kind of mercilessness they themselves had suffered. They described children who struggled to find the confidence and pride they needed in parents when those parents evidently couldn't cope, and did nothing but criticise, or tried to shield them from everything. But how could you help a child to develop confidence in the world and to make sense of it when experience had shown you that the world was not safe and made no sense? What looked overprotective to outsiders, what felt suffocating and relentless to their children, was only their sensible – essential – caution.

The hostility and fragility of victims inhibited post-Holocaust research. In China the political taboo had also closed off the subject. These speakers were all foreign. The audience was Chinese. The listeners scribbled notes, took pictures of the screen; there was urgency, but a palpable discomfort, that the experts could not miss, and they drew on the weight of European history to defuse their subject as well as to explain it. More and more, said a speaker, there was a need to talk about traumatic events, and especially the Cultural Revolution. They saw an increasing number of patients trying to make sense of what had happened to them and their families. In his eyes I saw his doubt: was he making a connection? He added carefully: 'In Germany it took a long time before people were willing and able to face the terrible violence of the Second World War which people, especially Jews, were exposed to. For a long time there was simply silence because people wanted to forget.'

The young woman next to me shifted in her seat. 'Why do they keep reminding us about this?' she hissed at his next mention of the Cultural Revolution. It wasn't clear what she resented: whether the point was so obvious that she felt patronised; or whether it was not our place, as foreigners, to inspect her nation's dirty laundry; or whether, though she had come to this seminar, and surely knew what it would contain, she did not want to think about it at all. Some things are worse when you see them clearly. People wanted to tame the subject, to treat it coolly and neutrally. But it was so dense that it closed up around you, so expansive that you could not escape; it had a microclimate of its own. If you knew what it really meant, perhaps you would never venture into it.

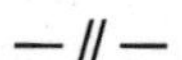

Dr Meng was the same age as the woman in the trauma session – in her early thirties, with long hair that shone. She was poised and elegant. I was not; I'd spent half an hour walking back and forth in search of a cafe which was, I'd at last found, twenty yards from my original starting point. I apologised and she began. She had thought she had chosen her subject, but perhaps it had chosen her. She knew of no personal connection to the Cultural Revolution. Only as her work progressed – as she saw how deep and wide the movement went – had she thought to ask her grandparents.

'And so then I knew that something had happened in my family.' She smiled. 'I understood why I chose this subject. I needed to do something for my family. Maybe something for myself. I realised that the Cultural Revolution was here' – she pointed at the table with one finger. 'And I was here' – she pointed at another spot. 'I can't go around it. I have to go through it.'

Dr Meng's parents didn't know or care about the subject, and it was because they didn't know that she had chosen it. The trauma had contained and consumed both the first and second generation. They existed inside it; there was no one but themselves there. For them, there was no one else. There was nothing else. The third generation were also affected. 'But we can do something. We have something in our lives besides the influence of trauma. We are outside it. For me, for my generation, it's history. I have my own life.' She took a delicate sip of chrysanthemum tea and gazed out of the cafe window for a moment, seeming suddenly shy. She thought her profession was doing something good, but how could they all be certain? 'I just . . . hesitate, especially for someone who's older. Talking is good for young people, but I don't know whether it is so good for them. There's no time for them to deal with things. I want to ask you a question – I don't know if you'll understand what I mean . . .' She unfolded a paper napkin and sketched a set of interlocking wheels. 'What is the meaning of trauma for humans? You can say there is trauma because things are always like this. A perpetual motion machine.' She stabbed at her drawing with the pencil. 'Round and round and round, and another generation will begin. But perhaps you could also say trauma keeps human beings moving along. Progressing.'

I was taken aback. Trauma had stunted or warped so many of the lives I had encountered. But she had a kind of Darwinian conception of the species as a whole groping its way forward. From a moral perspective, of course, humans should take responsibility. But if this suffering and endurance were part of a natural process, through which humans en masse might advance, becoming better and happier and stronger, perhaps all her work was in a way irrelevant. 'In this sense, at least, we need to do nothing – just follow the natural course?' She looked at me doubtfully. She really wanted an answer.

A few days later, back in Beijing, I thought of Dr Meng. I had detoured on my way home from the office, tempted by the gates of Ritan Park, and had climbed up to the little pavilion that stood on a mound at its heart. The welcome patch of green and gold around me was encircled by high-rises. Way above, an eagle-shaped speck hung in the sky; in the last of the sunshine I could just make out the kite's thread, held by an old man nearby. There were couples photographing themselves before the sunset, and children giggling as they clambered across the rocks below me. Further down, by the soupy lake, a man was practising the saxophone with more diligence than skill. It was a moment of small happinesses, personal pleasures pursued side by side. Things that were tiny in a city of 20 million, almost anomalous in this metropolis of cars and fumes and hustle and noise – and tiny, too, against the scale of the wreckage. Perhaps it was only a veneer, but it was at least a veneer. China was a land of raw suffering and need, driven by impulses it could not understand because it could not speak about so much that mattered. But I felt a kind of awe at its endurance. That people could fly kites, play music, laugh, love and even trust was a kind of miracle. A man who had watched his father's murder could be a caring, attentive parent; a man thrashed almost to death could thirst for life. A nation that had torn itself apart could rest, and play. Life went on.

All the while, the psychotherapists were gathering the whispers they heard beneath the country's song. They didn't know what they would do with the material, only that they must save it. They hurried to rescue stories before they died with their narrators, and before they themselves, the collectors, had departed. Those who had trained so long to heal and help were acknowledging defeat. They excavated the truth to rebury it – archaeologists stashing their treasures underground again. But within this realism persisted a profound, irrational, even radical optimism. Some day, the terrain might not be so treacherous. Some day, these time capsules would be disinterred: 'In a hundred years, a stranger will find them. Someone will go back.'

ELEVEN

> In spite of my own convictions when it came to the matter of hope, I had no way of blotting out its existence . . . Hope is something that lies in the future . . .
>
> **Lu Xun**

New Year 2015 arrived. I loved the fresh beginning. I loved the hubbub of crammed train stations, the edgy relief and anticipation of people pouring home in their tens of millions. I relished feasting with friends in the emptied city, half an eye on the TV gala – a peculiar concoction of pop stars and ball gowns, slapstick and Party dogma. Most of all I loved the pyrotechnics. My first spring festival I barely slept; from the twenty-eighth floor I could watch the fireworks bursting across the skyline. They bloomed through the night, red and golden and green, hour after hour. The rockets loosed by our neighbours shook the room. It was deafening and dazzling and glorious, and for days afterwards I edged through streets, dodging firecracker bursts. But year by year it grew quieter, and though my lungs and eardrums were grateful, and the capital's tally of injuries shrank, I missed the exuberant, loud, garish, almost untamed Beijing. This was the quietest New Year yet, so muted it was as if the city doubted that spring was coming. Soon, I would be gone.

I had arrived, in 2008, in a world which was constantly remaking itself – a place charged with possibility. I didn't believe that wholesale reform would magically result from the market, the internet or the march of history, but I watched in admiration and surprise as people scratched out space for themselves. Over seven years the pace of material development had become if anything more dizzying: more money, more people, more cars, more skyscrapers. There were four new billionaires each week. There were more ports, and roads, and railways. Even the museums were fast multiplying. There were more planes and warships, a long-awaited aircraft carrier. China was no longer biding its time. It built up disputed islets in the South China Sea and soon would come a naval base in Djibouti, a ninety-nine-year lease on a port in Sri Lanka, and the grand, sprawling Belt and Road Initiative for infrastructure spanning Europe, Central Asia and Africa. Even Earth could not bound China's ambitions: its spacecraft carried taikonauts into the heavens. Yet to me it felt as though the country was shrinking, indefinably but undeniably becoming denser and more suffocating. The rowdy, combustible place I fell for had hushed. The state was ever more confident and combative; the people seemed more anxious. More activists disappeared into prison, the lawyers of dissidents were targeted, then the lawyers of lawyers themselves were seized. It had always been tough to speak to officials, but now others too were growing wary. Fewer people would take my calls and some contacts stopped returning them, or spoke so cautiously that their quotes were too cryptic to be deciphered by a reader. Strangers spoke less freely to me – the suspicion of foreigners, never dead, had stirred again, and when I stopped at a market for a story on inflation, a vendor angrily rebuffed my questions about the price of cabbages: 'If we tell you, we'll be like foreign spies,' she replied, quite seriously.

Though the shift towards repression preceded Xi's ascension, he has imposed an extraordinary level of control, curtailing the freedoms won so painfully over decades. He has also amassed personal power in a way that few thought possible. In 2016, the fiftieth anniversary of the Cultural Revolution, he was hailed as the core of the Party, cementing what was evident to everyone: his concentration of authority within concentric rings – his grip upon the Party, its hold upon the country, and China's might in the world. The collective rule of his technocratic 'red engineer' predecessors was over. Their stabilisation of political power, ensuring the regular turnover of leaders, would fall by the wayside too. In 2022 he embarked upon indefinite rule with a norm-breaking third term and no successor in sight. When he had abolished the presidential term limit, four years earlier, official media said it did not mean that he was leader for life. But they quoted experts suggesting that the country needed 'consistent' leadership until, say, the middle of the century. By then Xi would be ninety-six. Mao died at eighty-two.

In a tiny village, tannoys once more blared out Party propaganda; in another, officials urged Christians to swap their posters of Jesus for portraits of Xi. He has portrayed Party loyalty as not merely a belief but a faith, so perhaps the religious melding was not entirely out of place. He is at once powerful and reassuring, a remote authority and a kindly presence with his avuncular smile. He understands better than anyone since Mao how to deploy mass emotion, how to tell his people a story, give them a purpose. Propaganda has called Xi the people's leader and helmsman: the titles are pure Mao. The message amasses in speeches and songs, on the news and in Party publications: *It should be lifelong, a whole life – that's what the hearts of the ordinary people are saying. Be a man like Xi Dada. Xi Jinping is a visionary. If you want to marry, marry someone like Xi. He has obtained the heartfelt love and respect of the entire Party, army and people. He is like our parents. Chairman Xi, General Secretary of People's Feelings.*

The echoes of the Cultural Revolution clang louder. China once more stakes a claim to global leadership. At home no one is too big to be toppled; tycoons and senior Party figures are felled. Conversations between friends are policed again; businesspeople as well as dissidents are called in over private chats on social media. There is intolerance not only of outright dissent but also of normal intellectual discussion. There is increasing suspicion of minorities and their cultures, and encouragement of tattling on neighbours. Underground churches, in the past mostly tolerated, are shuttered and scattered, their pastors seized. Even Marxist students who reach out to help striking labourers are detained. Undergraduates report on their lecturers for straying beyond the political limits; among the victims is a historian of the Cultural Revolution, who finds her office door plastered with accusations – uncannily reminiscent of those big-character posters. Not long afterwards, she moves abroad.

Both Chinese and Western friends are departing, for Europe, the United States and other parts of Asia. Hong Kong was once a haven. But the freedoms promised to it after handover are first ground down and then crushed outright: the ruthless response to unprecedented protests bringing one in four people onto the streets in a vain attempt to defend its limited autonomy. Authorities prosecute peaceful activists for sedition; the police raid news media, freezing their assets and arresting staff. Teachers, lecturers, lawyers and judges are targeted by pro-Beijing media. There is far worse in Xinjiang, where perhaps a million 'unreliable' residents, almost all Uighur or other Muslim minorities, have been herded into camps. They call them vocational training centres, for 'transformation through education', but with their barbed wire and control towers they look like what they are: prisons, for people held without charge or trial. Some of the detainees' children are sent to de facto orphanages. Women report forced sterilisations and sexual violence. Mosques and other cultural sites are razed. These are abuses 'of a scope and scale not seen in China since the Cultural Revolution', warns one human rights group. The camps are the cowsheds of their time, imposed for similar crimes: having family members abroad; reciting a religious verse. State television shows thankful inmates – though they call them students – who voice gratitude at having learned the error of their ways. (Teachers, writes the Education Bureau of the region's capital, Urumqi, are the engineers of the human soul – a phrase first used by Stalin, more recently by Xi, and redolent of Mao's great campaign to remould the hearts and minds of his people.) When the internment camps are closed, detention facilities and new jails spring up in their place. Beyond the bars of the internment camps, Xinjiang is a digital gulag of mass biometric data collection and facial recognition systems, where QR codes with family records are posted at the household's door, while cadres live with families to keep watch even at their hearths.

— // —

Yet Xi is only half Mao: it is impossible to picture him bragging about his monkey spirit. (Donald Trump, with his love of disruption and discord, his ability to channel the public's id, was in that regard a more Maoist leader.) Just before the Tiananmen Square protests were suppressed in 1989, Xi addressed underlings in his region: 'Wasn't the Cultural Revolution the manifestation of "big democracy"? This kind of "big democracy" is not in accordance with science, not in accordance with the rule of law, but instead in accordance with superstition, in accordance with stupidity, and the result is major chaos.' In many ways it is as if he has sought to root out the effects of the Cultural Revolution, and cultivate instead older systems of order and discipline. He has visited Confucius's birthplace to call for the promotion of traditional culture – inherited, he said, by the Party. In truth, his ideas seem (as Mao's did) to owe more to Legalism, a deeply hierarchical philosophy which expects the worst of people, regarding them not as bound by virtue but rulable through strict laws and hard punishments. He has looked to the past for inspiration, rooting his rule in a Chinese structure of behaviour and thought and obedience which the Party claims stretches back five thousand years – so long, it seems, that it not only was, and is, but must be. And he looks to the future for the new, efficient, means to do so.

The tools the party-state never abandoned – the ability to peer into each life, or exert pressure via friends or family – have been upgraded for the twenty-first century. It does not need to slice open envelopes to find out what you write to friends. It does not need the old ladies of the neighbourhood to tell it whom you met, though they still have their use. Gathering and processing information is increasingly easy and economical. Facial recognition technology allows officers to track individuals without trailing them on foot. A patchwork of social credit systems rate people for their public virtue as they would be for their spending and borrowing. Share 'fake news', commit traffic infringements, and already you may struggle to book train tickets, rent a flat or buy a car. The new networks of relationships are digital, but they hark back to the webs that once bound Chinese citizens in place, creating a simulacrum of trust, attractive to many in a society where so little of the real thing exists. Perhaps no one will need to send the cops to badger an old Red Guard's landlord. The algorithms will do their work. You may only realise what officials have done once they want you to know. And people will fall into line, as people do everywhere. Even the capital's street life is neatened, straightened. Teams march into the alleyways to brick up the windows and doors chipped out over decades. Concrete erases the strata of the past: blank walls stretch out, with none of the mess and clutter that mean Beijing to me. Propaganda posters plaster the city, one message standing for them all: *The Communist Party is good – people are happy.*

Some are – probably many; possibly most. In the wake of 2008's financial crash, Trump's rise and, later, early stages of the pandemic, it isn't hard to see why people in China might not envy the West its elected leaders. But Xi has also tapped into potent strains of discontent, notably the brewing rage towards an ostentatious elite. (Once, as I passed an Aston Martin which had just crashed into an Audi, an old man caught my eye and muttered: 'It would be better if rich people just died.') The attacks on corruption go far beyond the token efforts made by previous leaders, even if high-profile political families remain notably untouched, and they resonate far beyond the ranks of neo-Maoists. In time, Xi will promise 'common prosperity', putting pressure on big companies to donate chunks of their profits. The pledge to tackle soaring inequality has obvious appeal. But the more ambitious aspects – cheaper housing and childcare, a property tax – appear to be quietly shelved as the economy slows. It is unclear how far the intended tilt towards redistribution might go. It is certain that state control over the economy is growing, as it is over every aspect of life in China.

Yet, as Xi is not Mao, so his people are not Mao's people. 'During the Cultural Revolution, Mao Zedong was one brain controlling 800 million Chinese people,' the philosopher and activist Xu Youyu has observed, while now 'at least half have their own minds'. There are, in private, faint murmurings of discontent. When a scholar publishes a scathing essay, it spreads surreptitiously but rapidly: 'The Party media is going to great lengths to create a new Idol, and in the process it is offering up to the world an image of China as Modern Totalitarianism . . . We need to ask how a vast country like China, one that was previously so ruinously served by a Personality Cult, simply has no resistance to this new cult.' But the author is detained for a week, then fired from his job and barred from leaving Beijing, and the public space is more constrained than ever. Repression will soon move from the familiar realms – religion, academia, law, civil society, minorities – to areas of society and culture that the Party gradually retreated from after Mao's time, targeting everyone from entrepreneurs to entertainers.

China's state media did not cover the fiftieth anniversary of the Cultural Revolution. But an editorial appeared the next day, 17 May, in the *People's Daily*, the Party's mouthpiece – a twenty-four-hour gap which rendered it safer and more tolerable; propaganda orders were secret, but the thinking behind them was often both transparent and utterly implausible in its tortured logic. The piece didn't, of course, address or even mention such details as persecutions, struggle sessions and murders. It was like publishing an article on 9/12 about the Twin Towers' collapse, without any reference to deaths or even the aeroplanes. It described the movement as 'a significant bend in the course of our country's development history', and explained that the Party took a solemn attitude towards errors: 'One is to admit it. The second is correct analysis. The third is resolute correction. This makes mistakes, and mistakes together with the Party's successful experience, a precious historical textbook.'

There was, in this sense, no such thing as a setback. In absorbing and interpreting the calamity, the Party had actually propelled the nation along the path to its future; history was always moving forward. Even this terse and misleading account was itself pushing China towards its destiny. What the Party was actually admitting remained entirely unclear.

Just before the anniversary, a friend had shown me photographs of Peng Qi'an's museum in Shantou – though it took a while to recognise. The statues of famous victims were caged by scaffolding and sheet metal; they would later be cemented in. Propaganda banners swathed the building, which this time appeared irrevocably shut. Garish red posters plastered over the sombre memorial walls read

CHINESE DREAM in great golden characters, Xi's promise of a glorious future covering up the past. Around the same time, Yu Xiangzhen's blog vanished from all four of the platforms hosting it. She no longer writes about her youth. Wang Xilin, the composer, has remarried and moved to Germany. Xu Weixin, the painter, is working on portraits of figures involved in reform and opening, a politically less complicated era of China's recent past. There was less time than we thought.

In 2021, Xi declared that the Party had been 'chosen by history and the people' as it celebrated its centenary. Diplomats and state media recite the same theme: that the great rejuvenation has entered an 'irreversible historical process'. Yet Xi's vision is of a glory bounded by new perils and growing hostility, where vigilance is more essential than ever: 'By learning from history, we can understand why powers rise and fall,' he said.

The history he speaks of thrives by erasing another. The sociologist Michel Bonnin once wrote of unofficial memory in China as 'an archipelago whose little islands are threatened by the vast surrounding ocean of official oblivion'. In the year of the centenary the waters surged again. The authorities launched a website and hotline to report acts of historical nihilism; China's internet regulator soon boasted that it had overseen the deletion of more than 2 million posts containing 'harmful' discussion of history. An official Party history dramatically condensed its coverage of the Cultural Revolution, removing references to the damning 1981 verdict. Deng Xiaoping's warning against one-man rule vanished from historical texts. It became a criminal offence to slander China's martyrs and heroes; multiple arrests, charges and at least one conviction followed. As 2021 ended, five young Maoists were jailed, under another charge, for circulating articles attacking Deng and other reformist leaders.

Around the same time, Xi oversaw a plenum approving a resolution on the Party's Major Achievements and Historical Experience in a Century of Struggle – only the third leader to pass such a statement on the Party's history in its hundred years. Mao did so in 1945 to underscore and cement his dominance and the defeat of his opponents. Deng did so in 1981 to negate the Cultural Revolution while shoring up his own position, ensuring the Party's survival and setting it on a new course. Xi has done it to enshrine himself as a leader of the same stature as those men, able to control the narrative as they did, and as the natural heir to the Party and all that it stands for. Under Mao, we are told, China stood up. Under Deng, it became rich. Under Xi, it grows strong. He is not merely the guardian of its mission; he is, in a sense, the culmination of that journey – the document states explicitly that it is needed, among other things, for 'resolutely upholding Comrade Xi Jinping's core position'. To criticise Xi is more dangerous than ever: it is to criticise the Party itself.

Though the Cultural Revolution's legacy is more relevant – more evident – than ever, this book could not be written if I were to begin it today. There is, in fact, an inverse relationship between utility and acceptability: what makes the era's lessons so vital is also what makes them impermissible. It was safer when it felt like an anomaly, or at least the full stop at the end of Maoism. But now primary-school children carry books with Xi's image upon the cover and settle down to study Xi Jinping Thought, learning that 'Grandpa Xi Jinping has always cared for us, and wishes for us to strive to grow into worthy builders and inheritors of socialism.' And so these stories belong to another age – not the decade of the movement itself but the time when people, at least a few, found a space to share them.

I am half a world away now, back in London, getting used to another alien country. The first time I returned, after moving to China, the drive from Heathrow startled me – how suddenly quaint all the houses appeared, as though they had shrunk in a year of absence; how neat and inconsequential my homeland looked through my new eyes. Now the landscape itself has shifted and what surprises me is not just that shift but my sudden recognition. There are manufactured fights over empire and slavery, the flag is hoisted, judges and experts denounced. Division is not a result but the purpose, for all this is instrumental. I know this, I realise – I know this language: Who are our enemies? Who are our friends? This is, as Mao thought, the most important question. I'm not truly surprised, either, when the pandemic upends our lives. I'm disbelieving – almost angered – by the shock of friends who thought our world was solid, that the worst couldn't happen. Yet in my heart lies the same lingering instinct, something I would like to call hope but that may just be incomprehension – complacency bred in a life unbounded by disasters waiting to strike. A belief that patience and strength can see you through to better days.

On my wall, as I write, hangs another image from the Cultural Revolution. It's an original, harder to buy these days, due to both their growing sensitivity and increased commercial value. It's a slick, professional poster, painted socialist-realist style. In the Soviet Union, Andrei Sinyavsky observed of such work that it was 'half-classicist half-art, none too socialist, and not at all realistic'; this soft and vague and hazy image is the Cultural Revolution in the mode of a dinner party, graceful and pleasant. Characters printed along the bottom instruct the reader to be healthy for the revolution's sake. But it appears less a command than an appeal: the painting could be selling milk, or soap, or sportswear. It is literally rose-tinted, an almost dreamy image of children running towards an unseen future under a melted ice-cream sky of palest pink and vanilla and peach. Their red armbands are worn over cheerful scarlet and purple sweaters. Their eyes are locked on the horizon.

The optimism the image evokes, the belief in a brighter Communist dawn, had died long before it was created – after the brutality of Red August; the chaos and contradictions exemplified by Lin Biao's dramatic end; the stultified, stagnant later years. The picture is a giant lie, even a repulsive one, and yet it tells an inadvertent truth. It is dated at the bottom: 1975. The end of the Cultural Revolution was still a year or more away, with Mao's death in September 1976 and the Gang of Four's overthrow. Still, the straitjacket has loosened, just a little. The very worst is over. These runners are young – thirteen, perhaps, the age at which the painter captured Yu Xiangzhen. They have known no other world. But I like to imagine that they sense something lying just beyond the horizon. They have no idea what it is, why it matters; only that it is there, and they must reach it. They would be adults now, with children of their own, and perhaps grandchildren too. Here they are frozen in youth and motion, the energy coursing through their bodies. Joy and freedom surge in their limbs. Pumping legs carry them endlessly forward –

Not one of them looks back.

SOURCES

Throughout this book I have drawn upon *Mao's Last Revolution* by Roderick MacFarquhar and Michael Schoenhals (2006), a magisterial account of the Cultural Revolution and particularly helpful on developments at the top of the Party. For those seeking a brief version, *The Cultural Revolution: A Very Short Introduction* by Richard Curt Kraus (2012) is a good beginning which lives up to its name but packs in a great deal. *The Cultural Revolution: A People's History, 1962–1976* by Frank Dikötter (2016) offers a lengthier but very readable analysis.

I had finished this book when *The World Turned Upside Down* by Yang Jisheng (2021) was published but was able to benefit from his analysis and extraordinary detail in revising it. *Mao: The Real Story* by Alexander V. Pantsov and Steven I. Levine (2012) was also helpful.

An astonishing window into the era is offered by Li Zhensheng in *Red-Color News Soldier* (2003), a collection of pictures he took and hid as a photographer for a Party newspaper during the movement.

Finally, *Pieces of Light: How the New Science of Memory Illuminates the Stories We Tell About Our Pasts* by Charles Fernyhough (2013) is a highly accessible introduction to the science of memory.

PERMISSIONS

Epigraph quotations are credited as follows:

pages vii and 41: From Nietzsche's *On the Use and Abuse of History for Life*, from Ian C. Johnston's translation, by permission of Richer Resources Publications, 2010.
page 23: Translation by permission of Frederick C. Teiwes and Warren Sun.
page 67: From *Without the Freedom to Remember, There Can Be No Freedom to Forget*, by permission of Chang Ping, translation by permission of Louisa Chiang.
page 91: Excerpt from Theodor W. Adorno, *Marginalien zu Mahler*, in: ders., *Gesammelte Schriften in 20 Bänden – Band 18: Musikalische Schriften V* © Suhrkamp Verlag, Frankfurt am Main, 1984. All rights reserved by and controlled through Suhrkamp Verlag, Berlin. Translation by Susan H. Gillespie from *Essays on Music* (2002) by permission of University of California Press.
page 151: Translation by permission of Brendan O'Kane.
page 173: By permission of John F. Burns.
page 205: From *1984* by George Orwell (1948), by permission of the estate of the late Sonia Brownell Orwell and HarperCollins Publishers Ltd.
page 225: From 'Preface to *Outcry*', Lu Xun (1923) *Jottings Under Lamplight* by Lu Xun, edited by Eileen J. Cheng and Kirk A. Denton, Cambridge, Mass.: Harvard University Press, Copyright © 2017 by the President and Fellows of Harvard College. Used by permission. All rights reserved.
page 243: From *Roses without Blooms, Part II* by Lu Xun, *Jottings Under Lamplight* by Lu Xun, edited by Eileen J. Cheng and Kirk A. Denton, Cambridge, Mass.: Harvard University Press, Copyright © 2017 by the President and Fellows of Harvard College. Used by permission. All rights reserved.

NOTES

Prologue

4 *To stand out was not an advantage* In *What Really Matters: Living a Moral Life Amidst Uncertainty and Danger* (2006), Arthur Kleinman quotes a physician victimised in the Cultural Revolution: 'To survive in China you must reveal nothing to others . . . Let your public self be like rice in a dinner: bland and inconspicuous, taking on the flavor of its surroundings while giving off no flavor of its own.'

7 *Mao's control of his party had been weakened by his Great Leap Forward* See *Tombstone* by Yang Jisheng (2008) and *Mao's Great Famine* by Frank Dikötter (2010).

8 *A second wave of 'rebel' Red Guard groups formed* *Fractured Rebellion: The Beijing Red Guard Movement*, Andrew Walder's detailed study of Red Guards (2009), has upended the conventional wisdom that the rebel groups were formed by those with less social capital, suggesting that instead the process was much more complex and less predictable.

8 *In Daxing District . . . entire families were murdered* See *Collective Killings in Rural China During the Cultural Revolution* by Yang Su (2011), Tan Hecheng's devastating *The Killing Wind: A Chinese County's Descent Into Madness During the Cultural Revolution* (2017) and Song Yongyi, 'Chronology of Mass Killings During the Chinese Cultural Revolution (1966–1976)', Online Encyclopedia of Mass Violence: https://www.sciencespo.fr/mass-violence-war-massacre-resistance/en/document/chronology-mass-killings-during-chinese-cultural-revolution-1966-1976.html.

10 *'a great madness, having nothing in common . . .'* 'The Soviet Embassy reports on the deterioration of Chinese–North Korean relations as a result of the Cultural Revolution in China', https://digitalarchive.wilsoncenter.org/document/114570, cited in a conference presentation

by Dr James Person of the Johns Hopkins University School of Advanced International Studies.

10 *the most 'sinister' aspect of one supposed conspiracy* *Mao's Last Revolution.*

11 *'All physically strong bodies . . .'* Preface to *Outcry*, Lu Xun, in *Jottings Under Lamplight*, edited by Eileen J. Cheng and Kirk A. Denton (2017).

11 *'The problem of selfishness in China . . .'* *From the Soil: The Foundations of Chinese Society* by Fei Xiaotong, with introduction and epilogue by Gary G. Hamilton and Wang Zheng (1992).

12 *'Our society is ethically hollow . . .'* *The Cowshed: Memories of the Chinese Cultural Revolution* by Ji Xianlin (2016) is a powerful and insightful first-person account of the era.

13 *It existed for the most part as an absence* Susanne Weigelin-Schwiedrzik describes the debate on the Cultural Revolution as 'at the same time everywhere and nowhere' in 'Coping with the Cultural Revolution: Contesting Interpretations', *Political Science*, 1 September 2008.

14 *China's first gay beauty pageant* Perhaps predictably, police shut the event down an hour before it was due to start.

15 *A survivor told me of her ordeal* Author's interview with Liu Tianyou. For more on the retreat, see Sun Shuyun's *The Long March* (2006).

15 *An octogenarian recounted dances and card games* Author interviews with Sidney Rittenberg. See 'Sixty years on: veterans of Chairman Mao's China remember', *Guardian*, 30 September 2009, and his extraordinary memoir, *The Man Who Stayed Behind*, co-authored by Amanda Bennett (1993).

15 *A photographer described how she had captured the moment* Author interview with Hou Bo, Mao's personal photographer. See 'Sixty years on: veterans of Chairman Mao's China Remember'.

15 *The daughter of Mao's secretary* Author interview with Hu Muying.

15 *The lawyer appointed to defend Mao's wife* Author interview with Zhang Sizhi.

17 *Its radicalism arguably birthed* See Guobin Yang in *The Red Guard Generation and Political Activism in China* (2016).

17 *'violently intrudes upon the present . . .'* Elena Cherepanov, *Understanding the Transgenerational Legacy of Totalitarian Regimes* (2020).

18 *But the memoirs and histories I read* The Cultural Revolution is probably best known through memoirs such as Nien Cheng's *Life and Death in Shanghai* (1986) and Ji Xianlin's strikingly candid – and more reflective – *The Cowshed* (first published in China in 1998). As I began to read more widely on the subject, I discovered the work of scholars such as Ba Jin (in the immediate aftermath) and (more recently) Xu Youyu exploring the broader meaning of the era. While I was working on this book, Cambridge University Press published *Red Shadows: Memories and Legacies of the Chinese Cultural Revolution*, edited by Patricia M. Thornton, Peidong Sun and Chris Berry (2017), which explores the long-lasting consequences of the movement in essays on subjects ranging from clothing choices to Educated Youth.

18 *Yet online, or in more daring publications* See, for example, 'Former Red Guard breaks silence on murder', Bo Gu, NBC, 27 September 2011.

18 *Even English-language state media* See, for example, 'Xu Xing rejects mainstream fame in quest for truth', Liang Chen, *Global Times*, 11 April 2014.

20 *'What we need in the present is constructed . . .'* Fei Xiaotong, *From the Soil.*

21 *within months would attack 'historical nihilism'* 'China takes aim at Western ideas', Chris Buckley, *New York Times*, 19 August 2013.

21 *'denigrate the country's past . . .'* 'We won't allow Britain's history to be cancelled', Oliver Dowden, *Daily Telegraph*, 15 May 2021.

22 *what we are willing to accept, and what we are willing to do* No one has put this better than the late congressman John Lewis in his posthumous essay 'Together, you can redeem the soul of our nation', *New York Times*, 30 July 2020: 'Democracy is not a state. It is an act.'

One

While descriptions are largely based on my interviews with Yu Xiangzhen, I have at times drawn upon her blog posts. The recollections of other former Red Guards and their families were also helpful in forming a picture of the time.

25 *'a blank sheet of paper . . .'* Mao, 'Introducing a Cooperative', 15 April 1958.

25 *The Communist Party's victory and control across this fractured country* Tony Saich's new book, *From Rebel to Ruler: One Hundred Years of the Chinese Communist Party* (2021), documents the Party's truly extraordinary rise from a small, secret gathering of thirteen young Chinese men to, a century later, a behemoth running a superpower.

25 *as welcome and astonishing* Clearly many – and not only Kuomintang supporters – were also anxious about the Communist Party's victory. (During the Civil War, for example, the Party had laid siege to cities such as Changchun, starving the inhabitants into submission.) In his book *The Tragedy of Liberation: A History of the Chinese Revolution, 1945–57* (2013) Frank Dikötter estimates that, by 1951, close to 2 million people – including small children – had been murdered on political grounds. Nonetheless there was real enthusiasm about the country's prospects, including among those who did not support the Party; many intellectuals returned from overseas to contribute – only to suffer in the anti-rightist movement and Cultural Revolution. (As one of the most eminent of those, the economist and linguist Zhou Youguang, told me: 'History misled us.')

26 *In 1958, Mao launched the Great Leap Forward* See *Tombstone* by Yang Jisheng and *Mao's Great Famine* by Frank Dikötter.

27 *'but it is the tiger spirit which is dominant . . .'* *The Cultural Revolution at the Margins: Chinese Socialism in Crisis* by Wu Yiching (2014).

27 *'being trained as our successors . . .'* May 16 communiqué, quoted in *Mao's Last Revolution.*

30 *Worshipping Chairman Mao was not a choice* The quasi-religious aspects of Mao's personality cult are well documented. Daniel Leese notes in *Mao Cult: Rhetoric and Ritual in China's Cultural Revolution* (2011) that people were urged to 'boundless worship'. In some villages there were shrines to him.

30 *'spiritual atom bomb . . .'* First used by the *People's Liberation Army Daily* in an editorial and later by Lin Biao and others. See *Mao Cult.*

31 *The girls . . . sailed back and forth* Traffic chaos was narrowly averted when Zhou Enlai vetoed a demand that red, the revolutionary colour,

should mean making progress at the lights instead of stopping; but Yang Jisheng notes in *The World Turned Upside Down* that traffic police were told to use Little Red Books instead of batons, because only Mao's Thought could show the way.

33 *The targets of the raid were executed soon after* See *Turbulent Decade* by Yan Jiaqi and Gao Gao (1996).

33 *'or writing an essay . . .'* *Quotations from Chairman Mao Tse-tung* aka the Little Red Book (1966).

36 *the centre had to stop it* Free travel and board ended in late 1966, though an official edict to end the touring was further off.

Two

Many of the details in this chapter are drawn from *The Chinese Cultural Revolution: A History* by Paul Clark (2008), which transformed my perceptions of the movement, setting out a convincing case for taking the art of this period seriously despite its obvious shortcomings. I also found *Art in Turmoil: The Chinese Cultural Revolution, 1966–76*, edited by Richard King (2010), extremely helpful. After interviewing Wang, I discovered that Liao Yiwu has written movingly about his life in *The Corpse Walker: Real-Life Stories, China From the Bottom Up* (2008).

42 *a damning critique of a drama* See *Mao's Last Revolution.*

43 *'freaks and monsters . . . in our press, radio, magazines . . .'* *Important Documents on the Great Proletarian Cultural Revolution in China* (1970).

43 *Gu Shengying, a brilliant and renowned young pianist* Ding Zilin writes movingly about her schoolfriend's life and death in the essay 'Three People Deeply Imprinted on My Memory', 8 April 2001: www.hrichina.org/en/content/4665.

43 *'while we buried 46,000'* Mao Zedong at the second plenary session of the Eighth Communist Party Congress Central Committee (1958).

45 *what was needed, too, was a 'cultural army'* Talks at the Yenan Forum on Literature and Art, Mao Tse-tung, Foreign Languages Press (1967, fourth edition).

45 *'There is in fact no such thing as art for art's sake . . .'* Talks at the Yan'an

Forum, 1942, in *Quotations from Chairman Mao Tse-tung*.

56 *His wife Jiang Qing* See Ross Terrill's *The White-Boned Demon: A Biography of Madame Mao Zedong* (1984).

56 *'Only a solitary flower bloomed . . .'* Ba Jin, *Random Thoughts*, translated by Geremie R. Barmé (1984).

58 *Li devoted himself to re-establishing classical music* See *Rhapsody in Red: How Western Classical Music Became Chinese* by Sheila Melvin and Jindong Cai (2004).

60 *'Proper limits have to be exceeded in order to right a wrong . . .'* Gao was mischievously quoting a famous remark by Mao Zedong on the peasant movement in Hunan in the 1920s, itself a rejection of an old Chinese phrase on not acting excessively.

60 *'cut off from the world and forced to become original'* Author interview with the musicologist Professor John Robison, of the University of South Florida. He has since published *Wang Xilin, Human Suffering, and Compositional Trends in Contemporary China* (2021).

63 *In the West, a universe away, it was the year of Twiggy* Although, paradoxically, Maoism would prove remarkably popular within Western counterculture in this era, standing 'not just for earnest anti-imperialism but also for youthful rebellion', as Julia Lovell notes in *Maoism: A Global History* (2019).

65 *'send constructive and positive messages'* Liu Qibao, then head of the propaganda department of the Party's central committee, quoted by state news agency Xinhua, 14 September 2014.

Three

67 *On a rare blue-sky day* Not so rare these days; air quality has dramatically improved in Beijing.

67 *hangs the portrait of Mao* He was not the first to be honoured; a portrait of Sun Yat-sen was hung there after his death, and later one of Chiang Kai-shek (from 1945 to 1949) – photographs of the gate in that era are distinctly disconcerting to the modern viewer. In 1953 Mao's image was replaced by one of Stalin for a day, to mark the Russian leader's death. Since then it has been Mao all the way.

67 *stretching 4.5 by 6 metres* 'Reclusive painter keeps Mao spirit alive on Tiananmen', Haze Fan and Maxim Duncan, Reuters, 30 June 2011.

68 *Mao both took up and transformed this geography* *Remaking Beijing: Tiananmen Square and the Creation of a Political Space* by Wu Hung (2005) offers a helpful account of the capital's political geography and the history of Mao's portrait.

68 *the twin Museums of the Chinese Revolution and Chinese History* See 'The Red Line: Creating a Museum of the Chinese Revolution' by Chang-tai Hung, *The China Quarterly*, no. 184 (December 2005).

68 *When China rebuilt it* See 'At China's grand new museum, history toes party line', Ian Johnson, *New York Times*, 3 April 2011; 'From Mao to Modern', Aric Chen, *Architectural Record*, 15 February 2012.

69 *Foreigners mainly associate it with the bloody crackdown* For an eyewitness account of the bloodshed, see 'Who Died in Beijing, and Why' by Robin Munro, *The Nation*, 11 June 1990. Though student victims received most of the international attention, many if not most of those who died were Beijing residents who had joined the movement, hoped to protect the demonstrators, or simply came out to see what was happening. For more on the legacy of the protest movement and massacre, see *The People's Republic of Amnesia* by Louisa Lim (2014), which focuses on the Party's attempt to erase the events.

69 *Since 1989 the Party has redoubled its commitment* *Never Forget National Humiliation: Historical Memory in Chinese Politics and Foreign Relations* by Zheng Wang (2012) describes the intensification of patriotic education and explores its causes.

70 *Xi's first public act* 'Xi Jinping pledges "great renewal of Chinese nation"', Wu Gang and Yan Shuang, *Global Times*, 30 November 2012.

72 *Not long after my arrival in China a terrible earthquake struck Sichuan* Details of the earthquake and its aftermath are taken from my own coverage at the time.

73 *shortly after he was punched in the head by police* Ai was planning to attend the trial of Tan Zuoren, who had investigated the schoolchildren's deaths, when he and other volunteers were detained.

74 *generally good support from the public* For obvious reasons, gauging the public mood in China is not easy. The best independent assessment

of attitudes is the series of surveys conducted by Harvard University's Ash Center for Democratic Governance and Innovation between 2003 and 2016, summarised in 'Understanding CCP Resilience: Surveying Chinese Public Opinion Through Time' by Edward Cunningham, Tony Saich and Jesse Turiel (July 2020): https://ash.harvard.edu/files/ash/files/final_policy_brief_7.6.2020.pdf. The authors find that satisfaction with the centre is much higher than with local officials; by 2016 they recorded a 93.1 per cent rate of satisfaction with Beijing, remarkable to anyone who has encountered widespread cynicism among ordinary people. They conclude: 'Although state censorship and propaganda are widespread, our survey reveals that citizen perceptions of governmental performance respond most to real, measurable changes in individuals' material well-being.' That means, however, that satisfaction and support must be consistently reinforced. And, of course, it is impossible to know what support there would be without all the censorship and propaganda.

75 *Your censors went into overdrive* Propaganda orders are secret, and often delivered verbally, but *China Digital Times* (https://chinadigitaltimes.net) does an excellent job of tracking censorship.

75 *'For Chinese people, history is our religion'* 'In China, "History Is a Religion"', Zheng Wang, *The Diplomat*, 16 June 2014.

76 *It sees history not as a record* Gao Xiang, the head of the Chinese Academy of History – founded by Xi Jinping in 2019 to promote the Party's vision of history – has written: 'History researchers shouldn't be cold-eyed observers of times and trends' and that historical research must 'guide governance and nurture people'. See 'China Repackages Its History in Support of Xi's National Vision', Chun Han Wong and Keith Zhai, *Wall Street Journal*, 15 June 2021.

76 *the* Records of the Grand Historian, *from the first century* BC, *describe an ambitious Qin dynasty eunuch* See 'Pointing at a Deer and Calling It a Horse', Victor Mair, Language Log, 30 August 2020: www.languagelog.ldc.upenn.edu.

77 *'The empire long divided . . .'* Luo Guanzhong, *Romance of the Three Kingdoms* (fourteenth century); translation Moss Roberts (1991).

77 *There was no doubt that anti-Japanese sentiment was real* The best-known

account is the devastating *The Rape of Nanking: The Forgotten Holocaust of World War II* by Iris Chang (1997), which helped to catapult the atrocities back to international attention.

77 *Critics pointed to the hypocrisy* The author and historian Ye Yonglie noted that Japan's history of erasing its invasion of China had been attacked as its 'textbook problem', continuing: 'China, in fact, has its own "textbook problem" . . . The Cultural Revolution occurred in China, but research on the Cultural Revolution occurs abroad!' Ye Yonglie, 'Textbook Problem' (2006), translated by Joel Martinsen for *Danwei*.

78 *More Britons believe the empire was a source of pride than shame* A YouGov survey in 2014 found that 59 per cent saw the empire more as a source of pride, against 19 per cent who saw it more as a source of shame; by 2020 only 32 per cent saw it more as a source of pride, but the rest had swung to 'don't know' rather than to shame. 'How Unique Are British Attitudes to Empire?' on www.yougov.co.uk, 11 March 2020. For a more honest reckoning with Britain's colonial history, see David Olusoga's *Black and British: A Forgotten History* (2016) and Howard W. French's revelatory *Born in Blackness: Africa, Africans, and the Making of the Modern World, 1471 to the Second World War* (2021).

78 *As children we learned more about the abolition of slavery* Eric Williams once observed that 'The British historians wrote almost as if Britain had introduced Negro slavery solely for the satisfaction of abolishing it.'

79 *a flood of memoirs and novels had laid bare trauma and oppression* See, for example, *Mao's Harvest: Voices from China's New Generation*, edited by Helen F. Siu and Zelda Stern (1983).

79 *'from now on and for quite some time . . .'* Guobin Yang, *The Red Guard Generation and Political Activism in China.*

80 *'In 2000 Song Yongyi . . .'* '"Enemy of the people" historian Song Yongyi gives as good as he gets', Verna Yu, *South China Morning Post*, 19 February 2013.

80 *'How fortunate we are that history . . .'* and *'Their father is dead . . .'* Quoted in the obituary of Liu Shaoqi's widow, Wang Guangmei, John Gittings, *Guardian*, 20 October 2006.

80 *Xi Jinping would hail him as a 'glorious model'* 'Xi salutes late leader Liu

Shaoqi's high spirit', An Baijie, *China Daily*, 24 November 2018.

81 *'The aim of summarising the past . . .'* See *China's Cultural Revolution, 1966–1969*, edited by Michael Schoenhals (1996).

83 *Peng, an official, was placed on a death list* Details of Peng Qi'an's story are drawn from interviews with museum volunteers who were kind enough to speak to me in some detail about the institution, their experiences and the pressure it has faced over the years, as well from as the following articles: 'Cultural Revolution memories under threat', Peh Shing Huei, *Straits Times*, 12 December 2011; 'China's Cultural Revolution museum a well-kept secret', Mark MacKinnon, *Globe and Mail*, 22 July 2010; 'China's first Cultural Revolution museum exposes Mao's war on "bourgeois culture"', Clifford Coonan, *Independent*, 21 February 2006; 'Chinese museum looks back in candor', Edward Cody, *Washington Post*, 3 June 2005; 'Museum keeps Cultural Revolution memories alive', Zhou Yan, Lai Yuchen and Chen Ji, Xinhua, 2 August 2013.

83 *The writer Ba Jin* See 'A Museum of the "Cultural Revolution"', Ba Jin, 15 June 1986. http://www.cnd.org/cr/english/articles/bajin.htm.

87 *Document Number Nine* A translation is available at www.chinafile.com/document-9-chinafile-translation.

89 *Soon afterwards, researchers noticed* 'Denying Historians: China's Archives Increasingly Off-Bounds', Maura Cunningham, *Wall Street Journal*, 18 August 2014. Authorities are also deleting historical journal articles; see 'China rewrites history with new censorship drive', Ben Bland, *Financial Times*, 4 September 2017.

89 *more than a hundred social media accounts were closed* 'Your public account is history', David Bandurski, *China Media Project*, 21 January 2015.

89 *In Shantou, Peng cancelled the commemoration service* 'Enforced Silence at China's Cultural Revolution Museum', Felicia Sonmez, AFP, 15 August 2014.

For more on China's selective memory, and the tacit acceptance of official censorship and the rewriting of history, see Yan Lianke, 'On China's state-sponsored amnesia', *New York Times*, 1 April 2013. The novelist writes:

'Gradually we become accustomed to amnesia and we question people who ask questions.' Chan Koonchung's dystopian novel *The Fat Years* (2009) is a compelling exploration of collective amnesia in China.

Four

Bian Zhongyun's killing is one of the most notorious events of the Cultural Revolution. My description is based primarily on Hu Jie's extraordinary documentary *Though I Am Gone* (2006), which centres around lengthy interviews with Bian's widower, Wang Jingyao. (Hu Jie has produced a series of remarkable historical documentaries; his work is discussed in more depth in Philip Pan's 2008 book *Out of Mao's Shadow*.) It also draws upon accounts given by Song Binbin and her friends in *Remembrance*, my interview with her friends and their own research, and Wang Youqin's work. At the time of writing, Professor Wang was completing her new book *Victims of the Cultural Revolution: Testimonies of a Tragedy* (2023).

101 *She had apologised* Zhu Liudi and Zhang Han, *Beijing News*, 13 January 2014. For English-language coverage, see, for example, 'Bowed and remorseful, former red guard recalls teacher's death', Chris Buckley, *New York Times*, 13 January 2014.

101 *But as the years passed a number came forward* See, for example, 'Red Guards Apologize Forty-four Years Later', *Southern Weekend*, 4 November 2010.

102 *In time, he founded his own digital magazine* *Remembrance* was co-founded with He Shu, another historian of the era. For more on *Remembrance*, see 'China's Brave Underground Journal', Ian Johnson, *New York Review of Books*, 4 December 2014.

105 *'If bad people beat good people, the good people achieve glory . . .'* *Fractured Rebellion: The Beijing Red Guard Movement* by Andrew G. Walder, Harvard University Press (2009).

106 *Song had been scared to intervene more decisively . . .* Song's article in *Remembrance* in 2014, based on her speech at the school.

115 *Song's friends had talked of South Africa's Truth and Reconciliation Commission* See *Country of My Skull* by Antjie Krog (1998) and

A Human Being Died That Night by Pumla Gobodo-Madikizela (2003). 'Trauma and Transitional Justice in Divided Societies' by Judy Barsalou, United States Institute of Peace special report 135 (2005), was also useful, as was 'Reconciliation After Violent Conflict: A Handbook', edited by David Bloomfield, Teresa Barnes and Luc Huyse, a report by the International Institute for Democracy and Electoral Assistance (2003).

116 *Wang, who had spent a lifetime remembering* In the conclusion of *The Red Guard Generation and Political Activism in China*, I was struck to read Guobin Yang's moving description of the involvement of one of Wang and Bian's daughters in running events related to the history of the Educated Youth: 'a project of preserving and understanding history and memory with a silent bravery'.

Five

My account of what happened in Chongqing in the Cultural Revolution is based primarily on interviews with several former Red Guards there and others who lived through the era, including historian He Shu. I discovered Guobin Yang's *The Red Guard Generation and Political Activism in China* only after finishing this book but wish I had read it earlier; he does a valiant job of disentangling the extraordinarily complex events in the city. Xujun Eberlein has written evocatively about her experiences of growing up in Chongqing at that time at www.xujuneberlein.com. Much of the detail on Bo Xilai comes from my own reporting at the time; for an overview of his career, and the scandal that brought him down, see *The Bo Xilai Scandal: Power, Death and Politics in China* by Jamil Anderlini (2012) and Carrie Gracie's lengthy BBC article 'Murder in the Lucky Holiday Hotel', www.bbc.co.uk/news/resources/idt-sh/Murder_lucky_hotel, 17 March 2017.

For more about the Party, read Richard McGregor's *The Party: The Secret World of China's Communist Rulers* (2010) and Tony Saich's *From Rebel to Ruler*, mentioned above. Another late discovery, which I read shortly after finishing this book, was Jude Blanchette's *China's New Red Guards: The Return of Radicalism and the Rebirth of Mao Zedong* (2019), which offers a good overview of the revival of Maoism.

119 *More than five hundred of the victims* 'Red Guards cemetery reveals scars yet to heal', Peng Yining, *China Daily*, 8 April 2010. Philip Pan's *Out of Mao's Shadow* also discusses the Shapingba cemetery.

123 *the supposed May 16 conspirators* According to *Turbulent Decade* by Yan Jiaqi and Gao Gao, so many were affected that a saying became common: 'Every household has a May 16 [member]; if not a relative, then certainly a friend.'

124 *Though Deng would dominate until his death* *Deng Xiaoping and the Transformation of China* by Ezra F. Vogel (2011) is an exhaustive exploration of Deng's later life and work.

124 *It is not hard to imagine the emotions engendered* Though young protestors in 1989 explicitly rejected comparisons to the Red Guards.

127 *Bo Xilai, when released from the brutal prison camp* For more detail of Bo's experiences in the Cultural Revolution, see 'Children of Mao's wrath vie for Power in China', Chris Buckley, Reuters, 22 June 2012.

129 *Those who had lived through the Cultural Revolution had recognised the danger* 'The Maoist Revival and the Conservative Turn in Chinese Politics', Willy Lam, *China Perspectives*, no. 2012/2, discusses the tactics of Bo and others, adding astutely: 'The possibilities are reasonably high that Bo Xilai's downfall notwithstanding, much of the restitution of Maoist norms will continue into the Xi Jinping era.'

129 *Academics wrote about the 'Chongqing model'* 'The Chongqing Model One Decade On', Yueran Zhang, *Made in China Journal*, vol. 6, issue 1 (January 2021).

133 *'For the past thirty years the Great Cultural Revolution has been marginalised and demonised . . .'* Mobo Gao's *The Battle for China's Past: Mao and the Cultural Revolution* (2008) offers a passionate defence of the movement, arguing that it was a liberation for those at the bottom of Chinese society. Dongping Han's work covers similar territory; see, for example, 'Impact of the Cultural Revolution on Rural Education and Economic Development: The Case of Jimo County', *Modern China*, vol. 27, no. 1 (January 2001), which argues that educational reforms had a positive side, for instance with the mass expansion of education in rural areas.

137 *For the dispossessed and marginalised* *Proletarian Power: Shanghai in*

the Cultural Revolution by Elizabeth J. Perry and Li Xun (1997) is an important study of the way that workers seized the opportunities of the moment, suggesting that 'Arguably, the truly extraordinary thing about the Cultural Revolution was less the oppressive political atmosphere imposed from on high than the diversity of organised popular responses which exploded from below.' *The Cultural Revolution at the Margins: Chinese Socialism in Crisis* by Yiching Wu (2014) is an intriguing exploration of the genuinely radical moments of the era – and their suppression – which gave me a much better sense of the possibilities within a destructive movement.

140 *Jiang's case is known as the birth of defence in China* See 'The Creation of Defence in China', Judith Bout, *Books & Ideas*, 17 December 2012, https://booksandideas.net/The-Creation-of-Defence-in-China.html, and my interview with Zhang Sizhi, who was assigned to defend Jiang (though she rejected his representation).

142 *Even China's economic growth owed nothing* There are, in fact, more sophisticated discussions about the contribution of the Cultural Revolution to China's economy today. In *The Chinese Cultural Revolution Reconsidered: Beyond Purge and Holocaust*, edited by Kam-yee Law (2003), Mark Lupher argues that the reforms seen under Deng were 'not a reaction against the Cultural Revolution, but the consequences of changes that occurred during the preceding decade', which restructured power. In the same volume, Christine Wong argues that the rural industrialisation it brought led subsequently to the rapid growth of Town and Village Enterprises.

145 *'and such historical tragedies as the Cultural Revolution may happen again . . .'* For more on the reaction to Wen Jiabao's remarks, see 'In China, political past, present and future collide', David Bandurski, *China Media Project*, 19 March 2012.

Six

I am indebted to Michel Bonnin's comprehensive work *The Lost Generation: The Rustication of China's Educated Youth (1968–1980)*, first published in English in 2013, for key details in this chapter (not least the unimprovable newspaper warning about things that 'do not lead to socialism'), as well as its illuminating oversight of the era. In addition to my interviewees in Chongqing, former Educated Youth (and their family members) elsewhere informed this chapter.

156 *There's a story – as implausible as it sounds – of Deng Xiaoping meeting Shirley MacLaine* MacLaine was the source of the anecdote; see for instance *From the Center of the Earth: The Search for the Truth about China* by Richard Bernstein (1982).

157 *In the early nineties, an exhibition* 'China's Zhiqing Generation: Nostalgia, Identity, and Cultural Resistance in the 1990s', Guobin Yang, *Modern China*, vol. 29, no. 3 (July 2003).

158 *He grew into manhood in Liangjiahe* 'Tracing the myth of a Chinese leader to its roots', Edward Wong, *New York Times*, 16 February 2011.

158 *Xi had begun to highlight those years of hardship* A 2004 interview about his experiences went viral following his ascension to the top job. See 'Flea Bites and Wading in Sewage: Xi Jinping's Account of Working Among Peasants Goes Viral', Zhuang Pinghui, *South China Morning Post*, 12 June 2014.

158 *'When I arrived at the Yellow Earth . . .'* 'The Creation Myth of Xi Jinping', John Garnaut, *Foreign Policy*, 19 October 2012.

159 *'On the whole special train . . .'* 'Communist Party History and Xi's Learned (and Unlearned) Lessons', Joseph Torigian, *China Perspectives*, no. 2018/1–2.

163 *They all knew this one* 'Music, Memory and Nostalgia: Collective Memories of Cultural Revolution Songs in Contemporary China', Lei X. Ouyang, *The China Review*, vol. 5, no. 2 (fall 2005), explores the fondness with which music of the period is still remembered.

166 *the deep conservatism in parts of the countryside* Though in other cases, urbanites were shocked by graphic sexual discussions among the farmers.

170 *and, by 1978, open protest* See, for example, '"We Want to Go Home!" The Great Petition of the *Zhiqing*, Xishuangbanna, Yunnan, 1978–1979', Bin Yang, *The China Quarterly*, no. 198 (June 2009).

Seven

Daniel Leese's *Mao Cult*, a fascinating account of the personality cult and its development, was particularly helpful in writing this chapter.

174 *'It takes all the running you can do, to keep in the same place . . .'* Lewis Carroll, *Through the Looking-Glass* (1871).

174 *'Mao images are everywhere . . .'* Simon Leys, *Chinese Shadows* (1977).

175 *his personal photographer told me once* Author interview with Hou Bo.

176 *Billions of the badges were made* See 'Badges of Chairman Mao Zedong' by Bill Bishop at wp.sinocism.com. Clint Twist's maozhang.net website offers a taste of the dazzling variety of designs.

180 *The rich in China are nouveau riche* That said, recent research suggests that the descendants of the pre-revolutionary elite have done markedly better than average despite all Mao's efforts. See 'The Grandchildren of China's Pre-revolutionary Elite are Unusually Rich', *The Economist*, 9 June 2022, https://www.economist.com/graphic-detail/2022/06/09/the-grandchildren-of-chinas-pre-revolutionary-elite-are-unusually-rich.

183 *When one of China's former top generals was arrested* 'PLA General "Profited from Military Housing Projects, Land Deals"', Wang Heyan, Caixin Global, 15 January 2014.

Eight

The Tragedy of Lin Biao: Riding the Tiger During the Cultural Revolution by Frederick C. Teiwes and Warren Sun (1996) was helpful, as was their book *The End of the Maoist Era: Chinese Politics During the Twilight of the Cultural Revolution, 1972–1976* (2007). *The Culture of Power: The Lin Biao Incident in the Cultural Revolution* by Qiu Jin (1999) offers an insider's view of events; the author is the daughter of Wu Faxian, the air force chief, who was close to Lin and was purged after his death, and her book draws upon his unpublished memoirs as well as interviews with former senior officials and their families.

189 *students in Harbin* 'Outcry as Chinese students recreate Red Guard persecution for yearbook photos', Anne Yi, *South China Morning Post,*

20 June 2014.

191 *others pitied him* Li Zhisui, one of Mao's personal physicians, believed Lin suffered from hypochondria. See Li Zhisui, *The Private Life of Chairman Mao* (1994).

192 *Lin's family panicked* His son, Lin Liguo, made an amateurish attempt at plotting Mao's assassination by sabotaging his train, but its route was changed. Lin Liguo appears to have hoped the family could flee to Guangzhou and launch a coup from there; in the end, they appear to have sought to flee to the Soviet Union.

192 *There were documents and meetings and broadcasts and headlines* In *Mao Cult*, Daniel Leese notes how Lin had to be erased before the new narrative could be imposed, including through his physical removal from millions of artworks, with authorities telling underlings to scrape off, cut out or paint and glue over images and inscriptions. The attacks on Lin would segue into the bizarre 'Criticise Lin – Criticise Confucius' campaign, linking the dead and disgraced leader to the ancient philosopher. It was essentially an attack on the premier, Zhou Enlai, but appears to have been almost as baffling to many ordinary people at the time as it seems today.

194 *Lin's portrait was added to the Chinese Military Museum* 'Lin Biao regains his place in army history', Xinhua, 17 July 2007.

200 *She had made an unexpected call* '"Mao Plot" general's daughter "calls for historical reckoning"', AFP, 6 November 2014.

Nine

210 *But Daihong caught meningitis* Frank Dikötter writes in *The Cultural Revolution: A People's History* that almost 160,000 people died in the outbreak fuelled by the mass migration.

214 *the daughter of one provincial governor was coerced* See Li Zhensheng's *Red-Color News Soldier*.

215 *Destroying Confucianism in China* The social and economic shifts in China have been so immense that the transformation of personal life has often been overlooked. One of my favourite books on China is Yunxiang Yan's extraordinary *Private Life under Socialism: Love,*

Intimacy, and Family Change in a Chinese Village, 1949–1999 (2003), which explores the rise of the private family, and of individualism within those families, as well as shifts from a 'vertical' focus on parent–child relationships to 'horizontal' ties between husband and wife (though feminists have argued that he overemphasises the power of women marrying into households).

215 *One collection of the purported writings of model soldier Lei Feng* Someone called Lei Feng probably existed, but the broader story, including the lengthy diary apparently found after his early death – full of declarations of devotion to Mao, and details of his selfless deeds – has long been regarded with deep scepticism, not least because of the quantity of professional photographs taken of this humble soldier before his death at twenty-two. More recently, he has come to be regarded as something between a depoliticised Good Samaritan and a somewhat kitsch figure.

217 *'She would be alive if she hadn't been [my] "stinking wife"'* Ba Jin, *Random Thoughts*.

217 *a Chinese historian told me* Author interview with Yin Hongbiao.

218 *he and his father had burned the family photographs after her disgrace* This was not uncommon. Zhang Yimou's 2014 film *Coming Home* includes a scene of photographs which have been cut up to remove the rightist father's image.

222 *a relic of Mao's planned economy: the household registration system* While there have been gradual and piecemeal reforms, Chinese authorities have ignored repeated calls for it to be scrapped, for a variety of reasons including the ability to reduce population movement, prevent slums from developing and avoid annoying the urban middle class, who do not want any further competition for quality services. For more on reform of the hukou, or household registration, see, for example, 'Is China Abolishing the Hukou System?' by Kam Wing Chan and Will Buckingham, *The China Quarterly*, no. 195 (September 2008). The costs are profound: a gulf between urban and rural dwellers, and between those born in cities and those who have migrated there; family separation and breakdown; and behavioural and educational problems among the more than 30 million left-behind children, often left with

family members who may be unable to care for them, rendering them vulnerable to bullying and abuse by adults. Around one in three children have lived without at least one parent for a prolonged period. See, for example, 'China raises a generation of "left-behind" children', April Ma, CNN, 5 February 2014, and 'The plight of China's "left-behind" children', *The Economist*, 8 April 2021.

223 *Given a drastic shortfall in female births* Prenatal scans and sex-selective abortion (illegal, but widely practised due to a preference for boys) led to 120 boys being born for every 100 girls, although the gap has closed to 110 boys more recently. In 2011 an expert predicted to me that 30 to 50 million men would fail to find wives in the subsequent two decades, equivalent to every man in the UK remaining a bachelor. The authorities, and some experts, are concerned about the resulting potential for social unrest.

223 *the state feminist organisation, the All-China Women's Federation, has been zealous* Leta Hong Fincher's *Leftover Women* (2014) is an eye-opening and influential account of the authorities' promotion of traditional gender roles and other aspects of the resurgence of gender inequality.

Ten

Understanding the Transgenerational Legacy of Totalitarian Regimes by Elena Cherepanov was especially helpful in its insights, while *Haunting Legacies* by Gabriele Schwab (2010) is a thoughtful and challenging account of the transmission of violent legacies. *Landscapes of the Chinese Soul: The Enduring Presence of the Cultural Revolution*, edited by Tomas Plänkers (2014), is a collection of psychoanalytically oriented interviews with survivors of the era and their children.

Professor Sverre Varvin, professor emeritus at Oslo Metropolitan University, was also kind enough to share his expertise on trauma; he has since co-authored *Psychoanalysis in China* (2014).

225 *I met a novelist for coffee* Author interview with the writer Tang Min.

229 *'We'll be all right as long as we keep going'* Ba Jin, *Random Thoughts*.

230 *'The path runs from the self to the family . . .'* Fei Xiaotong, *From the Soil.*

230 *'wanderers, strangers, people without roots . . .'* Philip A. Kuhn, *Soulstealers: The Chinese Sorcery Scare of 1768* (1990).

230 *'Was surviving the revolution a stroke of good or ill fortune?'* Ji Xianlin, *The Cowshed.*

233 *'nine tenths useless and one tenth distortion'* See *Psychology in Contemporary China* by L. B. Brown (2013).

233 *The country was searching for a purpose beyond wealth* *Deep China*, by Arthur Kleinman, Yunxiang Yan, Jing Jun, Sing Lee, Everett Zhang, Pan Tianshu, Wu Fei and Guo Jinhua (2011), makes a persuasive case that 'a pivotal transformation in the moral context and in the personhood of the Chinese' has been obscured by the magnitude of its economic transformation, noting: 'In the past, the self-identity of the Chinese individual was defined by preordained social relations . . . Only in the post-Mao reform era has the individual found the social conditions that would enable the quest and construction of self-identity.'

234 *The country now had perhaps 100 million Christians* Ian Johnson's *The Souls of China: The Return of Religion after Mao* (2017) is a superb exploration of religion in the country, and what has driven its resurgence.

234 *Yet alongside these tendencies ran an expansive, allusive tradition* I am indebted to Dr Richard Wu's presentation at the Shanghai conference for these insights.

234 *'The name that can be named is not the enduring and unchanging name'* *The Tao Te Ching*, translated by James Legge (1891), Oxford University Press.

236 *'The "trauma process" is not about . . .'* Susanne Weigelin-Schwiedrzik, 'Coping with the Cultural Revolution: Contesting Interpretations'.

236 *the series of disasters that had swept* Yu Hua's novella *To Live* (2003) is a vivid and harrowing portrayal of the succession of traumas and the devastation they wrought.

237 *'layer after layer of the patient's psyche . . .'* 'My Recollections of Sigmund Freud' by the Wolf-Man in *The Wolf-Man and Sigmund Freud*, edited by Muriel Gardiner (1971).

237 *The speakers in Shanghai spoke of parents* See, for example, the discussion of a father–son relationship in the wake of the movement in 'The Cultural Revolution: A Traumatic Chinese Experience and Subsequent Transgenerational Transmission – Some Thoughts About Inter-Cultural Interpretation' by Friedrich Markert, *International Journal of Applied Psychoanalytic Studies*, vol. 8, issue 3 (2011).

Eleven

245 *The collective rule of the 'red engineers' Rise of the Red Engineers* by Joel Andreas (2009) explores the emergence of China's technocrats and how Mao's attacks on the old educated elite and peasant revolutionaries in the Cultural Revolution fused them into a powerful new class.

245 *But then they quoted experts* Intriguingly, the articles in question have now vanished from the *Global Times* website.

246 *Underground churches, in the past mostly tolerated* See, for example, the trial of pastor Wang Yi for inciting subversion of state power: 'China sentences Wang Yi, Christian pastor, to 9 years in prison', Ian Johnson and Paul Mozur, *New York Times*, 30 December 2019.

246 *Even Marxist students who reach out* 'Inside China's crackdown on young Marxists', Yuan Yang, *Financial Times*, 13 February 2019.

246 *Undergraduates report on their lecturers* Professor Peidong Sun's experience is outlined in 'Spied on. Fired. Publicly shamed. China's crackdown on professors reminds many of Mao era', Alice Su, *Los Angeles Times*, 27 June 2020.

246 *Hong Kong was once a haven* For more on the protests and subsequent crackdown, see *City on the Edge: Hong Kong Under Chinese Rule* by Ho-fung Hung (2022), *Indelible City: Dispossession and Defiance in Hong Kong* by Louisa Lim (2022), and *The Impossible City: A Hong Kong Memoir* by Karen Cheung (2022).

246 *perhaps a million 'unreliable' residents* 'Up to one million detained in China's mass "re-education" drive', Amnesty International, September 2018. (Others have put the figure even higher.)

246 *Some of the detainees' children* 'Uighur children fall victim to China anti-terror drive', Emily Feng, *Financial Times*, 10 July 2018.

246 *Women report forced sterilisations* 'China cuts Uighur births with IUDs, abortion, sterilization', Associated Press, 29 June 2020.

246 *Mosques and other cultural sites are razed* 'Thousands of Xinjiang mosques destroyed or damaged', Helen Davidson, *Guardian*, 25 September 2020.

246 *'of a scope and scale . . .'* '"Eradicating Ideological Viruses": China's Campaign of Repression Against Xinjiang's Muslims', Human Rights Watch, 9 September 2018.

247 *Teachers, writes the Education Bureau* 'In China's crackdown on Muslims, children have not been spared', Amy Qin, *New York Times*, 28 December 2019.

247 *'Wasn't the Cultural Revolution the manifestation of "big democracy"?'* 'Communist Party History and Xi's Learned (and Unlearned) Lessons', Joseph Torigian, *China Perspectives*, no. 2018/1–2.

247 *In truth, his ideas seem . . . to owe more to Legalism* For an introduction to Legalism, see *Chinese Thought: From Confucius to Cook Ding* by Roel Sterckx (2019).

249 *Some are – probably many* See the research of the Ash Center at Harvard University, mentioned above.

249 *Xi will promise 'common prosperity'* See, for example, Ryan Hass, 'Assessing China's "common prosperity" campaign', Brookings, 9 September 2021.

249 *'During the Cultural Revolution, Mao Zedong was one brain . . .'* 'An Interview with Xu Youyu: "The Worst Is Yet to Come"', by Cao Yaxue, *China Change*, 31 October 2018.

249 *faint murmurings of discontent* For more on the reaction within the Party, see *Xi Jinping: The Backlash* by Richard McGregor (2019).

249 *'The Party media is going to great lengths . . .'* 'Imminent Fears, Immediate Hopes' by Xu Zhangrun, translated by Geremie R. Barmé, *China Heritage*, 1 August 2018.

250 *But an editorial appeared the next day* 'Excerpt from *People's Daily* on the Cultural Revolution', *New York Times*, 18 May 2016.

251 *'an archipelago whose little islands . . .'* Michel Bonnin, 'The Threatened History and Collective Memory of the Cultural Revolution's Lost Generation', *China Perspectives*, no. 2007/4.

251 *It became a criminal offence* 'Shutting down historical debate, China makes it a crime to mock heroes', Steven Lee Myers, *New York Times*, 2 November 2021.

251 *An official Party history* 'Party All the Time: The CCP in Comparative and Historical Perspective', Patricia Thornton, *The China Quarterly*, no. 248 (November 2021).

251 *As 2021 ended, five young Maoists* 'Five Mao fanatics jailed over articles "smearing former Chinese leaders"', Guo Rui and William Cheng, *South China Morning Post*, 11 January 2022, https://www.scmp.com/news/china/politics/article/3162988/five-mao-fanatics-jailed-over-articles-smearing-former-chinese.

252 *'Grandpa Xi Jinping . . .'* 'Xi Jinping Thought, for children', *The Economist*, 2 September 2021.

253 *'half-classicist half-art . . .'* Andrei Sinyavsky, 'On Socialist Realism' (1961), translated by George Dennis, www.dissentmagazine.org.

ACKNOWLEDGEMENTS

I could not have written *Red Memory* without the contributions of so many people throughout my years in China and beyond. It is the product of countless hours of interviews with those who lived through the era; I am indebted to all of those who were generous with their time and insights and who trusted me with their stories. I am conscious of the responsibility, especially given this subject's sensitivity, and hope I have done them justice.

Because I interviewed many people multiple times, I have in places condensed conversations for the sake of clarity and to avoid boring readers with repetition or unnecessary detail – while, of course, ensuring that quotes do not appear out of context. In two chapters, on the Educated Youth and on psychotherapy, I have changed the names and minor but potentially identifying details of interviewees at their request.

Written testimonies by some of those to whom I spoke also contributed. Interviews and conversations with scores of people who are not quoted directly, but whose experiences and knowledge were invaluable, have shaped this book. I have also drawn upon the wealth of scholarship on the era, much of it carried out by courageous Chinese researchers, often with little reward or recognition. I would urge anyone who wants to know more to explore the compelling books and papers listed in the endnotes. Together, all these sources explain what happened, how people survived it, and how they are attempting to make sense of it today.

— // —

Thank you to Bill Bishop and Carol Chow, for the conversations which set me on this path; without them, this book would never have been written. Bill's newsletter, *Sinocism*, is essential reading for anyone following China closely.

Thank you to all those who assisted me with research for this book. The expertise of scholars and analysts in and outside the country has enriched my understanding of China and the Cultural Revolution.

My reporting in China for the *Guardian* would have been impossible without the dedication and skill of our news assistants. Their job is demanding, difficult and wholly underappreciated. In particular, I owe a great deal to Chen Shi, Cecily Huang and Luna Lin: their knowledge, insights and love for their country taught me an enormous amount, while their good humour and friendship saw us through tedious journeys and peculiar encounters.

Thank you too to Sun Shuyun, for her generosity to a China neophyte before my move and after my arrival; to Pingke, probably the best-read person I know, for hours of conversation and coffee; to Jo Lusby for advice; to Yu Xiaodong for challenging me; to A for some of the most interesting conversations of my seven years in China; and to all those, too many to name, who shared their friendship and hospitality. Thank you to Beijing colleagues, in particular Lucy Hornby, Carrie Gracie, Tyra Dempster, Kim Jensen, Peh Shing Huei, Gady Epstein, Leo Lewis, Comino Tamura (an honorary member of the press corps), Rob Schmitz and William Wan.

Jo Cooke, Maria Yacoob and Naga Munchetty have always been frank and supportive in equal measure; I am grateful on both counts. Amy Shapiro, a model of perseverance, offered encouragement when I most needed it. Thank you also to Rachel Corp and Laurence Lee, JJ and Matt Smith, a friend from Sheffield to Shenyang.

I have been lucky enough to have studied with outstanding teachers, in particular George Beeley, Clare Wenham, Tim Shakesby and Graham McCann (who first introduced me to Nietzsche's *On the Use and Abuse of History for Life*)), and the ever-patient Song Laoshi and Zhang Laoshi.

Thank you to current and former *Guardian* colleagues, for variously hiring, editing, challenging, encouraging and inspiring me, especially Katharine Viner, Alan Rusbridger, Rebecca Allison, Aditya Chakrabortty, Vikram Dodd, Emma Graham-Harrison, Joseph Harker, Charlotte Higgins, Martin Hodgson, Lily Kuo, Raekha Prasad, Randeep Ramesh, Mark Rice-Oxley, Judith Soal (whose psychoanalytic expertise proved especially helpful), Jon Watts, Michael White and Jamie Wilson.

Special gratitude is due to the friends who were kind enough to read parts of this book; of course, all errors and omissions are entirely my own.

None of this would have been possible without Karolina Sutton's faith in this book and the clarity of her advice. Everyone told me I was lucky to work with my editor, Laura Hassan; they were right. Thank you too to Sophie Portas, Josh Smith, Jess Kim, Anne Owen, Hannah Knowles and all at Faber for their support; also to Silvia Crompton for her painstaking copy-editing. I am immensely grateful to Tina Bennett, to Tom Mayer for his thoughtful editing, and all at W. W. Norton.

My extraordinary parents have always been an unstinting source of love and support. So have Holly and Alun; one of the luckiest aspects of my life is having you in it. Another is that you have brought Stuart, Anne, Ariane, Rorie, Zara and Ivor into the family. Thank you also to Pe Ann and to Pearl, Thiam, Charissa, Elizabeth and Andy for their welcome and their love.

Finally, thank you to Zan, who brings me so much joy; and to

Dan Chung for all that you have taught me, and for all our adventures. Everything is better with you.